American Attitudes

American Attitudes

Who Thinks What about the Issues That Shape Our Lives

BY SUSAN MITCHELL

New Strategist Publications, Inc.
Ithaca, New York

New Strategist Publications, Inc.
P.O. Box 242, Ithaca, New York 14851
607/273-0913
www.newstrategist.com

ISBN 1-885070-17-9

Printed in the United States of America

For my son, Sam Beck.

Table of Contents

Chapter 1. The Public Arena

Chapter 2. Government and Politics

Chapter 3. Race and Immigration

Chapter 4. Religion

Chapter 5. Work and Money

Chapter 6. Marriage and Family

Chapter 7. Women's Roles

Chapter 8. Personal Outlook

Chapter 9. Sexual Attitudes and Behavior

Tables

Chapter 1. The Public Arena

Chapter 2. Government and Politics

Chapter 3. Race and Immigration

Chapter 4. Religion

Chapter 5. Work and Money

Chapter 6. Marriage and Family

Chapter 7. Women's Roles

Chapter 8. Personal Outlook

Chapter 9. Sexual Attitudes and Behavior

Introduction

Change has been a constant in the United States for over 200 years, but the pace of change has accelerated since the middle of this century. New technologies have radically altered the way we live and work. The traditional household of the 1950s, made up of a stay-at-home mother, working father, and children, has fractured into dual-income families, single parents, and single-person households. We are more racially and ethnically diverse than ever before.

It is no surprise, then, that over the past 20 years Americans have changed their minds about many issues. The biggest changes came about in opinions about race and the roles of women. Twenty years ago, far more Americans believed in separate societies for blacks and whites and traditional roles for men and women. Since then, men and women, blacks and whites, old and young, the most and the least educated have changed their minds about race and women's roles.

Racial tension is still very real in the 1990s, but overtly racist attitudes and forms of discrimination are greatly diminished. Few Americans now favor laws that exclude blacks from white neighborhoods or prevent people of different races from marrying. The idea that blacks have less innate ability than whites has lost credibility with Americans.

Likewise, most Americans matter-of-factly accept women's participation in politics and business. Compared with 20 years ago, far fewer Americans now believe women should be homemakers, leaving politics and breadwinning up to men.

Most Americans are still religious, but there is more religious diversity than there was 20 years ago, when Protestants were in the majority. Especially among the young, a growing share of people say they have no religious preference. Americans are less confident of religious leaders and less "fundamentalist" in their interpretation of the Bible.

Americans continue to be concerned about crime. They have a much more negative view of the nation's leaders—especially elected officials—than they did in

1976. Most people think income differences in America are too large but they are divided on whether or not government should do something about it.

The public wants government to spend less, but still assigns a long list of responsibilities to government. Most people think it is government's responsibility to provide housing for the poor, financial aid for low-income college students, health care for the mentally and physically ill, and support for the elderly. Americans also want government to help industry develop new technologies and create jobs.

Most Americans say they are pretty happy and in good health. But they are more likely to feel rushed all the time than they were in the early 1980s. Americans are split on whether people are helpful and fair. Most no longer trust others.

Americans are less likely to say their marriages are very happy than they were 20 years ago, but most believe their family life is very successful. They are less likely to think large families are ideal—the majority of Americans now consider two children the right number.

People are slightly more likely than they were 20 years ago to be dissatisfied with their financial situation. The proportion of those who say hard work is the key to success is slightly higher than in the past. Most people are satisfied with their jobs and would continue to work even if they didn't need the money.

Sexual mores have changed since the 1970s. Support for sex education in the schools is as high as it has ever been. The growing acceptance of premarital sex and homosexuality continue the liberalization of attitudes that began in the "free love" era of the 1960s. Attitudes toward adultery and pornography, however, have become more conservative.

Men and Women

Men and women agree on many issues, and even when they disagree, the differences of opinion are often not as large as they are between other demographic segments. But on some issues, men and women disagree sharply.

Both men and women believe taxes are too high on those with middle incomes. Both worry that the courts let criminals off too easily. They are concerned about the environment and threats to individual privacy. They are about equally likely to say they would vote for a black or female presidential candidate.

Women are more likely to view pornography and prostitution as detrimental to society and to believe they should be entirely illegal. Men are more accepting of premarital sex and sex between people in their early teens. Men and women are about equally likely to favor sex education in the schools.

Conventional wisdom holds that women are more liberal than men and on some questions women are more likely to take a point of view that would be considered "liberal." They are less supportive of the death penalty and more supportive of gun control, for example. They are more likely to believe that discrimination is the cause of the lower socioeconomic status of blacks. Women are more likely than men to want government to play an active role in solving a variety of problems, such as providing health care and alleviating poverty.

Men and women are about equally likely to view hard work rather than luck as the key to success. They both believe they are better off than their parents were at the same age, but women are less likely to think their children will be better off than they are now.

Men and women have changed their attitudes toward women's roles, and there is little disagreement about women's abilities and rights in the political and business arenas. But men are less likely to support affirmative action for women and more likely to believe that men will lose out in the workplace because of it. Women are more likely to believe they can combine motherhood and career successfully, but the sexes are equally likely to say both husband and wife should contribute to the household income.

Women are more religious than men. They are more likely to have a religious preference and to pray and attend religious services regularly. They are also more likely than men to take the Bible literally.

Blacks and Whites

The different experiences of blacks and whites over hundreds of years have clearly left their mark on attitudes. Blacks and whites hold different opinions about many issues relating to race, and the differences do not stop there. They disagree on many pocketbook issues as well.

It should surprise no one that blacks and whites see most race issues differently. Blacks are more likely to support busing, fair housing laws, and a black presidential candidate. Both blacks and whites are concerned about the consequences of more immigrants coming to the U.S. Blacks are especially concerned that new immigrants will take jobs away from citizens.

Blacks are more likely to be liberal Democrats and to believe government should spend more on social programs and do more to solve the nation's problems. Whites are more likely to support the death penalty, but both races favor requiring a police permit for anyone wanting to buy a gun.

On average, blacks have lower incomes than whites and this disparity is reflected in opinions on a number of issues. Blacks are more likely to say they consider themselves working class and that taxes on low-income people are too high. They are also more likely to say they are unhappy with their financial situation.

Life is generally easier for whites than for blacks, and consequently whites are more likely to say they are very happy, to find life exciting, and to say they are in excellent health. Blacks have much less faith in other people than do whites—they are far more likely than whites to say people take advantage of others, are not trustworthy, and are selfish.

Blacks are more traditionally religious than whites. They are more likely than whites to be Protestants, while whites are more likely to be Catholics. Blacks are more likely to pray daily and to interpret the Bible literally. They are also more likely to have a great deal of confidence in religious leaders.

Whites are more likely to say their marriages are very happy and that they feel very or completely successful in their family life. Blacks are more likely to value personal freedom over marriage.

Blacks and whites hold similar views regarding women's roles. Both races support women's participation in business and politics. Blacks have a more positive attitude toward working mothers than whites do, however.

The Generations

The generation gap is alive and well. Times have changed, attitudes have changed, but the generations do not see eye to eye. And they never will. On many issues, each ten-year age group is increasingly likely to agree or disagree. On other issues, there is a dividing line at age 50 or 60, with a wide difference of opinion separating baby boomers and Generation Xers from older generations. Younger generations are more comfortable with much of the ongoing social change than are older generations. Even when the attitudes of older Americans have changed, a generation gap often remains.

People of different ages are in general agreement on issues relating to crime and about the role of government in helping the poor. Younger generations are more likely to say they are liberal and politically independent. Older generations are more interested in politics, however.

The enormous changes in attitudes about race over the last 20 years are apparent in the differences of opinion between young and old. On many race issues, older generations hold more traditional views. They are more likely to say "blacks shouldn't push where they aren't wanted," to oppose fair housing laws, and to support laws against interracial marriage. Younger generations, themselves more racially diverse, are more comfortable with the idea of a black president and busing. Young people are more likely to believe different racial and ethnic groups should maintain their distinct customs rather than blend in.

The women's movement shaped the attitudes of younger generations about women's roles. Baby boomers and younger adults are less likely than older people to believe men and women should adhere to traditional roles at home, at work, and in politics. Younger generations are more likely to believe both husband and wife should contribute to the family income. The young have a more positive view of working mothers.

There are also generation gaps in religious attitudes. The young are more diverse in their religious preferences and more likely to have no religion. Older generations are more traditionally religious, praying and attending religious services more frequently than the young. Older Americans are also more likely to interpret the Bible literally.

Older generations continue to be appalled by many of the changes in sexual mores, while the young are more accepting of homosexuality, premarital sex, pornography, and sex education in the schools.

When it comes to work and money, attitudes are linked to life stages. The young are least satisfied with their personal finances but most likely to say their financial situation is improving. Older Americans are most satisfied with their personal finances but least likely to say their finances are improving. Younger people are more likely to consider themselves working class while older people are more likely to say they are middle class.

The Role of Education

Education clearly influences attitudes on some issues, such as the environment, but its role is less clear in other areas. The relationship between age and education (younger Americans are better educated) or income and education (the well-educated have higher incomes) make it difficult to ascertain whether education, age, or socioeconomic status is the most important determinant of attitudes.

Education strongly influences opinions about women's roles. Those with less education (who are also more likely to be older) are more likely to favor traditional sex roles and to believe in affirmative action for women.

People with more education generally have higher incomes, and this factor undoubtedly influences their outlook on questions about work and money. College graduates are more satisfied with their financial situation than those with less education and they are more likely to say their financial situation has gotten better over the last few years. They are also more likely to say they are very successful in their work.

People with less education are more likely to believe government has a responsibility toward the poor and the old and that it should help create and save jobs. They are also more likely to believe government should reduce income differences in America. Yet college graduates are more likely than those with less education to identify themselves as liberals.

Attitudes about racial issues are also linked to the extent of people's education. The college educated are more supportive of fair housing laws, more likely to vote for a black president, and more likely to view a lack of education as the cause of the socioeconomic differences between blacks and whites. Those with less education are more likely to support laws against interracial marriage, more likely to believe "blacks shouldn't push where they are not wanted," and more likely to believe immigrants hurt the economy and society.

There are also differences in religious outlook and practice by educational level. Those with less education are more likely to support school prayer, to interpret the Bible literally, and to have a great deal of confidence in religious leaders. They also are more conservative about sexual mores, more likely to condemn premarital and homosexual sex, and more likely to believe pornography should be illegal.

Education makes a big difference in personal outlook. Those with more education are more likely to be very happy, to have excellent health, and to find life exciting. They are more likely to think others are trustworthy, fair, and helpful.

Regardless of education, most Americans say they have very happy marriages, but the proportion of people who say they are very or completely successful in their family life rises with education.

About This Book

The second edition of *American Attitudes* examines the changing opinions of Americans and analyzes the social and demographic trends behind those changes.

The data in *American Attitudes* are from the General Social Surveys (GSS) of the University of Chicago's National Opinion Research Center (NORC). NORC is the oldest nonprofit, university-affiliated national survey research facility in the nation. It conducts the GSS through face-to-face interviews with an independently drawn, representative sample of 1,500 to 3,000 noninstitutionalized English-speaking persons aged 18 or older who live in the United States. The sample size for the 1996 survey, on which this book is based, was approximately 2,900 persons. The NORC took the first GSS in 1972 and then conducted it annually through 1994 (except for the years 1979, 1981, and 1992). It now conducts the survey every two years, and 1996 is the latest year for which data are available.

Until publication of the first edition of *American Attitudes* two years ago, social scientists and other researchers were the only ones with ready access to the wealth of information in the GSS, available only to those with the computing skills to mine the data. New Strategist's biennial publication of *American Attitudes* now gives the public regular access to this rich database. The book contains cross-tabulations—performed by the author—of the latest attitudinal data by sex, age, race, and education. Whenever possible, responses to the same attitudinal questions are shown at ten-year intervals back to the 1970s, allowing readers to see how attitudes have changed over the past two decades and to track attitudinal changes within 10-year age cohorts. The book also includes the author's insightful examination of why Americans think the way they do and how their opinions might change in the future.

American Attitudes is organized into nine chapters: Public Arena, Government and Politics, Race and Immigration, Religion, Work and Money, Marriage and Family, Women's Roles, Personal Outlook, and Sex and Morality. Each chapter includes tables and text describing the differences and similarities in the attitudes of Americans by demographic characteristic in 1996, 1986, and 1976. The author selected the questions presented in this book from the hundreds included in the GSS for their timeliness and ability to present a broad perspective on the attitudes of Americans toward the most important public and private issues. Not every question in the 1996 survey was also asked in the 1976 and 1986 surveys. In those cases, the author substituted responses from the closest available year. Although some were edited for space or clarity, the questions that appear above every table in the book are generally worded as they appear in the survey. GSS researchers have changed the wording of some questions over the years (for example, substituting "black" for "Negro"), but these changes do not affect the continuity of the results.

The GSS is an invaluable road map to American thought, but it is important to remember that the mental landscape can be foggy at times. Many factors, such as current events and the wording of questions, can influence opinion. Some attitudes and behaviors are notoriously hard to measure, such as those surrounding race and sexuality. Respondents may give answers they consider socially acceptable rather than honest responses. It is hard to know, for example, if everyone who answers yes to the abstract question, "Would you vote for a black presidential candidate?" would actually do so in the voting booth.

Nevertheless, a well-designed and properly executed survey, such as the GSS, minimizes these problems. And by looking at broad categories of Americans, it is possible to get a feeling for where we agree and disagree as a nation. The longitudinal nature of many of the survey questions offers an especially valuable look at how attitudes have changed over the past two decades and, by examining the attitudes of younger age groups, what the future may hold.

For more information about the General Social Survey, contact the National Opinion Research Center, University of Chicago, 1155 East 60th Street, Chicago, IL 60637; telephone (312) 753-7500. GSS data are also distributed by the Roper Center for Public Opinion Research, P.O. Box 440, Storrs, CT 06268; telephone (203) 486-4440.

About the Author

Susan Mitchell is a demographic writer, author, and consultant whose areas of expertise are demographics and social and consumer trends. Her books include *American Generations—Who They Are, How They Live, What They Think* (first and second editions), *Generation X: The Young Adult Market*, and *American Attitudes—Who Thinks What About the Issues That Shape Our Lives* (first and second editions).

Mitchell's articles on demographic trends have appeared in many publications, including *American Demographics, The Boomer Report, Marketing Tools, Natural Health, The Numbers News, Market:Europe*, and *American School Board Journal*. She is frequently cited as a trend expert in publications such as *The New York Times, The Wall Street Journal, Time, Money*, and *Entrepreneur*, and she has appeared on *The Today Show* and *The Oprah Winfrey Show* to discuss the baby-boom generation.

Mitchell is a graduate of the University of Wisconsin at Madison and was an adjunct faculty member and frequent guest lecturer in the sociology department at Ithaca College in Ithaca, NY. She lives in Clinton, Mississippi.

Chapter 1

The Public Arena

Everyone has an opinion about "public arena" issues—gun control, the death penalty, taxes, the environment, and so on. These opinions can be well-informed or seriously misinformed. Often, they are inflamed by the media or by politicians. Gun control is considered controversial, for example, but the public is remarkably united on this issue, and the overwhelming majority says people should have to obtain a police permit before buying a gun.

Concern about crime unites people on other issues as well. Most people support the death penalty and feel their local courts are not harsh enough on criminals. But most people would rather see a guilty person go free than an innocent person wrongly convicted.

As medicine pushes into new frontiers, Americans are facing difficult questions. About half of Americans think genetic screening will ultimately be beneficial, but one-quarter fear it will do more harm than good and one-quarter say they don't know what to think. Americans lean toward not allowing people to sell one of their kidneys for transplant, but there is much uncertainty about this issue. Although surrogate motherhood and physician-assisted suicide provoked tremendous debates when they first came to the attention of the public, majorities now favor allowing these practices.

Americans continue to be united in their concern for the environment. Majorities favor preventing development of areas inhabited by endangered species. They also believe that on some issues, including the environment, international bodies should have the right to enforce solutions.

Economic issues are still likely to provoke debate at a town meeting. The majority thinks income differences in the U.S. are too large. But Americans are divided on whether the rich pay too much or too little in taxes, although most believe those with middle and low incomes are overtaxed. The plurality of adults say our economic system just needs a little tinkering, but almost as many believe it needs fundamental changes. The jury is still out on NAFTA, with the largest percentage of people saying they don't know if it benefits the U.S. or not.

Americans believe the information government has about citizens, combined with computer technology that makes it possible to bring all this information together, poses a threat to individual privacy. One of the reasons for this belief may be the lack of confidence Americans have in their government. The vast majority has only some or hardly any confidence in Congress or the White House. Few have a great deal of confidence in these branches of government.

Most of the nation's major institutions do not fare much better. Fewer than one-quarter of Americans have a great deal of confidence in organized labor, the press, education, or major companies. They are divided, however, on whether organized labor has too much power or about the right amount. A plurality believes business and industry have too much power.

On most public-arena questions, men and women are near agreement, but they disagree in a few areas. Women feel more vulnerable to crime in their own neighborhoods and they are more in favor of requiring permits before people can purchase guns. Men are more likely to support the death penalty, but they are also more likely to believe it is worse to convict the innocent than to free the guilty.

Men have a lower opinion of politicians. They are more likely than women to say they have hardly any confidence in Congress and the executive branch. They are also more likely to have hardly any confidence in the press and in organized labor. This lack of trust is undoubtedly one reason why men are more likely to say labor unions are too powerful. Men have more confidence than women in the Supreme Court, the military, and the scientific and medical communities.

Gaps in opinion are much wider between blacks and whites than between men and women. Whites are more likely to support the death penalty and to believe the courts are not harsh enough on criminals. Whites are also more likely to support physician-assisted suicide and to believe genetic screening will do more good than harm.

Blacks are more likely than whites to say tax rates on low-income people are too high and to believe our economic system needs fundamental changes. Whites are more likely to have a great deal of confidence in the medical and scientific communities, the military, the Supreme Court, and major companies. Most blacks and whites say they have only some confidence in labor unions, but blacks are considerably more likely to say labor unions have too little power.

Different age groups often have different opinions about public arena issues. Different generations don't always see eye-to-eye on medical ethics, for example. The older people are, the less accepting they are of surrogate mothers and physician-assisted suicide. Older people are also more likely to believe labor unions have too much power. The proportion of people saying our economic system needs fundamental changes declines with age, however.

Generation Xers (under age 30) are more likely than older people to have a great deal of confidence in the medical and scientific communities and the military. Generations Xers and people aged 70 or older are more likely than other age groups to have a great deal of confidence in financial institutions, education, and organized labor.

Differences of opinion by education frequently find those with a college education disagreeing with people who have less education. College graduates are more likely than those with less education to say they have a great deal of confidence in the scientific community, the Supreme Court, and major companies. People who did not complete college are more likely to have hardly any confidence in Congress, the executive branch of the federal government, and banks and financial institutions. College graduates are more likely than those with less education to believe labor unions have about the right amount of power.

College graduates stand apart from those with less education on other issues as well. They are more likely to believe it is worse to convict an innocent person than to free a guilty one. They are more likely to believe our economic system is basically sound but in need of some minor changes, while those without a college degree are more likely to say the system needs fundamental changes. College graduates are also more likely to believe the practice of hiring surrogate mothers should be permitted.

On some issues, opinions change with rising levels of education. The proportion of people who favor gun control is lowest among those without a high school diploma, higher among high school graduates, and highest among college graduates. Similarly, both the proportion of those who say international bodies should have the right to enforce solutions to some of the world's problems and the percentage of those who say some environments should be protected from development rise with education. The percentage of those who say taxes on people with low incomes are too high, on the other hand, declines with rising levels of education.

Confidence in Leaders

Few of the nation's leaders inspire a great deal of confidence.

The confidence Americans have in their leaders is eroding. Most people say they have only some confidence in the leaders of the nation's major institutions. A minority (and in some cases, a very small minority) has a great deal of confidence in leaders.

Americans are most likely to say they have a great deal of confidence in the leaders of medicine, the scientific community, and the military. They have the least confidence in the executive branch of the federal government and in Congress.

Men are more likely than women to have a great deal of confidence in the Supreme Court, major companies, the scientific community, medicine, and the military. Men are also more likely than women to have hardly any confidence in the executive branch of the federal government, Congress, organized labor, and the press.

Blacks and whites assess some institutions very differently. Whites are far more likely than blacks to say they have a great deal of confidence in the scientific community, the military, the Supreme Court, and major companies. Blacks are more likely to have a great deal of confidence in education.

The youngest and the oldest adults are more likely than other age groups to have a great deal of confidence in various institutions. This is especially true for the military, banks and financial institutions, and education.

College graduates are considerably more likely than those with less education to have a great deal of confidence in the leaders of the scientific community, the Supreme Court, and major companies. People who did not complete high school are more likely to say they have a great deal of confidence in the military, education, the press, organized labor, and Congress.

Confidence in Leaders, 1996

"As far as the people running the following institutions are concerned, would you say you have a great deal of confidence, only some confidence, or hardly any confidence at all in them?"

(percent responding by sex, race, age, and education, 1996)

	executive branch of federal government			Congress			Supreme Court		
	great deal	only some	hardly any	great deal	only some	hardly any	great deal	only some	hardly any
Total	**10%**	**45%**	**42%**	**8%**	**46%**	**43%**	**28%**	**50%**	**17%**
Men	10	43	45	8	43	46	33	45	18
Women	10	46	39	7	49	40	24	54	16
Black	12	42	39	9	46	40	18	56	19
White	9	45	43	7	46	44	29	49	16
Aged 18 to 29	11	46	37	10	47	38	31	45	18
Aged 30 to 39	8	46	44	6	48	43	25	56	15
Aged 40 to 49	9	45	43	5	45	46	27	53	15
Aged 50 to 59	11	42	45	7	44	45	30	49	16
Aged 60 to 69	10	47	41	8	44	46	27	45	23
Aged 70 or older	15	40	38	11	47	36	30	44	13
Not high school grad.	14	38	38	13	36	41	25	38	21
High school graduate	9	42	46	7	45	46	24	53	19
Bachelor's degree	11	55	33	6	59	34	39	51	8
Graduate degree	12	54	32	7	54	38	47	40	10

(continued)

(continued from previous page)

	financial institutions			major companies			organized labor		
	great deal	only some	hardly any	great deal	only some	hardly any	great deal	only some	hardly any
Total	**25%**	**56%**	**16%**	**23%**	**59%**	**14%**	**11%**	**51%**	**29%**
Men	26	55	17	27	57	12	13	48	34
Women	24	57	16	20	61	15	10	53	25
Black	23	52	20	12	60	22	14	52	25
White	24	57	16	25	59	12	11	51	31
Aged 18 to 29	33	53	13	28	59	11	16	60	18
Aged 30 to 39	20	60	18	20	66	13	10	57	27
Aged 40 to 49	20	57	20	21	61	15	9	50	33
Aged 50 to 59	24	55	19	27	53	16	9	45	38
Aged 60 to 69	21	61	14	23	54	15	8	41	41
Aged 70 or older	35	48	12	22	54	13	14	40	29
Not high school grad.	28	47	17	18	49	21	18	44	22
High school graduate	24	56	18	22	62	13	11	53	28
Bachelor's degree	25	63	11	30	60	9	8	48	37
Graduate degree	32	52	13	32	53	13	5	48	40

	scientific community			medicine			education		
	great deal	only some	hardly any	great deal	only some	hardly any	great deal	only some	hardly any
Total	**39%**	**45%**	**7%**	**44%**	**45%**	**9%**	**23%**	**58%**	**18%**
Men	45	43	5	48	42	8	23	56	19
Women	34	46	9	41	48	9	22	59	17
Black	25	46	18	39	48	10	30	53	16
White	41	46	6	45	45	9	21	59	19
Aged 18 to 29	45	43	7	55	37	7	28	54	17
Aged 30 to 39	39	49	4	44	50	6	18	65	17
Aged 40 to 49	38	46	9	40	48	11	19	59	20
Aged 50 to 59	39	44	10	42	45	12	25	55	20
Aged 60 to 69	36	46	8	37	52	9	22	57	19
Aged 70 or older	35	37	9	44	41	11	31	50	16
Not high school grad.	30	35	14	49	36	11	35	46	17
High school graduate	35	49	8	44	46	9	22	58	19
Bachelor's degree	56	41	2	46	46	8	20	60	18
Graduate degree	53	41	2	44	47	8	19	65	14

(continued)

(continued from previous page)

	the press			the military		
	great deal	only some	hardly any	great deal	only some	hardly any
Total	**11%**	**48%**	**39%**	**37%**	**48%**	**11%**
Men	10	45	43	44	45	10
Women	11	50	35	32	51	12
Black	12	41	42	27	53	15
White	10	48	39	38	48	10
Aged 18 to 29	14	45	37	45	42	11
Aged 30 to 39	8	51	39	33	55	11
Aged 40 to 49	11	48	40	30	50	17
Aged 50 to 59	11	44	43	37	48	11
Aged 60 to 69	5	45	42	45	46	6
Aged 70 or older	13	49	30	41	46	6
Not a high school graduate	17	41	33	46	39	8
High school graduate	10	49	39	37	50	11
Bachelor's degree	9	52	39	36	50	12
Graduate degree	10	54	37	32	49	18

Note: Numbers may not add to 100 because "don't know" and no answer are not included.
Source: General Social Survey, National Opinion Research Center, University of Chicago

Confidence in the Executive Branch of Government

Confidence rises and falls with the popularity of the person who occupies the White House.

President Clinton may be riding high on his approval ratings despite the scandal surrounding him, but he has not been able to boost public confidence in government to the degree President Reagan did. Only 10 percent of Americans had a great deal of confidence in the executive branch of the federal government in 1996 compared with a much higher 21 percent in 1986. Fully 42 percent say they have hardly any confidence in the executive branch, up from 24 percent in 1986.

Forty-five percent of men say they have hardly any confidence in the executive branch of the federal government compared with 39 percent of women. Whites are more likely than blacks to say they have hardly any confidence in the executive branch—43 percent of whites compared with 39 percent of blacks.

People aged 70 or older are most likely to have a great deal of confidence in the executive branch (15 percent). People in their 30s are least likely to feel this way (8 percent).

High school graduates have a more negative view of the executive branch than do those with more or less education. Fourteen percent of people who did not complete high school (a disproportionate number of whom are older) have a great deal of confidence in the executive branch compared with 11 to 12 percent of college graduates and only 9 percent of high school graduates.

Confidence in the Executive Branch of Government, 1976 to 1996

"As far as the people running the executive branch of the federal government are concerned, would you say you have a great deal of confidence, only some confidence, or hardly any confidence at all in them?"

(percent responding by sex, race, age, and education, 1976–96)

	a great deal			only some			hardly any		
	1996	*1986*	*1976*	*1996*	*1986*	*1976*	*1996*	*1986*	*1976*
Total	**10%**	**21%**	**13%**	**45%**	**53%**	**58%**	**42%**	**24%**	**25%**
Men	10	22	16	43	52	56	45	24	26
Women	10	19	12	46	54	60	39	23	24
Black	12	15	3	42	47	53	39	34	40
White	9	21	14	45	54	59	43	22	24
Aged 18 to 29	11	24	11	46	54	65	37	20	22
Aged 30 to 39	8	18	14	46	55	61	44	26	23
Aged 40 to 49	9	19	11	45	58	63	43	22	22
Aged 50 to 59	11	20	16	42	55	55	45	23	26
Aged 60 to 69	10	20	15	47	50	51	41	26	30
Aged 70 or older	15	24	14	40	43	48	38	24	31
Not high school grad.	14	19	10	38	49	51	38	26	32
High school graduate	9	19	15	42	56	61	46	24	22
Bachelor's degree	11	30	14	55	49	72	33	19	13
Graduate degree	12	23	21	54	51	52	32	25	26

Note: Numbers may not add to 100 because "don't know" and no answer are not included.
Source: General Social Surveys, National Opinion Research Center, University of Chicago

Confidence in Congress

Congressional leaders inspire little confidence.

Only 8 percent of the public has a great deal of confidence in Congressional leaders. Fully 43 percent say they have hardly any confidence in Congress, while the plurality of 46 percent say they have only some confidence. The percentage of those who say they have hardly any confidence in Congress rose sharply between 1976 and 1996.

Men are more likely than women to have hardly any confidence in Congress (46 percent compared with 40 percent of women). Both men and women were far more likely to say this in 1996 than in 1976. There is only a slight difference in the percentages of blacks and whites who say they have hardly any confidence in Congress. But as is the case in all demographic segments, the percentages of those with hardly any confidence were higher in 1996 than in 1976.

Americans aged 70 or older and those under age 30 are less likely than others to say they have hardly any confidence in Congress (36 percent of those aged 70 or older and 38 percent of people under age 30 compared with 43 to 46 percent of other age groups).

People with a high school diploma or less education are more fed up with Congress than are college graduates. From 41 to 46 percent of people with a high school diploma or less education say they have hardly any confidence in Congress compared with 34 to 38 percent of college graduates.

Confidence in Congress, 1976 to 1996

"As far as the people running Congress are concerned, would you say you have a great deal of confidence, only some confidence, or hardly any confidence at all in them?"

(percent responding by sex, race, age, and education, 1976–96)

	a great deal			only some			hardly any		
	1996	**1986**	**1976**	**1996**	**1986**	**1976**	**1996**	**1986**	**1976**
Total	**8%**	**16%**	**14%**	**46%**	**61%**	**58%**	**43%**	**20%**	**25%**
Men	8	17	15	43	56	53	46	25	30
Women	7	15	13	49	64	62	40	17	22
Black	9	15	12	46	57	56	40	22	28
White	7	16	14	46	62	58	44	20	25
Aged 18 to 29	10	22	11	47	60	63	38	17	24
Aged 30 to 39	6	12	12	48	63	62	43	22	25
Aged 40 to 49	5	15	15	45	61	59	46	22	24
Aged 50 to 59	7	14	15	44	64	54	45	20	27
Aged 60 to 69	8	12	16	44	63	52	46	20	30
Aged 70 or older	11	21	17	47	53	52	36	20	25
Not high school grad.	13	20	14	36	53	53	41	21	27
High school graduate	7	15	14	45	62	60	46	21	25
Bachelor's degree	6	16	12	59	66	63	34	17	23
Graduate degree	7	15	13	54	68	61	38	16	26

Note: Numbers may not add to 100 because "don't know" and no answer are not included.
Source: General Social Surveys, National Opinion Research Center, University of Chicago

Confidence in the Supreme Court

The college educated are most likely to have a great deal of confidence in the Court.

Half of Americans say they have only some confidence in the Supreme Court, 28 percent say they have a great deal of confidence in the Court, and 17 percent have hardly any. While this isn't an overwhelming vote of confidence, the Supreme Court still enjoys a higher rating than both Congress and the executive branch of government.

Men are more likely than women to say they have a great deal of confidence in the Supreme Court (33 percent compared with 24 percent of women). Twenty-nine percent of whites, but only 18 percent of blacks, have a great deal of confidence in the nation's highest court.

By age, the proportions of those who say they have a great deal of confidence in the Supreme Court vary only slightly. Except for people aged 70 or older, the figures were lower in 1996 than in 1976.

The college educated are more likely than those with less education to say they have a great deal of confidence in the Supreme Court. Conversely, people who did not complete college are more likely to say they have hardly any confidence in the Court. Only 8 to 10 percent of college graduates have hardly any confidence in the Supreme Court compared with 19 to 21 percent of those with less education.

Confidence in the Supreme Court, 1976 to 1996

"As far as the people running the Supreme Court are concerned, would you say you have a great deal of confidence, only some confidence, or hardly any confidence at all in them?"

(percent responding by sex, race, age, and education, 1976–96)

	a great deal			only some			hardly any		
	1996	*1986*	*1976*	*1996*	*1986*	*1976*	*1996*	*1986*	*1976*
Total	**28%**	**30%**	**35%**	**50%**	**52%**	**43%**	**17%**	**14%**	**15%**
Men	33	36	39	45	47	41	18	14	16
Women	24	25	32	54	56	46	16	14	14
Black	18	22	30	56	49	47	19	19	14
White	29	31	36	49	53	43	16	13	16
Aged 18 to 29	31	39	38	45	48	48	18	10	10
Aged 30 to 39	25	30	33	56	55	45	15	13	16
Aged 40 to 49	27	29	33	53	54	47	15	14	17
Aged 50 to 59	30	27	39	49	52	40	16	18	14
Aged 60 to 69	27	22	35	45	58	35	23	15	22
Aged 70 or older	30	23	30	44	46	40	13	18	18
Not high school grad.	25	22	27	38	48	41	21	21	20
High school graduate	24	29	36	53	55	46	19	13	14
Bachelor's degree	39	43	50	51	47	38	8	8	9
Graduate degree	47	45	51	40	49	38	10	5	10

Note: Numbers may not add to 100 because "don't know" and no answer are not included.
Source: General Social Surveys, National Opinion Research Center, University of Chicago

Confidence in Banks and Financial Institutions

The oldest and the youngest adults have the most confidence in banks.

Americans have relatively little confidence in government and business, and banks are no exception. Only one-quarter say they have a great deal of confidence in the leaders of banks and financial institutions. More than half have some confidence while 16 percent have hardly any. In 1976, 39 percent said they had a great deal of confidence, and just 10 percent said they had hardly any.

The proportions of people who have a great deal of confidence, only some, and hardly any are similar by demographic characteristics with a few exceptions. People under age 30 and those aged 70 or older are more likely than other age groups to say they have a great deal of confidence in the leaders of banks and financial institutions. One-third of those under age 30 and 35 percent of people aged 70 or older have a great deal of confidence compared with only 20 to 24 percent of other age groups.

College graduates are less likely than those with less education to say they have hardly any confidence in banks and financial institutions. Eleven to 13 percent of college graduates have hardly any confidence compared with 17 to 18 percent of those with less education.

Confidence in Banks and Financial Institutions, 1976 to 1996

"As far as the people running banks and financial institutions are concerned, would you say you have a great deal of confidence, only some confidence, or hardly any confidence at all in them?"

(percent responding by sex, race, age, and education, 1976–96)

	a great deal			only some			hardly any		
	1996	*1986*	*1976*	*1996*	*1986*	*1976*	*1996*	*1986*	*1976*
Total	**25%**	**21%**	**39%**	**56%**	**60%**	**48%**	**16%**	**17%**	**10%**
Men	26	20	38	55	59	47	17	19	13
Women	24	22	41	57	60	48	16	16	8
Black	23	18	27	52	60	43	20	17	24
White	24	21	41	57	59	48	16	18	9
Aged 18 to 29	33	21	31	53	60	56	13	18	12
Aged 30 to 39	20	14	36	60	64	50	18	20	11
Aged 40 to 49	20	21	36	57	60	49	20	18	12
Aged 50 to 59	24	23	43	55	60	45	19	15	10
Aged 60 to 69	21	20	51	61	60	40	14	17	6
Aged 70 or older	35	31	50	48	49	37	12	14	6
Not high school grad.	28	23	41	47	55	45	17	16	9
High school graduate	24	19	39	56	61	49	18	19	10
Bachelor's degree	25	24	39	63	62	52	11	14	9
Graduate degree	32	21	38	52	61	48	13	16	15

Note: Numbers may not add to 100 because "don't know" and no answer are not included.
Source: General Social Surveys, National Opinion Research Center, University of Chicago

Confidence in Major Companies

Most people have only some confidence in the nation's big businesses.

The majority of Americans (59 percent) say they have only some confidence in the leaders of big business. About one-quarter have a great deal of confidence. While these figures do not indicate a high opinion of big business, they are an improvement over 1976. In that year, 22 percent of the public had hardly any confidence in major companies, a proportion that had dropped to 14 percent by 1996.

Men are more likely than women to say they have a great deal of confidence in major companies (27 percent compared with 20 percent of women). A similar gap existed in 1976.

Whites have more confidence in big business than do blacks. Only 12 percent of blacks say they have a great deal of confidence in major companies compared with 25 percent of whites. But 22 percent of blacks say they have hardly any confidence in the leaders of major companies compared with only 12 percent of whites.

Differences by age are not pronounced. People in their 50s and those under age 30 are more likely than other age groups to say they have a great deal of confidence in the people running major companies. In 1976, the middle aged were more likely than other age groups to feel confident.

College graduates are more likely than those with less education to say they have a great deal of confidence in the people running major corporations. Thirty to 32 percent of college graduates have a great deal of confidence in big business compared with 18 to 22 percent of those who did not complete college. Only 9 to 13 percent of people with at least a high school diploma say they have hardly any confidence in major companies compared with a higher 21 percent of people who did not graduate from high school.

Confidence in Major Companies, 1976 to 1996

"As far as the people running major companies are concerned,
would you say you have a great deal of confidence, only some confidence,
or hardly any confidence at all in them?"

(percent responding by sex, race, age, and education, 1976–96)

	a great deal			only some			hardly any		
	1996	*1986*	*1976*	*1996*	*1986*	*1976*	*1996*	*1986*	*1976*
Total	**23%**	**24%**	**22%**	**59%**	**62%**	**51%**	**14%**	**10%**	**22%**
Men	27	29	26	57	59	49	12	10	22
Women	20	21	18	61	64	53	15	10	21
Black	12	12	12	60	60	52	22	22	26
White	25	26	23	59	62	51	12	8	21
Aged 18 to 29	28	27	19	59	63	53	11	7	26
Aged 30 to 39	20	20	18	66	67	57	13	11	20
Aged 40 to 49	21	27	25	61	59	53	15	11	19
Aged 50 to 59	27	23	28	53	63	49	16	11	18
Aged 60 to 69	23	26	24	54	59	47	15	10	21
Aged 70 or older	22	22	21	54	53	44	13	11	22
Not high school grad.	18	17	18	49	57	45	21	17	26
High school graduate	22	25	22	62	65	54	13	8	21
Bachelor's degree	30	33	33	60	58	52	9	7	12
Graduate degree	32	34	26	53	60	57	13	5	15

Note: Numbers may not add to 100 because "don't know" and no answer are not included.
Source: General Social Surveys, National Opinion Research Center, University of Chicago

Confidence in Organized Labor

The oldest and the youngest Americans have more confidence in organized labor.

The proportion of Americans who say they have some confidence in the leaders of organized labor changed only slightly between 1976 and 1996, climbing from 47 to 51 percent. The proportion of those who say they have hardly any confidence in organized labor fell from 33 to 29 percent during those years.

One-third of men say they have hardly any confidence in organized labor compared with one-quarter of women. Thirty-one percent of whites, but only 25 percent of blacks, have hardly any confidence in union leaders.

Generation Xers (aged 18 to 29) and the older members of the World War II generation (aged 70 or older) are more likely than other age groups to have a great deal of confidence in organized labor. Sixteen percent of those under age 30 and 14 percent of those aged 70 or older have great confidence compared with 8 to 10 percent of other age groups.

The proportion of people who say they have a great deal of confidence in organized labor declines with education. Eighteen percent of people who did not complete high school have a great deal of confidence compared with 11 percent of high school graduates and just 5 to 8 percent of college graduates. Among the college educated, 37 to 40 percent have hardly any confidence in organized labor compared with 28 percent of high school graduates and 22 percent of those who did not complete high school.

Confidence in Organized Labor, 1976 to 1996

"As far as the people running organized labor are concerned, would you say you have a great deal of confidence, only some confidence, or hardly any confidence at all in them?"

(percent responding by sex, race, age, and education, 1976–96)

	a great deal			only some			hardly any		
	1996	1986	1976	1996	1986	1976	1996	1986	1976
Total	**11%**	**8%**	**12%**	**51%**	**47%**	**47%**	**29%**	**39%**	**33%**
Men	13	8	13	48	43	45	34	45	38
Women	10	8	10	53	50	50	25	35	29
Black	14	13	14	52	45	47	25	31	29
White	11	7	11	51	47	47	31	40	33
Aged 18 to 29	16	11	14	60	58	52	18	27	27
Aged 30 to 39	10	6	11	57	54	50	27	37	30
Aged 40 to 49	9	4	7	50	46	51	33	46	35
Aged 50 to 59	9	9	10	45	40	45	38	49	38
Aged 60 to 69	8	10	11	41	41	46	41	42	35
Aged 70 or older	14	8	14	40	31	33	29	44	39
Not high school grad.	18	12	14	44	44	42	22	32	30
High school graduate	11	8	11	53	48	51	28	40	32
Bachelor's degree	8	3	5	48	47	47	37	47	43
Graduate degree	5	3	10	48	51	49	40	44	41

Note: Numbers may not add to 100 because "don't know" and no answer are not included.
Source: General Social Surveys, National Opinion Research Center, University of Chicago

Confidence in Science

College graduates are most likely to have a great deal of confidence in science.

Confidence in the scientific community has slipped since 1976. In that year, 43 percent of Americans said they had a great deal of confidence in the leaders of the scientific community compared with 38 percent who had only some confidence. In 1996, however, 45 percent had only some confidence and 39 percent had a great deal of confidence.

Men are far more likely than women to have a great deal of confidence in the scientific community. Forty-five percent of men, but only 34 percent of women, have a great deal of confidence in science.

There is also a large difference in opinions by race. While 41 percent of whites say they have a great deal of confidence in the scientific community, only 25 percent of blacks concur. Fully 18 percent of blacks have hardly any confidence in the nation's scientists compared with only 6 percent of whites.

Not surprisingly, people with college degrees (many of whom are themselves working in the sciences) are much more likely than those with less education to say they have a great deal of confidence in the scientific community. Fully 53 to 56 percent of college graduates have a great deal of confidence compared with only 30 to 35 percent of people with a high school diploma or less education. Among those who did not graduate from high school, 14 percent say they have no confidence in the scientific community as do 8 percent of those with a high school diploma. Only 2 percent of college graduates share that view, however.

Confidence in Science, 1976 to 1996

"As far as the people running the scientific community are concerned, would you say you have a great deal of confidence, only some confidence, or hardly any confidence at all in them?"

(percent responding by sex, race, age, and education, 1976–96)

	a great deal			only some			hardly any		
	1996	*1986*	*1976*	*1996*	*1986*	*1976*	*1996*	*1986*	*1976*
Total	**39%**	**39%**	**43%**	**45%**	**47%**	**38%**	**7%**	**8%**	**7%**
Men	45	47	46	43	43	36	5	5	7
Women	34	33	40	46	50	39	9	9	7
Black	25	22	21	46	51	43	18	16	16
White	41	41	45	46	47	37	6	6	7
Aged 18 to 29	45	45	45	43	45	39	7	6	8
Aged 30 to 39	39	44	49	49	49	34	4	5	6
Aged 40 to 49	38	41	44	46	48	39	9	7	8
Aged 50 to 59	39	33	38	44	53	41	10	9	9
Aged 60 to 69	36	34	36	46	48	39	8	9	8
Aged 70 or older	35	27	38	37	42	34	9	14	7
Not high school grad.	30	24	33	35	50	36	14	15	10
High school graduate	35	40	44	49	48	41	8	6	7
Bachelor's degree	56	55	61	41	41	31	2	3	3
Graduate degree	53	55	62	41	41	33	2	3	2

Note: Numbers may not add to 100 because "don't know" and no answer are not included.
Source: General Social Surveys, National Opinion Research Center, University of Chicago

Confidence in Medicine

Confidence in medicine has declined, but still is relatively high.

The medical community enjoys more public confidence than any other major institution. This is not saying a lot, however, because only 44 percent of Americans say they have a great deal of confidence in the leaders of the medical community. In 1976, a 54 percent majority felt this way. The decline in confidence is evident in almost every demographic segment.

Forty-eight percent of men say they have a great deal of confidence in medicine, but among women, the proportion is a smaller 41 percent. Whites are more likely than blacks to say they have a great deal of confidence in the medical community (45 percent of whites compared with 39 percent of blacks). In 1976, the gap between blacks and whites was smaller.

People under age 30 are more likely than their elders to have a great deal of confidence in medicine. Over one-half of this age group (55 percent) has great confidence compared with 40 to 44 percent of people aged 30 to 59 and aged 70 or older. People in their 60s are least likely to have a great deal of confidence in medicine (37 percent).

Confidence in Medicine, 1976 to 1996

"As far as the people running medicine are concerned,
would you say you have a great deal of confidence, only some confidence,
or hardly any confidence at all in them?"

(percent responding by sex, race, age, and education, 1976–96)

	a great deal			only some			hardly any		
	1996	*1986*	*1976*	*1996*	*1986*	*1976*	*1996*	*1986*	*1976*
Total	**44%**	**46%**	**54%**	**45%**	**45%**	**35%**	**9%**	**7%**	**9%**
Men	48	51	56	42	42	33	8	6	10
Women	41	42	52	48	48	37	9	8	9
Black	39	40	52	48	47	33	10	10	13
White	45	46	54	45	45	35	9	7	9
Aged 18 to 29	55	56	60	37	37	32	7	6	7
Aged 30 to 39	44	48	58	50	46	36	6	5	5
Aged 40 to 49	40	42	55	48	51	34	11	7	11
Aged 50 to 59	42	38	48	45	50	45	12	11	5
Aged 60 to 69	37	42	47	52	47	36	9	9	16
Aged 70 or older	44	41	49	41	43	29	11	11	16
Not high school grad.	49	42	49	36	44	35	11	12	13
High school graduate	44	46	57	46	45	35	9	7	7
Bachelor's degree	46	48	57	46	50	34	8	1	9
Graduate degree	44	49	51	47	45	44	8	5	5

Note: Numbers may not add to 100 because "don't know" and no answer are not included.
Source: General Social Surveys, National Opinion Research Center, University of Chicago

Confidence in Education

Grades are falling for educational leaders.

Americans were less likely in 1996 than in 1976 to say they have a great deal of confidence in the nation's educational leaders. In 1996, only one-quarter of the public had a great deal of confidence in education compared with 37 percent in 1976.

Most people (58 percent) still have some confidence in the leaders of the nation's educational systems, however. Only 18 percent say they have hardly any confidence.

The loss of confidence in education has been greater among whites than blacks. In 1976, 37 percent of whites had a great deal of confidence in education, but by 1996, the proportion had fallen to just 21 percent. Blacks are more likely to have a great deal of confidence in education (30 percent), but the proportion is much lower than it was in 1976, when 40 percent had a great deal of confidence.

Parents of school-aged children are least likely to have a great deal of confidence in education. Only 18 to 19 percent of people aged 30 to 49 have a great deal of confidence in education. The oldest and the youngest adults are most likely to say they have a great deal of confidence. Thirty-one percent of people aged 70 or older and 28 percent of those under age 30 have a great deal of confidence in education.

Ironically, people who did not complete high school are the ones most likely to say they have a great deal of confidence in educational leaders. Thirty-five percent have a great deal of confidence compared with 19 to 22 percent of people with more education.

Confidence in Education, 1976 to 1996

"As far as the people running education are concerned, would you
say you have a great deal of confidence, only some confidence,
or hardly any confidence at all in them?"

(percent responding by sex, race, age, and education, 1976–96)

	a great deal			only some			hardly any		
	1996	1986	1976	1996	1986	1976	1996	1986	1976
Total	**23%**	**28%**	**37%**	**58%**	**60%**	**45%**	**18%**	**11%**	**15%**
Men	23	28	39	56	59	43	19	11	16
Women	22	27	36	59	61	46	17	10	15
Black	30	35	40	53	49	44	16	14	13
White	21	26	37	59	62	45	19	10	16
Aged 18 to 29	28	30	41	54	58	45	17	11	12
Aged 30 to 39	18	24	37	65	66	47	17	10	14
Aged 40 to 49	19	23	35	59	64	47	20	12	17
Aged 50 to 59	25	34	35	55	53	49	20	10	13
Aged 60 to 69	22	26	34	57	61	42	19	9	20
Aged 70 or older	31	30	37	50	53	36	16	12	19
Not high school grad.	35	30	40	46	54	39	17	12	17
High school graduate	22	27	35	58	62	48	19	10	15
Bachelor's degree	20	25	35	60	67	51	18	7	13
Graduate degree	19	29	44	65	58	43	14	13	11

Note: Numbers may not add to 100 because "don't know" and no answer are not included.
Source: General Social Surveys, National Opinion Research Center, University of Chicago

Confidence in the Press

The news media's confidence rating has gone from bad to worse.

In 1976, only 28 percent of Americans had a great deal of confidence in the people running the press. By 1996, the percentage was even lower, at 11 percent.

People who did not graduate from high school are most likely to have a great deal of confidence in the press. But even in this group, only 17 percent have a great deal of confidence. Among those with at least a high school diploma, only 9 to 10 percent have a great deal of confidence in the press.

While few men and women have a great deal of confidence in the press, men are more likely than women to say they have hardly any confidence in it. Thirty-five percent of women say they have hardly any confidence in the press, while the figure is a higher 43 percent for men.

People in their 30s and those in their 60s are least likely to say they have a great deal of confidence in the press. Only 5 percent of those in their 60s and 8 percent of those in their 30s feel this way. In other age groups, 11 to 14 percent have a great deal of confidence in the press.

Confidence in the Press, 1976 to 1996

"As far as the people running the press are concerned,
would you say you have a great deal of confidence, only
some confidence, or hardly any confidence at all in them?"

(percent responding by sex, race, age, and education, 1976–96)

	a great deal			only some			hardly any		
	1996	*1986*	*1976*	*1996*	*1986*	*1976*	*1996*	*1986*	*1976*
Total	**11%**	**18%**	**28%**	**48%**	**54%**	**52%**	**39%**	**25%**	**18%**
Men	10	20	29	45	51	50	43	28	19
Women	11	17	27	50	57	53	35	24	17
Black	12	20	28	41	49	48	42	27	18
White	10	18	28	48	55	52	39	25	18
Aged 18 to 29	14	19	32	45	54	48	37	25	18
Aged 30 to 39	8	21	31	51	54	52	39	25	15
Aged 40 to 49	11	18	29	48	58	50	40	23	19
Aged 50 to 59	11	16	22	44	56	56	43	26	19
Aged 60 to 69	5	16	29	45	53	53	42	30	15
Aged 70 or older	13	18	22	49	51	55	30	26	20
Not high school grad.	17	18	28	41	52	51	33	24	17
High school graduate	10	19	29	49	53	53	39	27	17
Bachelor's degree	9	18	30	52	60	47	39	20	20
Graduate degree	10	14	23	54	59	64	37	26	11

Note: Numbers may not add to 100 because "don't know" and no answer are not included.
Source: General Social Surveys, National Opinion Research Center, University of Chicago

Confidence in the Military

Americans still have some confidence in the military.

Although confidence in the leaders of many institutions has declined considerably, the military is holding its own. Americans were about as likely in 1996 as they were in 1976 to say they had a great deal of confidence in the nation's military leaders. But only 37 percent have this opinion, while the plurality of 48 percent say they have only some confidence in the military.

Men have more confidence in the military than women. Forty-four percent of men, but only 32 percent of women, have a great deal of confidence in the military. The percentage of women having confidence in the military has declined since 1976 and the gap between men and women has grown.

Whites are more likely than blacks to say they have a great deal of confidence in the military, as was true in 1976. While 38 percent of whites say they have a great deal of confidence in the military, only 27 percent of blacks do.

Baby boomers (aged 30 to 49) are less likely than other age groups to have much confidence in the military. Among 30-to-49-year-olds, only 30 to 33 percent say they have a great deal of confidence compared with 37 percent of those in their 50s and 41 to 45 percent of older and younger age groups.

Confidence in military leaders declines with education. While 46 percent of people who did not complete high school say they have a great deal of confidence, the proportion drops to 32 to 27 percent among those with more education. Only 8 percent of people who did not complete high school say they have hardly any confidence in military leaders but this share rises to 18 percent among those with graduate degrees. The differences in opinion between college graduates and those with less education was smaller in 1996 than in 1976, however.

Confidence in the Military, 1976 to 1996

"As far as the people running the military are concerned, would you say you have a great deal of confidence, only some confidence, or hardly any confidence at all in them?"

(percent responding by sex, race, age, and education, 1976–96)

	a great deal			only some			hardly any		
	1996	*1986*	*1976*	*1996*	*1986*	*1976*	*1996*	*1986*	*1976*
Total	**37%**	**31%**	**39%**	**48%**	**52%**	**41%**	**11%**	**14%**	**13%**
Men	44	34	43	45	52	39	10	14	14
Women	32	30	36	51	53	43	12	14	12
Black	27	34	30	53	43	45	15	15	16
White	38	31	40	48	54	41	10	13	13
Aged 18 to 29	45	35	35	42	50	44	11	14	19
Aged 30 to 39	33	26	38	55	54	44	11	18	13
Aged 40 to 49	30	26	41	50	57	42	17	14	11
Aged 50 to 59	37	37	45	48	51	39	11	10	8
Aged 60 to 69	45	33	40	46	54	36	6	10	12
Aged 70 or older	41	37	37	46	46	37	6	11	14
Not high school grad.	46	41	41	39	43	36	8	12	11
High school graduate	37	31	42	50	55	41	11	12	13
Bachelor's degree	36	24	28	50	54	51	12	20	16
Graduate degree	32	18	23	49	60	48	18	20	28

Note: Numbers may not add to 100 because "don't know" and no answer are not included.
Source: General Social Surveys, National Opinion Research Center, University of Chicago

Power of Business and Industry

The plurality of Americans believe business is too powerful.

Forty-four percent of Americans say business and industry have too much power, while 38 percent say they have about the right amount of power. These figures are essentially unchanged from 1985.

Men are slightly more likely than women to say business has too much power (47 percent compared with 41 percent of women), but 12 percent of women say they can't choose among too much, about right, and too little power. Similar proportions of blacks and whites say business is too powerful, but whites are more likely to say business and industry have about the right amount of power (40 percent compared with 30 percent of blacks). Blacks are more likely to say business has too little power (10 percent compared with 5 percent of whites).

The oldest and youngest adults are less likely than other age groups to feel business and industry have too much power. One-third of people aged 70 or older and 38 percent of those under age 30 hold this opinion. People aged 40 to 59 are most likely to believe business has too much power (49 to 50 percent).

Forty-three to 46 percent of people with at least a high school diploma believe business and industry have too much power. Among those who did not complete high school, only 36 percent agree. Fully 18 percent of this group say they can't choose.

Power of Business and Industry, 1996

"Do you think business and industry have too much power or too little power?"

(percent responding by sex, race, age, and education, 1996)

	far too much	too much	about right	too little	far too little	can't choose	too much, total	too little, total
Total	**11%**	**33%**	**38%**	**6%**	**0%**	**8%**	**44%**	**6%**
Men	12	35	38	7	1	4	47	8
Women	10	31	38	5	0	12	41	5
Black	11	32	30	9	1	13	43	10
White	11	33	40	5	0	8	44	5
Aged 18 to 29	11	27	43	8	0	7	38	8
Aged 30 to 39	9	35	39	7	0	7	44	7
Aged 40 to 49	13	37	33	6	0	7	50	6
Aged 50 to 59	13	36	34	5	1	7	49	6
Aged 60 to 69	10	31	43	4	1	7	41	5
Aged 70 or older	8	25	37	2	1	20	33	3
Not a high school graduate	8	28	34	8	1	18	36	9
High school graduate	11	33	38	6	0	8	44	6
Bachelor's degree	11	35	41	4	0	7	46	4
Graduate degree	13	30	38	6	1	4	43	7

Note: Numbers may not add to 100 because no answer is not included.
Source: General Social Survey, National Opinion Research Center, University of Chicago

Power of Business and Industry, 1985 to 1996

"Do you think business and industry have too much power or too little power?"

(percent responding by sex, race, age, and education, 1985–96)

	too much/ far too much		about right		too little/ far too little		can't choose	
	1996	1985	1996	1985	1996	1985	1996	1985
Total	**44**%	**43**%	**38**%	**40**%	**6**%	**4**%	**8**%	**10**%
Men	47	46	38	44	8	6	4	4
Women	41	41	38	38	5	4	12	15
Black	43	31	30	32	10	10	13	15
White	44	44	40	41	5	4	8	10
Aged 18 to 29	38	28	43	55	8	5	7	8
Aged 30 to 39	44	52	39	37	7	2	7	9
Aged 40 to 49	50	54	33	30	6	7	7	9
Aged 50 to 59	49	49	34	39	6	4	7	9
Aged 60 to 69	41	46	43	34	5	4	7	12
Aged 70 or older	33	30	37	41	3	9	20	17
Not a high school graduate	36	37	34	34	9	11	18	17
High school graduate	44	46	38	43	6	3	8	6
Bachelor's degree	46	45	41	37	4	1	7	14
Graduate degree	43	46	38	50	7	2	4	2

Note: Numbers may not add to 100 because no answer is not included.
Source: General Social Surveys, National Opinion Research Center, University of Chicago

Power of Labor Unions

Opinions about the power of unions have changed.

In 1985 more than half of Americans (59 percent) believed unions had too much power. By 1996, however, only 39 percent still felt this way. Thirty-four percent say unions have about the right amount of power, and 13 percent believe they have too little.

Forty-two percent of men say unions have too much power, down from 60 percent in 1985. Women are less likely to feel this way, with 36 percent saying unions are too powerful. But women are also less likely than men to believe unions have too little power (11 percent compared with 16 percent of men).

A large difference exists in the opinions of blacks and whites about the power of labor unions. Only 29 percent of blacks say unions have too much power compared with 40 percent of whites. Nearly one-quarter of blacks believe labor unions have too little power compared with only 12 percent of whites.

The proportion of people who say unions have too much power rises with age. Among people under age 50, 36 to 37 percent feel unions are too powerful, but this share rises to 44 percent among people aged 60 or older.

A plurality of college graduates (40 percent) believe labor unions have about the right amount of power, but only 33 percent of high school graduates and 28 percent of those who did not complete high school agree. Among people who did not graduate from college, pluralities believe unions have too much power.

Power of Labor Unions, 1996

"Do you think labor unions in this country have
too much power or too little power?"

(percent responding by sex, race, age, and education, 1996)

	far too much	too much	about right	too little	far too little	can't choose	too much, total	too little, total
Total	**14%**	**25%**	**34%**	**11%**	**2%**	**12%**	**39%**	**13%**
Men	17	25	34	13	3	6	42	16
Women	12	24	34	10	1	16	36	11
Black	12	17	31	20	3	15	29	23
White	14	26	34	10	2	11	40	12
Aged 18 to 29	14	23	37	13	1	11	37	14
Aged 30 to 39	8	28	37	9	3	13	36	12
Aged 40 to 49	14	23	34	13	3	11	37	16
Aged 50 to 59	19	22	32	10	4	9	41	14
Aged 60 to 69	18	26	26	16	2	10	44	18
Aged 70 or older	18	26	30	8	1	16	44	9
Not a high school graduate	13	27	28	11	1	18	40	12
High school graduate	15	24	33	12	3	11	39	15
Bachelor's degree	12	26	40	8	3	12	38	11
Graduate degree	13	18	40	17	1	6	31	18

Note: Numbers may not add to 100 because no answer is not included.
Source: General Social Survey, National Opinion Research Center, University of Chicago

Power of Labor Unions, 1985 to 1996

"Do you think labor unions in this country have
too much power or too little power?"

(percent responding by sex, race, age, and education, 1985–96)

	too much/ far too much		about right		too little/ far too little		can't choose	
	1996	*1985*	*1996*	*1985*	*1996*	*1985*	*1996*	*1985*
Total	**39%**	**59%**	**34%**	**25%**	**13%**	**7%**	**12%**	**7%**
Men	42	60	34	30	16	7	6	2
Women	36	59	34	22	11	7	16	10
Black	29	31	31	31	23	13	15	15
White	40	62	34	25	12	5	11	6
Aged 18 to 29	37	49	37	32	14	8	11	8
Aged 30 to 39	36	62	37	24	12	7	13	5
Aged 40 to 49	37	64	34	25	16	4	11	5
Aged 50 to 59	41	58	32	28	14	9	9	6
Aged 60 to 69	44	60	26	21	18	9	10	5
Aged 70 or older	44	65	30	17	9	4	16	12
Not a high school graduate	40	56	28	23	12	9	18	10
High school graduate	39	62	33	24	15	7	11	5
Bachelor's degree	38	53	40	34	11	2	12	7
Graduate degree	31	62	40	29	18	4	6	2

Note: Numbers may not add to 100 because no answer is not included.
Source: General Social Surveys, National Opinion Research Center, University of Chicago

Taxes on Low Incomes

A majority of Americans say those with low incomes pay too much in taxes.

Fully 59 percent of people believe taxes on those with low incomes are too high. Only 28 percent feel taxes on low-income people are about right.

Blacks are most likely to say taxes on the poor are too high. Seventy percent of blacks hold this view compared with 57 percent of whites. Fully 37 percent of blacks, but only 19 percent of whites, say taxes on those with low incomes are much too high. Twenty-nine percent of whites say tax rates for low-income people are about right compared with 17 percent of blacks.

The percentage of people who believe those with low incomes pay too much tax falls with education. Two-thirds of those who did not complete high school (and who are most likely to have low incomes) say the poor pay too much in taxes, but this figure drops to 50 to 54 percent among college graduates. Conversely, the proportion of those who say taxes on the poor are about right rises with education, from 18 percent of those who did not complete high school to 34 to 35 percent of college graduates.

Baby boomers (aged 30 to 49) are more likely than other age groups to believe taxes on people with low incomes are about right (30 to 32 percent). Least likely to concur are people in their 60s (21 percent). Two-thirds of them believe taxes on the poor are too high compared with 55 percent of baby boomers.

Taxes on Low Incomes, 1996

"Generally, how would you describe taxes in America today? We mean all taxes together, including Social Security, income tax, sales tax, and all the rest. For those with low incomes are taxes too high, about right, or too low?"

(percent responding by sex, race, age, and education, 1996)

	much too high	too high	about right	too low	much too low	too high, total	too low, total
Total	**22%**	**37%**	**28%**	**3%**	**1%**	**59%**	**4%**
Men	23	38	28	3	1	61	4
Women	21	36	27	4	1	57	5
Black	37	33	17	3	2	70	5
White	19	38	29	3	0	57	3
Aged 18 to 29	22	40	25	5	0	62	5
Aged 30 to 39	18	37	32	3	0	55	3
Aged 40 to 49	22	33	30	4	1	55	5
Aged 50 to 59	25	37	26	2	1	62	3
Aged 60 to 69	31	36	21	4	0	67	4
Aged 70 or older	21	39	24	1	1	60	2
Not high school grad.	27	39	18	3	0	66	3
High school graduate	23	37	26	4	1	60	5
Bachelor's degree	16	38	35	3	1	54	4
Graduate degree	18	32	34	4	0	50	4

Note: Numbers may not add to 100 because "can't choose" and no answer are not included.
Source: General Social Survey, National Opinion Research Center, University of Chicago

Taxes on Low Incomes, 1987 to 1996

"Generally, how would you describe taxes in America today? We mean all taxes together, including social security, income tax, sales tax, and all the rest. For those with low incomes are taxes too high, about right, or too low?"

(percent responding by sex, race, age, and education, 1987–96)

	too high/ much too high		about right		too low/ much too low	
	1996	*1987*	*1996*	*1987*	*1996*	*1987*
Total	**59%**	**66%**	**28%**	**25%**	**4%**	**4%**
Men	61	65	28	26	4	4
Women	57	67	27	24	5	4
Black	70	75	17	10	5	6
White	57	64	29	27	3	3
Aged 18 to 29	62	64	25	25	5	5
Aged 30 to 39	55	68	32	25	3	4
Aged 40 to 49	55	67	30	25	5	3
Aged 50 to 59	62	66	26	26	3	3
Aged 60 to 69	67	61	21	31	4	2
Aged 70 or older	60	66	24	20	2	2
Not a high school graduate	66	72	18	17	3	3
High school graduate	60	63	26	27	5	4
Bachelor's degree	54	64	35	27	4	3
Graduate degree	50	64	34	29	4	4

Note: Numbers may not add to 100 because "can't choose" and no answer are not included.
Source: General Social Surveys, National Opinion Research Center, University of Chicago

Taxes on Middle Incomes

People in their 50s are most likely to believe taxes on the middle class are too high.

Most Americans are in the middle income range, so it is no surprise that they are more likely to say taxes are too high for those with middle incomes than for the rich or the poor. Sixty-two percent of the public says taxes on those with middle incomes are too high, while 30 percent says they are about right.

Blacks are more likely than whites to believe taxes on the middle class are far too high (21 percent compared with 14 percent of whites). The proportion of whites saying this was lower in 1996 than in 1987, when 67 percent said people with middle incomes pay too much.

People under age 30 and those aged 70 or older are more likely than other age groups to say taxes on middle-income people are about right. They are less likely than other age groups to say taxes are too high. Those most likely to believe taxes for middle-income people are too high are people in their 50s—the age group of peak earnings. Fully 72 percent of those in their 50s say taxes for those in the middle are too high.

Taxes on Middle Incomes, 1996

"Generally, how would you describe taxes in America today? We mean all taxes together, including Social Security, income tax, sales tax, and all the rest. For those with middle incomes are taxes too high, about right, or too low?"

(percent responding by sex, race, age, and education, 1996)

	much too high	too high	about right	too low	much too low	too high, total	too low, total
Total	**16%**	**46%**	**30%**	**2%**	**0%**	**62%**	**2%**
Men	16	46	30	2	0	62	2
Women	15	46	29	2	0	61	2
Black	21	42	25	4	0	63	4
White	14	47	30	2	0	61	2
Aged 18 to 29	11	43	37	3	0	54	3
Aged 30 to 39	14	50	29	1	0	64	1
Aged 40 to 49	19	48	23	4	0	67	4
Aged 50 to 59	21	51	22	1	0	72	1
Aged 60 to 69	20	40	33	2	0	60	2
Aged 70 or older	11	39	36	1	0	50	1
Not high school grad.	18	40	26	2	0	58	2
High school graduate	15	47	31	2	0	62	2
Bachelor's degree	14	54	28	2	0	68	2
Graduate degree	22	43	28	2	0	65	2

Note: Numbers may not add to 100 because "can't choose" and no answer are not included.
Source: General Social Survey, National Opinion Research Center, University of Chicago

Taxes on Middle Incomes, 1987 to 1996

"Generally, how would you describe taxes in America today? We mean all taxes together, including Social Security, income tax, sales tax, and all the rest. For those with middle incomes are taxes too high, about right, or too low?"

(percent responding by sex, race, age, and education, 1987–96)

	too high/ much too high		about right		too low/ much too low	
	1996	1987	1996	1987	1996	1987
Total	**62%**	**66%**	**30%**	**27%**	**2%**	**2%**
Men	62	63	30	31	2	2
Women	61	69	29	23	2	2
Black	63	61	25	24	4	5
White	61	67	30	27	2	2
Aged 18 to 29	54	64	37	29	3	2
Aged 30 to 39	64	69	29	25	1	2
Aged 40 to 49	67	74	23	22	4	2
Aged 50 to 59	72	73	22	23	1	1
Aged 60 to 69	60	56	33	35	2	2
Aged 70 or older	50	56	36	30	1	2
Not a high school graduate	58	60	26	26	2	3
High school graduate	62	69	31	26	2	1
Bachelor's degree	68	66	28	32	2	0
Graduate degree	65	73	28	22	2	2

Note: Numbers may not add to 100 because "can't choose" and no answer are not included.
Source: General Social Surveys, National Opinion Research Center, University of Chicago

Taxes on High Incomes

Americans are divided on whether taxes on the rich are too high or too low.

Thirty-four percent of people believe taxes on the rich are too high, but a similar proportion (35 percent) say taxes on the rich are too low. In 1987, the 55 percent majority believed the rich paid too little in taxes.

People aged 60 or older are less likely than younger people to believe taxes on the rich are too high. Only 26 to 27 percent of this age group say the rich pay too much in taxes compared with 33 to 35 percent of people under age 40 or in their 50s. People in their 40s are most likely to believe the rich pay too much in taxes (38 percent).

People with graduate degrees are more likely than those with less education to believe taxes on the rich are too low. Forty percent believe the rich should pay more compared with 32 percent of people with bachelor's degrees and 32 percent of people who did not complete high school. Thirty-seven percent of high school graduates feel taxes on the rich are too low.

Taxes on High Incomes, 1996

"Generally, how would you describe taxes in America today? We mean all taxes together, including Social Security, income tax, sales tax, and all the rest. For those with high incomes are taxes too high, about right, or too low?"

(percent responding by sex, race, age, and education, 1996)

	much too high	too high	about right	too low	much too low	too high, total	too low, total
Total	**11**%	**23**%	**22**%	**27**%	**8**%	**34**%	**35**%
Men	12	24	23	26	9	36	35
Women	9	23	22	28	8	32	36
Black	16	19	20	27	8	35	35
White	10	24	22	27	9	34	36
Aged 18 to 29	12	21	22	29	7	33	36
Aged 30 to 39	9	26	21	28	8	35	36
Aged 40 to 49	12	26	18	29	6	38	35
Aged 50 to 59	12	22	22	28	10	34	38
Aged 60 to 69	8	18	30	24	15	26	39
Aged 70 or older	7	20	27	20	8	27	28
Not high school grad.	12	22	17	23	9	34	32
High school graduate	10	24	22	27	10	34	37
Bachelor's degree	9	29	26	25	7	38	32
Graduate degree	13	16	22	35	5	29	40

Note: Numbers may not add to 100 because "can't choose" and no answer are not included.
Source: General Social Survey, National Opinion Research Center, University of Chicago

Taxes on High Incomes, 1987 to 1996

"Generally, how would you describe taxes in America today? We mean all taxes together, including Social Security, income tax, sales tax, and all the rest. For those with high incomes are taxes too high, about right, or too low?"

(percent responding by sex, race, age, and education, 1987–96)

	too high/ much too high		about right		too low/ much too low	
	1996	1987	1996	1987	1996	1987
Total	**34%**	**17%**	**22%**	**21%**	**35%**	**55%**
Men	36	19	23	23	35	54
Women	32	17	22	20	36	56
Black	35	23	20	18	35	45
White	34	16	22	21	36	57
Aged 18 to 29	33	17	22	22	36	53
Aged 30 to 39	35	17	21	18	36	59
Aged 40 to 49	38	22	18	17	35	57
Aged 50 to 59	34	15	22	24	38	55
Aged 60 to 69	26	15	30	24	39	52
Aged 70 or older	27	17	27	24	28	48
Not a high school graduate	34	21	17	21	32	47
High school graduate	34	17	22	20	37	57
Bachelor's degree	38	17	26	23	32	57
Graduate degree	29	19	22	24	40	55

Note: Numbers may not add to 100 because "can't choose" and no answer are not included.
Source: General Social Surveys, National Opinion Research Center, University of Chicago

Are Income Differences Too Large?

Most people believe there is too large a gap between rich and poor.

The income disparity between the rich and the poor has grown over the last decade. As the disparity has grown, an increasing number of Americans believes the gap is too large. In 1987 over half of Americans (55 percent) said differences in income are too large, but by 1996 the figure had risen to 64 percent.

The proportions of those who say the gap is too large are similar for all demographic groups, ranging from 60 to 68 percent. Larger differences by demographic characteristics are found in the proportions of those who say they do not agree and those who neither agree nor disagree.

Men are more likely than women to say they do not believe income differences are too large (23 percent compared with 17 percent of men). People in their 50s (who are in their peak earning years) are more likely than the youngest and the oldest age groups to disagree that differences in income are too large. Twenty-three percent of people in their 50s feel this way compared with 18 percent of people under age 30 or over age 60.

Are Income Differences Too Large? 1996

"Differences in income in America are too large—do you agree or disagree?"

(percent responding by sex, race, age, and education, 1996)

	strongly agree	agree	neither	disagree	strongly disagree	agree, total	disagree, total
Total	**32%**	**32%**	**12%**	**12%**	**8%**	**64%**	**20%**
Men	31	31	12	11	12	62	23
Women	33	33	13	12	5	66	17
Black	33	29	10	12	9	62	21
White	31	33	13	12	8	64	20
Aged 18 to 29	28	38	14	11	7	66	18
Aged 30 to 39	33	31	14	12	8	64	20
Aged 40 to 49	32	33	12	13	8	65	21
Aged 50 to 59	35	29	12	12	11	64	23
Aged 60 to 69	32	36	9	8	10	68	18
Aged 70 or older	35	25	10	12	6	60	18
Not high school grad.	35	30	9	10	8	65	18
High school graduate	34	31	12	12	8	65	20
Bachelor's degree	22	39	14	13	9	61	22
Graduate degree	34	28	14	12	10	62	22

Note: Numbers may not add to 100 because "can't choose" and no answer are not included.
Source: General Social Survey, National Opinion Research Center, University of Chicago

Are Income Differences Too Large? 1987 to 1996

"Differences in income in America are too large—do you agree or disagree?"

(percent responding by sex, race, age, and education, 1987–96)

	agree		neither		disagree	
	1996	*1987*	*1996*	*1987*	*1996*	*1987*
Total	**64%**	**55%**	**12%**	**21%**	**20%**	**19%**
Men	62	53	12	21	23	23
Women	66	57	13	22	17	15
Black	62	60	10	18	21	15
White	64	55	13	22	20	19
Aged 18 to 29	66	52	14	26	18	19
Aged 30 to 39	64	59	14	19	20	19
Aged 40 to 49	65	49	12	23	21	23
Aged 50 to 59	64	54	12	22	23	21
Aged 60 to 69	68	56	9	19	18	17
Aged 70 or older	60	64	10	18	18	11
Not a high school graduate	65	59	9	16	18	16
High school graduate	65	56	12	23	20	17
Bachelor's degree	61	48	14	22	22	28
Graduate degree	62	56	14	21	22	19

Note: Numbers may not add to 100 because "can't choose" and no answer are not included.
Source: General Social Surveys, National Opinion Research Center, University of Chicago

Are the Courts Too Harsh?

Few people think their local courts are too hard on criminals.

Few topics concern Americans more these days than crime. Asked whether their local courts are too harsh or not harsh enough with criminals, more than three-quarters of Americans answer, not harsh enough. This opinion is not a recent development, however. In 1976 fully 81 percent of Americans felt their local courts were too easy on criminals.

People were slightly less likely in 1996 than in 1976 to say the courts are not harsh enough. In 1986, however, Americans were more likely to think the courts were not harsh enough. In the mid-1980s crime rates were rising rapidly and lawmakers were just beginning to respond with tougher sentencing laws.

Both blacks and whites are far more likely to say the courts are not harsh enough than to say the courts deal too harshly with criminals. Twelve percent of blacks, however, say the courts are too harsh compared with only 3 percent of whites. Blacks are disproportionately likely to be caught up in the criminal justice system, which may account for this difference of opinion.

It is important to note that substantial percentages of respondents volunteered that their local courts are "about right" in the handling of criminals. If the question included "about right" as a standard response choice, the percentage of those who say the courts are not harsh enough might have been lower.

Are the Courts Too Harsh? 1996

"In general, do you think the courts in this area deal too harshly
or not harshly enough with criminals?

(percent responding by sex, race, age, and education, 1996)

	too harshly	not harshly enough	about right*	don't know
Total	**5%**	**77%**	**11%**	**7%**
Men	5	77	11	6
Women	4	78	10	8
Black	12	71	9	7
White	3	79	11	7
Aged 18 to 29	7	75	9	8
Aged 30 to 39	6	79	9	6
Aged 40 to 49	3	78	13	5
Aged 50 to 59	6	75	12	7
Aged 60 to 69	2	83	9	6
Aged 70 or older	2	75	12	11
Not a high school graduate	7	75	10	7
High school graduate	4	80	9	6
Bachelor's degree	5	75	11	7
Graduate degree	6	66	20	8

Volunteered response.
Note: Numbers may not add to 100 because no answer is not included.
Source: General Social Survey, National Opinion Research Center, University of Chicago

Are the Courts Too Harsh? 1976 to 1996

"In general, do you think the courts in this area deal too harshly
or not harshly enough with criminals?"

(percent responding by sex, race, age, and education, 1976–96)

	too harshly			not harshly enough			about right*		
	1996	*1986*	*1976*	*1996*	*1986*	*1976*	*1996*	*1986*	*1976*
Total	**5%**	**3%**	**3%**	**77%**	**85%**	**81%**	**11%**	**8%**	**10%**
Men	5	4	3	77	85	82	11	8	10
Women	4	3	3	78	86	80	10	8	10
Black	12	9	9	71	77	76	9	9	7
White	3	2	3	79	87	81	11	8	10
Aged 18 to 29	7	6	7	75	81	71	9	9	13
Aged 30 to 39	6	4	3	79	85	83	9	7	8
Aged 40 to 49	3	1	2	78	87	83	13	9	12
Aged 50 to 59	6	2	2	75	91	83	12	5	8
Aged 60 to 69	2	2	1	83	89	86	9	7	8
Aged 70 or older	2	2	1	75	83	87	12	10	9
Not high school grad.	7	6	3	75	81	82	10	9	9
High school graduate	4	2	4	80	89	83	9	6	9
Bachelor's degree	5	3	2	75	82	74	11	10	14
Graduate degree	6	1	3	66	78	72	20	15	16

*Volunteered response.
Note: Numbers may not add to 100 because "don't know" and no answer are not included.
Source: General Social Surveys, National Opinion Research Center, University of Chicago

Death Penalty

Blacks are least likely to support the death penalty.

As concern about crime has grown, so has support for the death penalty. Seventy-one percent of the public supports the death penalty for persons convicted of murder, up from 65 percent in 1976.

There is some variation in the level of support for the death penalty by demographic characteristics. Men are far more likely than women to support the death penalty, as was the case in 1976. Seventy-nine percent of men, compared with 65 percent of women, favor executions.

The death penalty garners the least support among blacks. Only 50 percent of blacks favor the death penalty compared with 75 percent of whites. This gap is slightly larger than it was in 1976.

People aged 70 or older are less likely than younger people to support the death penalty. Only 63 percent of the oldest Americans favor executions compared with 70 to 72 percent of those aged 18 to 59 and 76 percent of people in their 60s.

High school graduates are more likely than people who did not complete high school and those with college degrees to support the death penalty. Three-quarters of people with just a high school diploma favor executions compared with 62 to 67 percent of people with more or less education.

Substantial percentages of people say they don't know whether they favor or oppose the death penalty, reflecting the difficulty Americans have reconciling their concerns about crime with ethical and moral beliefs. Blacks, the elderly, women, and people who did not graduate from high school are most likely to say they don't know whether they favor or oppose the death penalty.

Death Penalty, 1996

"Do you favor or oppose the death penalty for persons convicted of murder?"

(percent responding by sex, race, age, and education, 1996)

	favor	*oppose*	*don't know*
Total	**71%**	**21%**	**7%**
Men	79	17	5
Women	65	25	10
Black	50	37	12
White	75	18	7
Aged 18 to 29	72	22	6
Aged 30 to 39	72	20	8
Aged 40 to 49	70	24	7
Aged 50 to 59	72	21	6
Aged 60 to 69	76	16	8
Aged 70 or older	63	25	11
Not a high school graduate	66	24	10
High school graduate	75	18	7
Bachelor's degree	67	26	7
Graduate degree	62	31	7

Note: Numbers may not add to 100 because no answer is not included.
Source: General Social Survey, National Opinion Research Center, University of Chicago

Death Penalty, 1976 to 1996

"Do you favor or oppose the death penalty for persons convicted of murder?"

(percent responding by sex, race, age, and education, 1976–96)

	favor			oppose		
	1996	1986	1976	1996	1986	1976
Total	**71%**	**71%**	**65%**	**21%**	**23%**	**30%**
Men	79	79	72	17	17	24
Women	65	66	60	25	28	34
Black	50	43	41	37	47	54
White	75	75	68	18	20	28
Aged 18 to 29	72	71	58	22	23	39
Aged 30 to 39	72	70	68	20	28	27
Aged 40 to 49	70	69	69	24	25	28
Aged 50 to 59	72	78	68	21	20	26
Aged 60 to 69	76	73	69	16	19	25
Aged 70 or older	63	68	65	25	22	27
Not a high school graduate	66	66	61	24	26	32
High school graduate	75	74	71	18	21	25
Bachelor's degree	67	68	61	26	27	35
Graduate degree	62	69	48	31	28	48

Note: Numbers may not add to 100 because "don't know" and no answer are not included.
Source: General Social Surveys, National Opinion Research Center, University of Chicago

Convict the Innocent or Free the Guilty?

Most people would rather see the guilty go free than convict an innocent person.

There is always a great outcry from the public when someone thought to be guilty of a crime walks free. But most people would prefer that if the justice system makes a mistake, it err on the side of freeing the guilty rather than convict an innocent person. Sixty percent of the public say it is worse to convict an innocent person, and only 23 percent believe it is worse for a guilty person to go free. It is a difficult question for many however—15 percent say they can't choose.

The sharpest disagreement is found by education. More than three-quarters of college graduates say it is worse to convict an innocent person compared with only 50 to 57 percent of those with a high school diploma or less education. While more than one-quarter of those with no more than a high school diploma say it is worse to let a guilty person go free, only 12 to 13 percent of college graduates agree.

Women are more likely than men to say it is worse to free the guilty. Men are more likely to say it is worse to convict an innocent person. About three in five blacks and whites say it is worse to convict the innocent. Blacks are more likely than whites to say they can't choose, while whites are more likely than blacks to say it is worse to free the guilty than to convict the innocent.

The middle-aged (aged 40 to 59) are more likely than other age groups to believe it is worse to convict the innocent. There has been a pronounced shift in opinion since 1985, however, especially among those aged 50 or older. The proportion of those who say it is worse to convict the innocent fell while the proportion of those who say it is worse to free the guilty rose.

Convict the Innocent or Free the Guilty? 1996

"All systems of justice make mistakes, but which do you think is worse—
to convict an innocent person or let a guilty person go free?"

(percent responding by sex, race, age, and education, 1996)

	convict innocent	free guilty	can't choose
Total	**60%**	**23%**	**15%**
Men	65	20	13
Women	57	25	16
Black	61	16	20
White	60	24	14
Aged 18 to 29	59	25	14
Aged 30 to 39	61	24	14
Aged 40 to 49	63	20	14
Aged 50 to 59	63	18	17
Aged 60 to 69	56	31	11
Aged 70 or older	56	20	20
Not a high school graduate	50	27	20
High school graduate	57	25	16
Bachelor's degree	77	12	11
Graduate degree	73	13	10

Note: Numbers may not add to 100 because no answer is not included.
Source: General Social Survey, National Opinion Research Center, University of Chicago

Convict the Innocent or Free the Guilty? 1985 to 1996

"All systems of justice make mistakes, but which do you think is worse—
to convict an innocent person or let a guilty person go free?"

(percent responding by sex, race, age, and education, 1985–96)

	convict innocent		free guilty		can't choose	
	1996	*1985*	*1996*	*1985*	*1996*	*1985*
Total	**60%**	**60%**	**23%**	**21%**	**15%**	**17%**
Men	65	66	20	19	13	13
Women	57	56	25	22	16	20
Black	61	54	16	27	20	19
White	60	61	24	20	14	17
Aged 18 to 29	59	52	25	27	14	19
Aged 30 to 39	61	60	24	19	14	22
Aged 40 to 49	63	59	20	21	14	20
Aged 50 to 59	63	68	18	17	17	14
Aged 60 to 69	56	64	31	23	11	10
Aged 70 or older	56	67	20	15	20	13
Not a high school graduate	50	56	27	27	20	14
High school graduate	57	61	25	22	16	16
Bachelor's degree	77	63	12	12	11	26
Graduate degree	73	79	13	10	10	12

Note: Numbers may not add to 100 because no answer is not included.
Source: General Social Surveys, National Opinion Research Center, University of Chicago

Afraid in Own Neighborhood?

Women, blacks, and the elderly are most likely to be afraid in their own neighborhoods.

Fear of crime is both objective and subjective. People who live in high-crime neighborhoods (as many of the poor do) have reason to be afraid. But even if they live in relatively safe neighborhoods, many people are still fearful because they feel personally vulnerable.

Forty-two percent of Americans say there is an area within a mile of their homes where they would be afraid to walk alone at night. The oldest Americans are more likely to feel this way than younger people (56 percent of those aged 70 or older compared with 39 to 41 percent of younger people). Many older people undoubtedly feel physically vulnerable and less able to defend themselves.

Many women, like the elderly, also feel vulnerable to crime. Over half of women (55 percent) are afraid to walk at night in their neighborhood. In contrast, only 26 percent of men have this fear.

Blacks, who are disproportionately likely to be poor, are more likely than whites to be afraid to walk at night in their neighborhood. Over half of blacks (56 percent) say this compared with 40 percent of whites.

Afraid in Own Neighborhood? 1996

"Is there any area right around here—that is, within a mile—
where you would be afraid to walk alone at night?"

(percent responding by sex, race, age, and education, 1996)

	yes	*no*
Total	**42%**	**57%**
Men	26	74
Women	55	44
Black	56	44
White	40	59
Aged 18 to 29	40	60
Aged 30 to 39	40	59
Aged 40 to 49	40	58
Aged 50 to 59	39	60
Aged 60 to 69	41	57
Aged 70 or older	56	41
Not a high school graduate	46	52
High school graduate	42	58
Bachelor's degree	37	62
Graduate degree	40	59

Note: Numbers may not add to 100 because "don't know" and no answer are not included.
Source: General Social Survey, National Opinion Research Center, University of Chicago

Afraid in Own Neighborhood? 1976 to 1996

"Is there any area right around here—that is, within a mile—
where you would be afraid to walk alone at night?"

(percent responding by sex, race, age, and education, 1976–96)

	yes			no		
	1996	*1985*	*1976*	*1996*	*1985*	*1976*
Total	**42%**	**40%**	**44%**	**57%**	**59%**	**56%**
Men	26	20	23	74	80	77
Women	55	56	61	44	42	39
Black	56	62	48	44	36	51
White	40	37	43	59	62	56
Aged 18 to 29	40	39	41	60	60	59
Aged 30 to 39	40	34	40	59	66	60
Aged 40 to 49	40	34	41	58	65	58
Aged 50 to 59	39	39	47	60	61	53
Aged 60 to 69	41	42	44	57	57	55
Aged 70 or older	56	60	56	41	37	43
Not a high school graduate	46	51	48	52	47	52
High school graduate	42	37	45	58	62	55
Bachelor's degree	37	39	31	62	61	69
Graduate degree	40	18	38	59	82	62

Note: Numbers may not add to 100 because "don't know" and no answer are not included.
Source: General Social Surveys, National Opinion Research Center, University of Chicago

Gun Control

The overwhelming majority of Americans favor requiring a permit to purchase a gun.

Americans clearly support requiring a police permit for anyone purchasing a gun. Fully 80 percent favor this kind of restriction on guns, up from 71 percent in 1976. The percentage of people who favor gun permits has grown since 1976 in all demographic segments.

Women are far more supportive of gun control than men. The rift between men and women was also evident in 1976. Since then, greater numbers of both men and women have come to support this form of gun control, but fully one-quarter of men still oppose gun permits compared with only 11 percent of women.

Strong majorities of all age groups support requiring a police permit to purchase a gun. The level of support for gun permits rises with education, however, with 83 to 84 percent of college graduates saying they favor gun permits compared with 75 percent of people who did not complete high school and 80 percent of those with only a high school diploma.

Gun Control, 1996

"Would you favor or oppose a law which would require a person
to obtain a police permit before he or she could buy a gun?"

(percent responding by sex, race, age, and education, 1996)

	favor	*oppose*
Total	**80%**	**18%**
Men	73	25
Women	86	11
Black	81	15
White	79	19
Aged 18 to 29	77	22
Aged 30 to 39	83	14
Aged 40 to 49	82	16
Aged 50 to 59	79	20
Aged 60 to 69	79	19
Aged 70 or older	81	17
Not a high school graduate	75	21
High school graduate	80	17
Bachelor's degree	84	15
Graduate degree	83	15

Note: Numbers may not add to 100 because "don't know" and no answer are not included.
Source: General Social Survey, National Opinion Research Center, University of Chicago

Gun Control, 1976 to 1996

"Would you favor or oppose a law which would require a person to obtain a police permit before he or she could buy a gun?"

(percent responding by sex, race, age, and education, 1976–96)

	favor			oppose		
	1996	*1985*	*1976*	*1996*	*1985*	*1976*
Total	**80%**	**73%**	**71%**	**18%**	**26%**	**27%**
Men	73	67	64	25	32	35
Women	86	78	77	11	20	20
Black	81	73	72	15	25	23
White	79	73	71	19	26	27
Aged 18 to 29	77	75	72	22	25	26
Aged 30 to 39	83	76	73	14	24	25
Aged 40 to 49	82	66	73	16	33	26
Aged 50 to 59	79	73	67	20	25	32
Aged 60 to 69	79	72	70	19	27	29
Aged 70 or older	81	74	72	17	21	26
Not a high school graduate	75	70	68	21	27	30
High school graduate	80	72	71	17	27	27
Bachelor's degree	84	80	79	15	20	20
Graduate degree	83	78	72	15	22	28

Note: Numbers may not add to 100 because "don't know" and no answer are not included.
Source: General Social Surveys, National Opinion Research Center, University of Chicago

Should Marijuana Be Legal?

Most people believe marijuana should not be legalized.

Sentiment for legalizing marijuana fell during the late 1970s and early 1980s but had risen back to 1976 levels by 1996. Slightly more than two-thirds of the public said marijuana should not be legal in both 1976 and 1996, a considerably smaller share than the 80 percent who felt this way in 1986.

Generational differences have always been evident on this issue, but the gap is smaller now than it was 20 years ago. In 1976 half of people under age 30 thought marijuana should be legal compared with only 10 percent of those aged 70 or older. In 1996, just 31 percent of people aged 18 to 39 said marijuana should be legal compared with 14 to 15 percent of those aged 60 or older.

Two-thirds of men say marijuana should remain illegal compared with a slightly larger 72 percent of women. Thirty percent of men, but only 22 percent of women, believe marijuana should be legalized.

People with less education are more likely to believe marijuana should continue to be illegal. Seventy-three percent of people who did not complete high school feel this way, a proportion that drops to 64 percent among those with graduate degrees.

Should Marijuana Be Legal? 1996

"Do you think the use of marijuana should be made legal or not?"

(percent responding by sex, race, age, and education, 1996)

	should	should not	don't know
Total	**26%**	**69%**	**5%**
Men	30	66	4
Women	22	72	6
Black	23	68	9
White	26	69	5
Aged 18 to 29	31	65	4
Aged 30 to 39	31	64	5
Aged 40 to 49	26	70	4
Aged 50 to 59	27	66	7
Aged 60 to 69	14	83	4
Aged 70 or older	15	78	7
Not a high school graduate	21	73	6
High school graduate	25	71	4
Bachelor's degree	28	67	5
Graduate degree	27	64	9

Note: Numbers may not add to 100 because no answer is not included.
Source: General Social Survey, National Opinion Research Center, University of Chicago

Should Marijuana Be Legal? 1976 to 1996

"Do you think the use of marijuana should be made legal or not?"

(percent responding by sex, race, age, and education, 1976–96)

	should			should not		
	1996	*1986*	*1976*	*1996*	*1986*	*1976*
Total	**26%**	**18%**	**28%**	**69%**	**80%**	**69%**
Men	30	23	32	66	74	63
Women	22	14	24	72	84	73
Black	23	21	34	68	74	60
White	26	18	27	69	80	70
Aged 18 to 29	31	26	50	65	71	46
Aged 30 to 39	31	26	28	64	72	69
Aged 40 to 49	26	10	21	70	89	76
Aged 50 to 59	27	10	14	66	86	84
Aged 60 to 69	14	16	23	83	83	71
Aged 70 or older	15	9	10	78	89	87
Not a high school graduate	21	13	19	73	84	78
High school graduate	25	18	29	71	80	68
Bachelor's degree	28	24	39	67	73	55
Graduate degree	27	23	54	64	78	43

Note: Numbers may not add to 100 because "don't know" and no answer are not included.
Source: General Social Surveys, National Opinion Research Center, University of Chicago

Physician-Assisted Suicide

Support for physician-assisted suicide for the terminally ill has grown.

Support for allowing the incurably ill to hasten the end of their lives has grown over the past few decades. The majority of Americans (68 percent) favor giving the incurably ill the option of having a doctor end their lives. This is a larger majority than the 59 percent who favored it in 1977.

Blacks, the elderly, and people who did not complete high school are not as willing as others to allow doctors to end the life of a terminally ill patient, however. Nearly half of blacks do not believe physicians should be allowed to help the terminally ill end their lives if they so wish, while 47 percent say it should be permitted. Historical experiences, such as the Tuskegee Syphilis Experiment—in which blacks with syphilis were not treated so that physicians could observe the progression of the disease—have left many blacks suspicious that practices such as physician-assisted suicide will be used against them.

Among people aged 60 or older, 57 to 61 percent support physician-assisted suicide compared with a higher 68 to 70 percent of people aged 30 to 59 and 75 percent of those aged 18 to 30. Between 1977 and 1996, Americans of all ages grew more supportive of physician-assisted suicide.

Support for physician-assisted suicide is lower among people who did not complete high school (a group in which older Americans are overrepresented). Only 55 percent of people without a high school diploma believe doctors should be able to end the life of a terminally ill patient if patient and family request it. This compares with 69 to 76 percent of those with at least a high school diploma.

Physician-Assisted Suicide, 1996

"When a person has a disease that cannot be cured, do you think doctors should be allowed by law to end the patient's life by some painless means if the patient and his family request it?"

(percent responding by sex, race, age, and education, 1996)

	yes	no
Total	**68%**	**28%**
Men	72	24
Women	65	31
Black	47	49
White	71	25
Aged 18 to 29	75	23
Aged 30 to 39	68	28
Aged 40 to 49	68	28
Aged 50 to 59	70	26
Aged 60 to 69	61	35
Aged 70 or older	57	35
Not a high school graduate	55	40
High school graduate	69	26
Bachelor's degree	76	23
Graduate degree	69	27

Note: Numbers may not add to 100 because "don't know" and no answer are not included.
Source: General Social Survey, National Opinion Research Center, University of Chicago

Physician-Assisted Suicide, 1977 to 1996

"When a person has a disease that cannot be cured, do you think doctors should be allowed by law to end the patient's life by some painless means if the patient and his family request it?"

(percent responding by sex, race, age, and education, 1977–96)

	yes			no		
	1996	**1986**	**1977**	**1996**	**1986**	**1977**
Total	**68%**	**66%**	**59%**	**28%**	**30%**	**36%**
Men	72	71	65	24	25	31
Women	65	62	55	31	35	39
Black	47	50	36	49	44	57
White	71	68	62	25	29	33
Aged 18 to 29	75	73	70	23	23	26
Aged 30 to 39	68	71	60	28	27	37
Aged 40 to 49	68	68	57	28	30	40
Aged 50 to 59	70	57	58	26	36	37
Aged 60 to 69	61	61	55	35	35	40
Aged 70 or older	57	53	45	35	41	43
Not a high school graduate	55	60	52	40	34	40
High school graduate	69	67	62	26	30	34
Bachelor's degree	76	70	61	23	23	34
Graduate degree	69	66	74	27	31	24

Note: Numbers may not add to 100 because "don't know" and no answer are not included.
Source: General Social Surveys, National Opinion Research Center, University of Chicago

Best Way to Assign Donor Organs

Eight in 10 people believe organs should go to those who have waited the longest.

The great majority of Americans (80 percent) believe scarce donor organs should go to the person who has been waiting the longest. Few believe organs should be auctioned to the highest bidder, assigned by lottery, or given to the person who can make the greatest contribution to society.

College graduates are more likely than those with less education to say donor organs should be assigned by lottery (10 to 11 percent compared with 2 to 5 percent of those with less education). People with a high school diploma are most likely to say organs should be given to those longest on the waiting list (83 percent compared with 79 percent of those without a high school diploma and 70 to 75 percent of college graduates).

Women are more likely than men to say organs should be assigned on a first-come, first-served basis (82 percent compared with 76 percent of men). Nearly equal proportions of blacks and whites say patients who have been waiting the longest should get donor organs.

Best Way to Assign Donor Organs, 1996

"When only one organ is available and several patients need it for survival, which of several procedures should be used to assign the organ: By auction (the organ is assigned to the patient who can pay the most for it); by first come, first served (assigned to the patient who has been waiting the longest); by lottery (assigned to a patient drawn at random); by merit (assigned to the patient who can make the greatest contribution to others and society)?"

(percent responding by sex, race, age, and education, 1996)

	auction	first come, first served	lottery	merit
Total	1%	80%	6%	8%
Men	2	76	7	10
Women	1	82	5	7
Black	2	79	4	6
White	1	80	6	9
Aged 18 to 29	1	81	6	9
Aged 30 to 39	1	82	6	7
Aged 40 to 49	2	81	5	7
Aged 50 to 59	1	75	10	7
Aged 60 to 69	1	82	6	6
Aged 70 or older	2	72	2	15
Not a high school graduate	1	79	2	10
High school graduate	1	83	5	7
Bachelor's degree	2	75	11	9
Graduate degree	1	70	10	9

Note: Numbers may not add to 100 because "don't know" and no answer are not included.
Source: General Social Survey, National Opinion Research Center, University of Chicago

Should People Be Allowed to Sell Kidneys?

Americans aren't ready to create a free market in kidneys.

The plurality of Americans (44 percent) say people with two healthy kidneys should definitely or probably not be allowed to sell one of them for transplant. About one-third say they probably or definitely should be allowed to sell a kidney.

Men are more inclined than women to believe people should probably or definitely be allowed to sell a kidney (38 percent compared with 31 percent of women). Blacks are more likely than whites to say it definitely should not be allowed (36 percent compared with 30 percent of whites).

Young adults (under age 30) are the only demographic segment in which more people say yes than no to selling kidneys. Only 30 percent of 18-to-29-year-olds believe selling a kidney definitely or probably should not be allowed, while 46 percent say it probably or definitely should be allowed. Over half of people in their 50s and 60s say selling kidneys definitely or probably should not be allowed, as do 42 to 47 percent of people aged 30 to 49 and 60 or older.

Should People Be Allowed to Sell a Kidney? 1996

"A body organ that is much in need and that people may contribute are kidneys. Most people can live with only one kidney, though their chances of survival are better if they have two. Do you believe that people with two healthy kidneys should be permitted to sell a kidney to a hospital or organ center to use for transplants?"

(percent responding by sex, race, age, and education, 1996)

	definitely not	probably not	perhaps	probably	definitely
Total	**31%**	**13%**	**17%**	**16%**	**18%**
Men	30	13	15	18	20
Women	31	13	19	14	17
Black	36	10	14	17	17
White	30	14	17	16	19
Aged 18 to 29	20	10	22	22	24
Aged 30 to 39	27	15	21	14	20
Aged 40 to 49	34	13	16	17	16
Aged 50 to 59	39	14	14	15	12
Aged 60 to 69	41	13	12	16	15
Aged 70 or older	34	11	13	11	19
Not a high school graduate	39	11	9	18	14
High school graduate	29	12	20	16	19
Bachelor's degree	28	17	19	15	19
Graduate degree	30	17	14	17	19

Note: Numbers may not add to 100 because "don't know" and no answer are not included.
Source: General Social Survey, National Opinion Research Center, University of Chicago

Genetic Screening

One-quarter of Americans don't know if genetic screening is helpful or harmful.

Half of Americans say they believe genetic screening will do more good than harm. One-quarter believe it will do more harm than good, while the remaining one-quarter say they just don't know.

Whites are more confident than blacks that genetic screening will ultimately be beneficial. Over half of whites (54 percent) say it will do more good than harm compared with 42 percent of blacks. But whites are also more likely to say genetic screening, on balance, will be harmful while blacks are far more likely to say they don't know yet.

Half of people aged 70 or older say they don't know what effects genetic screening will have. People under age 30 and those aged 50 to 69 are most likely to believe genetic screening will do more good than harm. While 57 to 58 percent of these age groups say genetic screening will be beneficial, only 48 to 50 percent of baby boomers (aged 30 to 49) agree. The proportion drops to 37 percent among people aged 70 or older.

College graduates are more likely than those with less education to say genetic screening will be beneficial. But the proportion of those who say it will be harmful also rises with education. The less education people have, the more likely they are to say they don't know whether genetic screening will be helpful or harmful.

Genetic Screening, 1996

"Some people say that genetic screening is a wonderful medical advance. Others think it may cause trouble. Based on what you know, do you think genetic screening will do more good than harm or more harm than good?"

(percent responding by sex, race, age, and education, 1996)

	more good than harm	more harm than good	don't know
Total	**51%**	**24%**	**25%**
Men	49	28	23
Women	53	21	27
Black	42	19	39
White	54	25	22
Aged 18 to 29	57	22	22
Aged 30 to 39	50	27	23
Aged 40 to 49	48	29	23
Aged 50 to 59	58	23	18
Aged 60 to 69	57	19	24
Aged 70 or older	37	12	51
Not a high school graduate	49	13	38
High school graduate	50	25	26
Bachelor's degree	61	24	15
Graduate degree	54	34	11

Note: Numbers may not add to 100 because "don't know" is not included.
Source: General Social Survey, National Opinion Research Center, University of Chicago

Surrogate Mothers

Most Americans have gotten used to the idea of surrogate mothers.

New technologies give rise to new questions. While the practice of hiring a woman to bear a child for a couple unable to have children ignited controversy when it first began, most Americans now accept it. Sixty percent say the practice of paying women to be surrogate mothers should be permitted. Only 32 percent believe it should be illegal.

While the solid majority (63 percent) of whites believe hiring a surrogate to carry a child should be permitted, blacks are divided on this issue. Forty-five percent of blacks say the practice should be forbidden while 47 percent say it should be permitted.

Younger generations are more comfortable with surrogate mothers than are older people. The proportion of those who say it should be illegal rises with age from only 24 percent among people aged 18 to 29 to 46 percent among those aged 70 or older. Among the oldest age group, 11 percent say they don't know if it should be permitted or outlawed.

People who did not complete high school are divided on the question of surrogate mothers; 47 percent say it should be forbidden and 43 percent say it should be permitted. The majority of those with at least a high school diploma believe the practice of hiring a surrogate mother should be permitted.

Surrogate Mothers, 1996

"Recently, some married couples who are unable to have children have paid women, called 'surrogate mothers,' to bear a child for them. When the child is born, the couple becomes its adoptive parents and the surrogate mother receives a fee. Do you think this practice should be permitted or forbidden under the law?"

(percent responding by sex, race, age, and education, 1996)

	forbid it	permit it	don't know
Total	**32%**	**60%**	**7%**
Men	30	63	7
Women	34	59	7
Black	45	47	7
White	30	63	7
Aged 18 to 29	24	69	7
Aged 30 to 39	28	64	7
Aged 40 to 49	31	63	6
Aged 50 to 59	36	57	6
Aged 60 to 69	42	50	8
Aged 70 or older	46	43	11
Not a high school graduate	47	43	10
High school graduate	32	61	7
Bachelor's degree	24	69	7
Graduate degree	27	67	6

Note: Numbers may not add to 100 because no answer is not included.
Source: General Social Survey, National Opinion Research Center, University of Chicago

Privacy and Personal Information

Concerns are growing about maintaining privacy in a high-tech age.

The government has access to a wealth of information about Americans from many different sources. Computer technology makes it easy to bring all that information together and build a dossier on individuals. Increasingly, Americans view this as a threat to their privacy. Thirty-six percent of Americans believe the federal government's ability to compile information about them poses a very serious threat to individual privacy, up from 29 percent in 1985. The proportion of those who say it is not a serious threat or not a threat at all fell from 34 percent in 1985 to 23 percent in 1996.

Two-thirds of Americans say it is a very serious or fairly serious threat to privacy. Blacks are more likely than whites to say personal information collected by the government is a very serious threat to privacy (46 percent compared with 35 percent of whites).

Younger generations are more comfortable with new technologies, which may be why young adults are less likely than older Americans to feel that their privacy is threatened. Only 29 percent of people aged 18 to 39 believe the government's ability to collect and combine information about people is a serious threat to privacy. The proportion rises to 37 percent among people in their 40s, however, and to 45 to 46 percent among people aged 50 or older.

Thirty-seven percent of people with a high school diploma or less education believe the combination of information and technology represents a very serious threat to privacy, as do 39 percent of people with graduate degrees. But people with bachelor's degrees are less likely to feel this way (27 percent).

Privacy and Personal Information, 1996

"The federal government has a lot of different pieces of information about people which computers can bring together very quickly. Is this a very serious threat to individual privacy, a fairly serious threat, not a serious threat, or not a threat at all to individual privacy?"

(percent responding by sex, race, age, and education, 1996)

	very serious threat	fairly serious threat	not a serious threat	not a threat at all	can't choose
Total	**36%**	**32%**	**19%**	**4%**	**7%**
Men	35	32	21	4	6
Women	37	31	18	4	8
Black	46	22	14	5	12
White	35	33	20	4	6
Aged 18 to 29	29	33	25	3	9
Aged 30 to 39	29	37	23	4	5
Aged 40 to 49	37	30	22	4	6
Aged 50 to 59	46	28	10	5	9
Aged 60 to 69	45	29	16	6	3
Aged 70 or older	45	26	7	8	11
Not a high school graduate	37	23	15	9	14
High school graduate	37	31	20	4	7
Bachelor's degree	27	46	21	2	4
Graduate degree	39	28	21	6	3

Note: Numbers may not add to 100 because no answer is not included.
Source: General Social Survey, National Opinion Research Center, University of Chicago

Privacy and Personal Information, 1985 to 1996

"The federal government has a lot of different pieces of information about people which computers can bring together very quickly. Is this a very serious threat to individual privacy, a fairly serious threat, not a serious threat, or not a threat at all to individual privacy?"

(percent responding by sex, race, age, and education, 1985–96)

	very serious threat		fairly serious threat		not a serious threat		not a threat at all	
	1996	*1985*	*1996*	*1985*	*1996*	*1985*	*1996*	*1985*
Total	**36%**	**29%**	**32%**	**28%**	**19%**	**25%**	**4%**	**9%**
Men	35	27	32	29	21	29	4	9
Women	37	31	31	28	18	22	4	8
Black	46	31	22	22	14	20	5	10
White	35	29	33	29	20	26	4	8
Aged 18 to 29	29	16	33	29	25	39	3	12
Aged 30 to 39	29	31	37	27	23	24	4	11
Aged 40 to 49	37	31	30	30	22	24	4	7
Aged 50 to 59	46	40	28	30	10	17	5	5
Aged 60 to 69	45	31	29	29	16	18	6	8
Aged 70 or older	45	37	26	22	7	19	8	5
Not a high school graduate	37	34	23	20	15	19	9	12
High school graduate	37	28	31	31	20	24	4	9
Bachelor's degree	27	28	46	31	21	31	2	7
Graduate degree	39	31	28	26	21	33	6	2

Note: Numbers may not add to 100 because "can't choose" and no answer are not included.
Source: General Social Surveys, National Opinion Research Center, University of Chicago

Environment Versus Development

Most people would give up economic development to protect endangered species.

Americans care about the environment. Three in 10 strongly agree that natural environments inhabited by scarce or endangered species should be left alone, even if that means foregoing the economic benefits that might come from development. The majority (57 percent) agrees strongly or somewhat.

Younger generations are more likely than their elders to want to see the habitats of endangered species protected even if that means giving up the economic benefits of commercial development. Thirty to 35 percent of people under age 60, compared with 22 percent of those aged 60 or older, agree strongly that certain natural environments should be protected from development.

The desire to protect the environment rises with education. Barely half of people who did not complete high school agree that the habitats of endangered species should be protected rather than developed. The proportion rises to 59 to 60 percent among college graduates.

Environment Versus Development, 1996

"Do you agree or disagree with this statement: Natural environments that support scarce or endangered species should be left alone, no matter how great the economic benefits to your community from developing them commercially might be."

(percent responding by sex, race, age, and education, 1996)

	strongly agree	somewhat agree	somewhat disagree	strongly disagree	don't know	agree, total	disagree, total
Total	**31%**	**26%**	**20%**	**17%**	**6%**	**57%**	**37%**
Men	30	27	21	19	3	57	40
Women	31	25	20	16	8	56	36
Black	31	26	18	16	8	57	34
White	30	26	20	17	5	56	37
Aged 18 to 29	32	24	17	21	5	56	38
Aged 30 to 39	35	27	17	15	5	62	32
Aged 40 to 49	32	27	22	17	2	59	39
Aged 50 to 59	30	24	22	18	6	54	40
Aged 60 to 69	22	25	29	15	8	47	44
Aged 70 or older	22	28	20	16	14	50	36
Not high school grad.	25	26	19	18	12	51	37
High school graduate	30	26	20	18	5	56	38
Bachelor's degree	34	25	23	14	3	59	37
Graduate degree	32	28	21	17	2	60	38

Note: Numbers may not add to 100 because "don't know" and no answer are not included.
Source: General Social Survey, National Opinion Research Center, University of Chicago

Opinion of U.S. Economic System

Few people believe our economic system is as good as it could be.

Most Americans believe our economic system needs some adjusting. A plurality (44 percent) says the U.S. economic system is basically OK but needs some tinkering. Another 37 percent of the public say it needs some fundamental changes. Only 7 percent says it is as good as it could be, while an equal proportion say it needs to be replaced entirely.

Men are more satisfied with our economic system than are women. Forty percent of women say the economic system is in need of fundamental changes compared with 34 percent of men. Ten percent of men, but only 5 percent of women, say our economic system is fine the way it is.

Blacks and whites are even farther apart on this issue. Almost half of blacks believe our economic system needs fundamental changes, but only 35 percent of whites agree. Whites are more likely to say the U.S. economic system is basically OK but needs some adjustments (47 percent compared with 30 percent of blacks).

The proportion of people who say our economic system needs fundamental changes falls with age. Only 29 percent of people aged 70 or older believe major changes are needed, but the proportion rises to 41 to 42 percent among those under age 40. Older Americans are most likely to say the system is fine as it is.

Over half of college graduates say our economic system just needs some adjustments, compared with 42 percent of high school graduates and 37 percent of people who did not complete high school. College graduates are also more likely than those with less education to say the system is the best we could have. People who did not graduate from college are far more likely to say the system needs to be replaced (10 percent compared with 1 to 3 percent of college graduates).

Opinion of U.S. Economic System, 1996

"On the whole, do you think our economic system is the best system we could possibly have, basically OK but in need of some tinkering, in need of some fundamental changes, or needs to be replaced by some other system?"

(percent responding by sex, race, age, and education, 1996)

	best system	OK, but needs work	needs fundamental changes	needs to be replaced	don't know
Total	**7%**	**44%**	**37%**	**8%**	**3%**
Men	10	46	34	8	2
Women	5	43	40	8	4
Black	3	30	49	13	4
White	8	47	35	7	3
Aged 18 to 29	3	43	42	11	1
Aged 30 to 39	4	45	41	7	2
Aged 40 to 49	7	48	34	9	2
Aged 50 to 59	13	40	39	5	3
Aged 60 to 69	10	48	33	6	2
Aged 70 or older	12	41	29	5	12
Not a high school graduate	8	37	35	10	9
High school graduate	5	42	41	10	2
Bachelor's degree	10	54	31	3	2
Graduate degree	12	54	31	1	1

Note: Numbers may not add to 100 because no answer is not included.
Source: General Social Survey, National Opinion Research Center, University of Chicago

International Governmental Bodies

Americans believe some problems must be solved internationally.

Two-thirds of Americans agree that international bodies should have the right to enforce solutions to some of the problems facing the world, such as environmental pollution. Only 10 percent do not agree.

There is some disagreement by education, however. Sixty-four percent of people who did not complete high school agree that international bodies should have enforcement power for some problems. This rises to 77 percent among people with graduate degrees.

Most likely to disagree are people in their 60s. Twenty-one percent of that age group disagrees that international bodies should have the right to enforce solutions compared with 13 percent of those aged 70 or older, 12 percent of those in their 50s, and 6 to 10 percent of those under age 50.

Blacks are less likely than whites to agree that international bodies should be able to enforce solutions to certain problems. Sixty-eight percent of whites agree compared with 58 percent of blacks. Blacks are not more likely than whites to disagree, but they are more likely to say they can't choose (11 percent compared with 5 percent of whites).

International Governmental Bodies, 1996

"For certain problems, like environmental pollution, international bodies should have the right to enforce solutions—do you agree or disagree?"

(percent responding by sex, race, age, and education, 1996)

	strongly agree	agree	neither	disagree	strongly disagree	agree, total	disagree, total
Total	**19%**	**48%**	**15%**	**8%**	**2%**	**67%**	**10%**
Men	20	49	13	10	4	69	14
Women	19	46	16	8	1	65	9
Black	17	41	18	8	2	58	10
White	19	49	14	9	2	68	11
Aged 18 to 29	20	50	18	5	1	70	6
Aged 30 to 39	21	48	16	8	1	69	9
Aged 40 to 49	17	48	15	8	2	65	10
Aged 50 to 59	21	49	9	9	3	70	12
Aged 60 to 69	15	43	12	15	6	58	21
Aged 70 or older	18	44	12	10	3	62	13
Not high school grad.	25	39	12	8	1	64	9
High school graduate	18	48	16	8	2	66	10
Bachelor's degree	20	50	12	9	3	70	12
Graduate degree	22	55	9	10	0	77	10

Note: Numbers may not add to 100 because "can't choose" and no answer are not included.
Source: General Social Survey, National Opinion Research Center, University of Chicago

Is NAFTA Good for the U.S.?

The jury is still out on the North American Free Trade Agreement.

A plurality of people (43 percent) say they don't know if America does or does not benefit from being a member of NAFTA. Twenty-eight percent believe NAFTA is beneficial while 20 percent say it is not.

Nearly half of women say they don't know if NAFTA is good for the country. One-quarter say it is beneficial. Men are more likely than women to believe NAFTA is beneficial (32 percent), but a plurality of men (35 percent) say they don't know if NAFTA is good or not.

Pluralities of both blacks and whites say they don't know if NAFTA is good for the country or not. Whites are considerably more likely to believe NAFTA is beneficial (29 percent compared with 17 percent of blacks). Twenty percent of blacks say they have not heard of NAFTA.

People in their 50s are more likely than other age groups to say NAFTA is beneficial. Pluralities in all age groups say they don't know if NAFTA is good for the country or not.

Support for NAFTA rises with education. Only 14 percent of people who did not complete high school believe the U.S. benefits from being a member of NAFTA. One-quarter of high school graduates agree. But the figure rises to 42 to 55 percent among college graduates. Pluralities of people with a high school diploma or less say they don't know whether NAFTA is beneficial or not.

Is NAFTA Good for the U.S.? 1996

"Generally speaking, would you say that America benefits or
does not benefit from being a member of NAFTA?"

(percent responding by sex, race, age, and education, 1996)

	benefits	does not benefit	don't know	never heard of NAFTA
Total	**28%**	**20%**	**43%**	**9%**
Men	32	27	35	5
Women	24	14	49	12
Black	17	13	48	20
White	29	22	41	7
Aged 18 to 29	28	14	46	12
Aged 30 to 39	28	18	46	7
Aged 40 to 49	30	22	40	7
Aged 50 to 59	34	23	36	7
Aged 60 to 69	22	27	44	5
Aged 70 or older	20	19	40	16
Not a high school graduate	14	11	49	24
High school graduate	24	23	43	9
Bachelor's degree	42	20	36	1
Graduate degree	55	14	28	2

Note: Numbers may not add to 100 because no answer is not included.
Source: General Social Survey, National Opinion Research Center, University of Chicago

Chapter 2

Government and Politics

Party loyalty is on the decline. Independents now outnumber both Democrats and Republicans. Nevertheless, most Americans are at least somewhat interested in politics and think they have a pretty good understanding of the important issues facing the nation. But a plurality of Americans say the average citizen doesn't have much influence on politics. They are divided on whether government does too much or too little, but most think government is too powerful.

Eight in 10 Americans favor cuts in government spending to help the economy. But it is clear that Americans still believe government plays an important role in our society and economy. If they had to choose between spending more on social programs such as health care and Social Security (even if it meant paying more taxes) and cutting taxes (even if it meant spending less on social programs), a plurality would choose to increase spending.

Although Americans have supported cutbacks in social programs, they still believe government should aid some segments of society. Solid majorities believe government should be responsible for helping the elderly, low-income students, and the mentally ill, and should provide decent housing for the poor. A plurality believes government should be primarily responsible for making sure people can pay for health care.

Most also see a role for government in areas where individual Americans have little control. Majorities believe the government should be responsible for preventing industries from damaging the environment, keeping prices under control, and making sure consumers have the information they need to make informed choices.

Most people think government should work with the private sector to improve the economy. Solid majorities favor government support for developing new technologies and for financing projects to create new jobs. Pluralities—but not majorities—favor government support of declining industries to protect jobs and want less regulation of business.

Americans are divided on whether or not it should be government's responsibility to reduce income differences between rich and poor or provide the unemployed with a decent standard of living. The plurality says improving the lot of the poor should be the combined responsibility of government and poor people themselves.

Women, blacks, and the less educated stand apart from men, whites, and the better educated on many issues. The former group is more likely to believe it should be government's responsibility to provide a decent standard of living for the elderly and the unemployed, provide housing for the poor, and reduce income differences between rich and poor. They are more likely to think government should control prices and wages and that it should save existing jobs and help create new ones.

One likely reason for these differences of opinion is socioeconomic status. On average, women have lower incomes than men, blacks have lower incomes than whites, and people with less education have lower incomes than those with more education. The lower the socioeconomic status, the more people favor government help—often because it helps them.

There are fewer differences of opinion by age than by other demographic characteristics. On some issues, however, the opinions of Generation Xers (under age 30) differ from those of older people. They are less likely to support cuts in government spending, for example. They are more likely to believe it should be government's responsibility to reduce income differences between rich and poor, provide jobs for everyone, and provide mental health care for the mentally ill. They are more likely to think government should control wages. Along with the oldest Americans, they are more likely to think it is government's responsibility to keep prices under control. Both Generation Xers and younger baby boomers (aged 30 to 39) are less likely to favor easing government regulation of business. They are also less likely to believe the average citizen has much influence on politics.

The younger the age group, the more likely its members are to think it is government's responsibility to give financial aid to low-income college students and to make sure people can pay for health care. The older people are, the more likely they are to be interested in politics. Whether younger generations will grow more interested in politics as they get older remains to be seen.

Interest in Politics

Interest in politics rises sharply with age.

The majority of Americans say they are at least somewhat interested in politics, but only 15 percent are very interested. Twenty-seven percent say they are not very or not at all interested.

Interest in politics rises sharply with age. Thirty percent of people aged 18 to 29 are fairly or very interested in politics. The proportion rises steadily with each older age group, peaking at 54 percent among people in their 60s. Only 9 percent of people under age 30 are very interested in politics, but this figure rises to 22 percent among people aged 70 or older.

Large differences exist in the level of interest in politics by education. Only 10 to 13 percent of people with no more than a high school diploma are very interested in politics compared with 20 to 25 percent of college graduates. Fully 16 percent of people who did not complete high school say they are not at all interested.

Politics holds more interest for men than women. While 44 percent of men are fairly or very interested in politics, only 38 percent of women are. Among blacks, 46 percent are fairly or very interested compared with 40 percent of whites.

Interest in Politics, 1996

"How interested would you say you personally are in politics?"

(percent responding by sex, race, age, and education, 1996)

	very interested	fairly interested	somewhat interested	not very interested	not at all interested
Total	**15%**	**25%**	**31%**	**19%**	**8%**
Men	19	25	31	15	9
Women	12	26	31	21	8
Black	17	29	27	12	10
White	15	25	32	20	8
Aged 18 to 29	9	21	33	23	10
Aged 30 to 39	13	20	38	19	7
Aged 40 to 49	15	27	30	18	8
Aged 50 to 59	18	31	29	16	5
Aged 60 to 69	20	34	21	17	8
Aged 70 or older	22	29	21	16	11
Not a high school graduate	10	24	26	17	16
High school graduate	13	24	32	22	8
Bachelor's degree	20	28	34	12	6
Graduate degree	25	32	32	11	0

Note: Numbers may not add to 100 because "can't choose" is not included.
Source: General Social Survey, National Opinion Research Center, University of Chicago

Understanding of Political Issues

College graduates are most likely to say they understand the important issues facing the nation.

Slightly more than half of Americans (54 percent) agree with the statement, "I feel that I have a pretty good understanding of the important political issues facing our country." Only 21 percent disagree, while 22 percent say they neither agree nor disagree. Those who neither agreed nor disagreed may feel they understand some issues well, but not others.

College graduates are most likely to say they have a good understanding of the important issues facing the nation. Two-thirds of those with bachelor's degrees and three-quarters of those with graduate degrees feel they understand the issues well. In contrast, a smaller 45 percent of high school graduates and 53 percent of those who did not complete high school say they understand the important issues.

Men are far more likely than women to say they have a good grasp of the issues. Among women, 48 percent agree that they understand the important issues, while 24 percent say they don't. But 60 percent of men say they understand the important issues, while only 17 percent say they don't.

Young adults are notorious for not following "hard" news and not participating in the political process. It is no surprise, then, that people aged 18 to 29 are least likely to say they have a good understanding of the issues facing the nation. Only 42 percent say they have a good understanding compared with 63 percent of people in their 60s and 54 to 58 percent of other age groups.

Understanding of Political Issues, 1996

"How much do you agree or disagree with this statement: I feel that I have a pretty good understanding of the important political issues facing our country?"

(percent responding by sex, race, age, and education, 1996)

	strongly agree	agree	neither	disagree	strongly disagree	agree, total	disagree, total
Total	**8%**	**46%**	**22%**	**18%**	**3%**	**54%**	**21%**
Men	10	50	20	15	2	60	17
Women	6	42	23	20	4	48	24
Black	10	43	18	19	3	53	22
White	7	47	22	18	3	54	21
Aged 18 to 29	6	36	30	21	4	42	25
Aged 30 to 39	8	46	19	19	4	54	23
Aged 40 to 49	7	49	21	18	3	56	21
Aged 50 to 59	8	50	23	15	2	58	17
Aged 60 to 69	11	52	18	14	2	63	16
Aged 70 or older	9	47	15	16	4	56	20
Not high school grad.	7	46	18	15	5	53	20
High school graduate	6	39	26	22	4	45	26
Bachelor's degree	11	55	17	14	1	66	15
Graduate degree	12	64	12	10	0	76	10

Note: Numbers may not add to 100 because "can't choose" is not included.
Source: General Social Survey, National Opinion Research Center, University of Chicago

Political Influence of Average Citizen

Only 3 in 10 Americans believe the average person can influence politics.

Fewer than one-third of Americans agree with the statement, "The average citizen has considerable influence on politics." Nearly half (46 percent) disagree. Nineteen percent say they neither agree nor disagree.

Blacks are more likely than whites to believe the average citizen has political influence (39 percent compared with 29 percent of whites). Forty-seven percent of whites don't agree compared with 37 percent of blacks.

People under age 40 are more cynical than older Americans. Only 26 percent of 18-to-39-year-olds think the average person has considerable influence on politics compared with 33 to 36 percent of people aged 40 or older. People aged 70 or older are less likely than younger age groups to disagree with the idea that the average person has considerable influence on politics.

People who did not complete high school are more likely than those with more education to think the average citizen has political influence. One explanation for this is that older Americans are disproportionately represented among the least educated.

Political Influence of Average Citizen, 1996

"The average citizen has considerable influence on politics—
do you agree or disagree?"

(percent responding by sex, race, age, and education, 1996)

	strongly agree	agree	neither	disagree	strongly disagree	agree, total	disagree, total
Total	4%	27%	19%	36%	10%	31%	46%
Men	5	25	19	36	11	30	47
Women	3	27	19	36	9	30	45
Black	7	32	13	28	9	39	37
White	3	26	19	37	10	29	47
Aged 18 to 29	3	23	18	37	12	26	49
Aged 30 to 39	4	22	23	37	12	26	49
Aged 40 to 49	4	30	18	36	10	34	46
Aged 50 to 59	5	28	21	32	9	33	41
Aged 60 to 69	5	30	13	38	8	35	46
Aged 70 or older	4	32	12	32	6	36	38
Not high school grad.	4	29	17	23	12	33	35
High school graduate	4	25	20	40	9	29	49
Bachelor's degree	5	29	15	37	11	34	48
Graduate degree	2	26	24	29	14	28	43

Note: Numbers may not add to 100 because "don't know" and no answer are not included.
Source: General Social Survey, National Opinion Research Center, University of Chicago

Political Leanings

The proportion of people who identify themselves as conservative has grown slightly.

In 1976, only 30 percent of Americans said they were conservative, but by 1996 the figure had grown to 35 percent. A similar percentage say they are moderate, while one-quarter identify themselves as liberal.

Men are more likely than women to say they are conservative (38 percent compared with 32 percent of women). Whites are more likely than blacks to identify themselves as conservative, but the difference is smaller than it was in 1976. In that year, 31 percent of whites, but only 13 percent of blacks, said they were conservative. By 1996, 36 percent of whites and 30 percent of blacks identified themselves as conservative.

If the definition of a conservative is "a liberal who has been mugged," there are quite a few crime victims among the baby-boom generation. In 1976, only 17 percent of 18-to-29-year-old boomers identified themselves as conservative while 42 percent said they were liberal. In 1996, one-third of 40-to-49-year-old boomers identified themselves as conservative and only 28 percent retained the liberal label.

Despite the conversion of some boomers, younger generations are still more likely than their elders to identify themselves as liberals. Among people under age 50, 25 to 28 percent say they are liberals, but this share drops to between 15 and 18 percent among people aged 60 or older.

College graduates are more likely to take the extreme position than are those with less education. While 34 to 35 percent of college graduates say they are liberals, this is true for only 19 to 21 percent of those with a high school diploma or less. Similarly, 38 to 39 percent of college graduates describe themselves as conservative compared with a smaller 29 to 33 percent of those without a college degree. Only 25 to 28 percent of college graduates say they are moderates compared with 37 to 40 percent of those with less education.

Political Leanings, 1996

"We hear a lot of talk these days about liberals and conservatives. On a seven-point scale from extremely liberal to extremely conservative, where would you place yourself?"

(percent responding by sex, race, age, and education, 1996)

	extremely liberal	liberal	slightly liberal	moderate, middle of the road	slightly conserv-ative	conserv-ative	extremely conserv-ative
Total	**2%**	**10%**	**12%**	**36%**	**16%**	**16%**	**3%**
Men	3	9	11	35	17	17	4
Women	2	12	12	37	14	15	3
Black	2	14	12	33	14	13	3
White	2	10	12	36	16	17	3
Aged 18 to 29	3	13	12	35	16	12	3
Aged 30 to 39	2	9	14	35	16	16	3
Aged 40 to 49	2	13	13	35	14	16	2
Aged 50 to 59	3	10	9	36	19	15	4
Aged 60 to 69	1	5	9	39	15	20	5
Aged 70 or older	1	10	7	38	11	19	3
Not high school grad.	2	8	9	37	11	15	3
High school graduate	2	9	10	40	15	15	3
Bachelor's degree	2	14	19	25	18	18	3
Graduate degree	3	18	13	28	18	17	3

Note: Numbers may not add to 100 because "don't know" and no answer are not included.
Source: General Social Survey, National Opinion Research Center, University of Chicago

Political Leanings, 1976 to 1996

"We hear a lot of talk these days about liberals and conservatives.
On a seven-point scale from extremely liberal to extremely conservative,
where would you place yourself?"

(percent responding by sex, race, age, and education, 1976–96)

	liberal (slightly to extremely)			moderate			conservative (slightly to extremely)		
	1996	*1986*	*1976*	*1996*	*1986*	*1976*	*1996*	*1986*	*1976*
Total	**24%**	**23%**	**26%**	**36%**	**39%**	**37%**	**35%**	**33%**	**30%**
Men	23	23	32	35	36	32	38	38	32
Women	26	22	23	37	42	41	32	29	27
Black	28	30	41	33	35	32	30	25	13
White	24	21	25	36	40	38	36	35	31
Aged 18 to 29	28	27	42	35	40	34	31	30	17
Aged 30 to 39	25	29	26	35	35	37	35	33	31
Aged 40 to 49	28	23	21	35	38	41	32	37	34
Aged 50 to 59	22	16	18	36	41	37	38	37	37
Aged 60 to 69	15	17	19	39	46	44	40	31	30
Aged 70 or older	18	14	23	38	41	34	33	33	33
Not high school grad.	19	22	22	37	42	38	29	26	28
High school graduate	21	21	26	40	43	42	33	33	29
Bachelor's degree	35	31	38	25	26	23	39	44	36
Graduate degree	34	32	48	28	20	13	38	47	38

Note: Numbers may not add to 100 because "don't know" and no answer are not included.
Source: General Social Surveys, National Opinion Research Center, University of Chicago

Political Party Identification

Independents outnumber Democrats and Republicans.

The Democrats win the White House. The Republicans win Congress. No one wins the loyalty of the American electorate. In 1996, the largest proportion of people identified themselves as independents (37 percent). Thirty-four percent said they were Democrats, down from 42 percent in 1976. Republicans have gained ground; 28 percent identified themselves as Republicans in 1996, up from 20 percent in 1976.

Blacks are the strongest supporters of the Democrats. Fully 65 percent of blacks think of themselves as Democrats compared with only 28 percent of whites. Thirty-seven percent of blacks, but only 10 percent of whites, say they are strong Democrats. One-third of whites, but only 4 percent of blacks, consider themselves Republicans.

Women are more likely than men to say they are Democrats. Among women, 39 percent are Democrats, 35 percent are independent, and 25 percent are Republican. Among men only 27 percent consider themselves Democrats, while 31 percent say they are Republicans, and 41 percent, independents. Both sexes were less likely to identify themselves as Democrats and more likely to say they were Republicans in 1996 than in 1976.

The youngest Americans (aged 18 to 29) are independent minded (47 percent). Only 23 percent of young adults identify themselves as Republicans while 27 percent say they are Democrats. The proportion of the public identifying itself as Democrats rises with age, reaching 49 percent among people aged 70 or older. One-quarter of the oldest Americans say they are strong Democrats compared with 11 to 17 percent of people aged 30 to 69 and just 7 percent of those aged 18 to 29. Among people under age 50, strong Republicans outnumber strong Democrats.

The Democrats have more support among the most and least educated, with 41 percent of people who did not complete high school and 37 percent of those with graduate degrees saying they usually identify themselves as Democrats. Only about one-third of people with a high school diploma or a bachelor's degree think likewise. Only 19 percent of people who did not complete high school say they usually consider themselves Republicans compared with 28 to 35 percent of people with at least a high school diploma.

Political Party Identification, 1996

"Generally speaking, do you usually think of yourself as a
Republican, Democrat, independent, or what?"

(percent responding by sex, race, age, and education, 1996)

	Democrat	independent	Republican
Total	**34**%	**37**%	**28**%
Men	27	41	31
Women	39	35	25
Black	65	30	4
White	28	37	33
Aged 18 to 29	27	47	23
Aged 30 to 39	29	37	31
Aged 40 to 49	35	37	28
Aged 50 to 59	37	33	28
Aged 60 to 69	35	32	33
Aged 70 or older	49	24	25
Not a high school graduate	41	40	19
High school graduate	32	39	28
Bachelor's degree	33	30	35
Graduate degree	37	29	31

Note: Numbers may not add to 100 because "other" and no answer are not included.
Source: General Social Survey, National Opinion Research Center, University of Chicago

Strength of Party Identification, 1996

"Generally speaking, do you usually think of yourself as a Republican, Democrat, independent, or what? If Republican or Democrat, would you call yourself a strong Republican/Democrat or not a very strong Republican/Democrat? If independent, do you think of yourself as closer to the Republican or Democratic Party?"

(percent responding by sex, race, age, and education, 1996)

	Democrat		independent			Republican	
	strong	*not very strong*	*lean Democrat*	*neither*	*lean Republican*	*strong*	*not very strong*
Total	**14%**	**20%**	**12%**	**16%**	**9%**	**17%**	**11%**
Men	11	16	13	16	12	19	12
Women	16	23	12	16	7	16	9
Black	37	28	11	15	4	3	1
White	10	18	12	15	10	20	13
Aged 18 to 29	7	20	16	21	10	16	7
Aged 30 to 39	11	18	11	18	8	20	11
Aged 40 to 49	14	21	13	15	9	18	10
Aged 50 to 59	17	20	11	13	9	16	12
Aged 60 to 69	17	18	10	12	10	20	13
Aged 70 or older	25	24	10	9	5	11	14
Not high school grad.	20	21	12	20	8	11	8
High school graduate	12	20	12	17	10	18	10
Bachelor's degree	13	20	12	11	7	21	14
Graduate degree	20	17	12	9	8	17	14

Note: Numbers may not add to 100 because "other" and no answer are not included.
Source: General Social Survey, National Opinion Research Center, University of Chicago

Political Party Identification, 1976 to 1996

"Generally speaking, do you usually think of yourself as a
Republican, Democrat, independent, or what?"

(percent responding by sex, race, age, and education, 1976–96)

	Democrat			independent			Republican		
	1996	*1986*	*1976*	*1996*	*1986*	*1976*	*1996*	*1986*	*1976*
Total	**34%**	**40%**	**42%**	**37%**	**34%**	**37%**	**28%**	**26%**	**20%**
Men	27	34	37	41	37	40	31	27	22
Women	39	43	46	35	31	34	25	25	20
Black	65	70	67	30	25	27	4	5	6
White	28	35	39	37	35	37	33	30	22
Aged 18 to 29	27	28	36	47	40	49	23	31	15
Aged 30 to 39	29	42	45	37	38	37	31	19	16
Aged 40 to 49	35	38	42	37	36	38	28	26	21
Aged 50 to 59	37	44	46	33	31	34	28	24	21
Aged 60 to 69	35	49	42	32	24	30	33	27	27
Aged 70 or older	49	42	44	24	22	25	25	33	31
Not high school grad.	41	50	52	40	30	32	19	20	17
High school graduate	32	37	39	39	36	40	28	26	21
Bachelor's degree	33	27	27	30	34	43	35	37	28
Graduate degree	37	44	31	29	31	36	31	26	31

Note: Numbers may not add to 100 because "other" and no answer are not included.
Source: General Social Surveys, National Opinion Research Center, University of Chicago

Power of the Federal Government

Younger generations are more likely to say the feds have too much power.

With so many politicians campaigning against "big government," it is no surprise that the percentage of Americans who say the federal government has too much power has grown. In 1996, 61 percent said the government had too much power, up from 54 percent in 1985. The proportion of those who say government has about the right amount of power fell from 35 to 28 percent during those years.

Two-thirds of men believe the federal government has too much power. Women are less likely to say this (57 percent). In a big change from 1985, 61 percent of both blacks and whites now say government is too powerful. In 1985, 55 percent of whites, but only 39 percent of blacks, said the government had too much power.

Opinion on this issue changes at age 60. Americans under age 60, who are too young to have experienced the Great Depression and World War II, have never had the positive experience of the power of the federal government that older Americans had. Among those under age 60, 62 to 65 percent say the government is too powerful. This share drops to 56 percent of people in their 60s and 49 percent of those aged 70 or older.

Power of the Federal Government, 1996

"Do you think the federal government has too much power or too little power?"

(percent responding by sex, race, age, and education, 1996)

	far too much	too much	about right	too little	far too little	can't choose	too much, total	too little, total
Total	**23%**	**38%**	**28%**	**3%**	**0%**	**4%**	**61%**	**3%**
Men	28	39	25	3	0	2	67	3
Women	19	38	30	3	1	6	57	4
Black	26	35	22	3	2	8	61	5
White	22	39	28	3	0	3	61	3
Aged 18 to 29	20	42	27	5	0	2	62	5
Aged 30 to 39	20	43	29	2	0	2	63	2
Aged 40 to 49	27	38	23	3	0	5	65	3
Aged 50 to 59	26	36	27	1	0	5	62	1
Aged 60 to 69	27	29	33	3	4	3	56	7
Aged 70 or older	21	28	30	4	1	11	49	5
Not a high school graduate	20	32	27	5	1	11	52	6
High school graduate	26	39	25	2	0	3	65	2
Bachelor's degree	19	44	29	2	0	3	63	2
Graduate degree	23	32	32	3	0	1	55	3

Note: Numbers may not add to 100 because no answer is not included.
Source: General Social Survey, National Opinion Research Center, University of Chicago

Power of the Federal Government, 1985 to 1996

"Do you think the federal government has too much power or too little power?"

(percent responding by sex, race, age, and education, 1985–96)

	too much/ far too much		about right		too little/ far too little		can't choose	
	1996	1985	1996	1985	1996	1985	1996	1985
Total	**61%**	**54%**	**28%**	**35%**	**3%**	**3%**	**4%**	**6%**
Men	67	53	25	39	3	4	2	2
Women	57	54	30	32	4	3	6	9
Black	61	39	22	29	5	8	8	12
White	61	55	28	36	3	3	3	5
Aged 18 to 29	62	42	27	42	5	6	2	7
Aged 30 to 39	63	58	29	39	2	2	2	1
Aged 40 to 49	65	64	23	31	3	2	5	2
Aged 50 to 59	62	60	27	30	1	3	5	5
Aged 60 to 69	56	53	33	34	7	1	3	8
Aged 70 or older	49	48	30	27	5	9	11	14
Not a high school graduate	52	46	27	33	6	7	11	11
High school graduate	65	58	25	34	2	3	3	4
Bachelor's degree	63	55	29	37	2	4	3	1
Graduate degree	55	62	32	36	3	0	1	2

Note: Numbers may not add to 100 because no answer is not included.
Source: General Social Surveys, National Opinion Research Center, University of Chicago

Tax or Spend?

Americans don't want to cut social spending to reduce taxes.

Nobody likes taxes, a fact politicians have successfully exploited since the first tax was imposed. "Tax and spend" is a pejorative used to damage political opponents. But faced with complex choices, Americans are not knee-jerk opponents of taxes. Given the choice between spending more on social programs such as health care and Social Security, even if it means higher taxes, and cutting taxes, even if it means less spending on social programs, the plurality of 46 percent chooses increased spending. Only 31 percent would rather see taxes cut. Twenty-two percent say they can't choose between the two options.

Men are more likely than women to want a tax cut (38 percent compared with 25 percent of women), while women are more likely to support more spending on social programs (50 percent compared with 41 percent of men).

Fifty-seven percent of blacks choose spending on social programs over cutting taxes, but only 44 percent of whites agree. Thirty-three percent of whites want tax cuts compared with 18 percent of blacks.

College graduates are more likely than those with less education to choose cutting taxes over spending more on social programs. While 27 to 29 percent of people with a high school diploma or less say they prefer tax cuts, the figure stands at 33 percent of people with graduate degrees and 44 percent of those with bachelor's degrees.

Tax or Spend? 1996

"If the government had a choice between reducing taxes or spending more on social programs like health care, social security, and unemployment benefits, which do you think it should do? (Taxes includes all taxes, social security, income tax, sales, tax, etc.) Reduce taxes, even if this means spending less on social programs or spend more on social programs, even if this means higher taxes?"

(percent responding by sex, race, age, and education, 1996)

	reduce taxes	spend more	can't choose
Total	**31%**	**46%**	**22%**
Men	38	41	20
Women	25	50	24
Black	18	57	24
White	33	44	22
Aged 18 to 29	31	41	26
Aged 30 to 39	32	49	18
Aged 40 to 49	34	42	24
Aged 50 to 59	28	48	23
Aged 60 to 69	30	52	17
Aged 70 or older	24	49	24
Not a high school graduate	29	42	26
High school graduate	27	48	24
Bachelor's degree	44	41	14
Graduate degree	33	45	18

Note: Numbers may not add to 100 because no answer is not included.
Source: General Social Survey, National Opinion Research Center, University of Chicago

Does Government Do Too Much?

Blacks are least likely to say government is doing too much.

Although politicians have been successfully running on a platform of "less govern-ment," a plurality of Americans (38 percent) place themselves in the middle of a scale ranging from "too much" to "too little." One-quarter say government should do more to solve the country's problems and one-third believe it is doing too many things that should be left to individuals and private businesses.

Far more men than women think government is doing too much. Only 28 percent of women say this compared with 39 percent of men. Women are more likely to take a position between "too much" and "too little."

Blacks are far more likely than whites to say government should do more. Only 21 percent of whites say this compared with 39 percent of blacks. Thirty-seven percent of whites say government is doing too much compared with 11 percent of blacks.

The proportion of people who feel strongly that government should do more declines sharply with education. Almost one-quarter of people who did not complete high school feel strongly that government is not doing enough, but this proportion drops to 12 percent among high school graduates and to 4 to 8 percent among college graduates. College graduates are more likely to feel strongly that government does too much.

Does Government Do Too Much? 1996

"Some people think that the government in Washington is trying to do too many things that should be left to individuals and private businesses. Others disagree and think that the government should do even more to solve our country's problems. Still others have opinions somewhere in between. Where would you place yourself on a scale of 1 to 5 or haven't you made up your mind on this?"

(percent responding by sex, race, age, and education, 1996)

	government should do more		agree with both		government is doing too much
	1	2	3	4	5
Total	**12%**	**12%**	**38%**	**17%**	**16%**
Men	11	13	33	18	21
Women	12	12	41	16	12
Black	23	16	40	6	5
White	9	12	37	19	18
Aged 18 to 29	11	14	43	20	8
Aged 30 to 39	12	17	37	16	15
Aged 40 to 49	12	11	35	20	16
Aged 50 to 59	11	11	35	15	23
Aged 60 to 69	15	7	35	12	26
Aged 70 or older	13	8	39	14	14
Not a high school graduate	23	10	36	10	11
High school graduate	12	13	38	16	16
Bachelor's degree	4	13	39	21	20
Graduate degree	8	17	27	23	18

Note: Numbers may not add to 100 because "don't know" and no answer are not included.
Source: General Social Survey, National Opinion Research Center, University of Chicago

Does Government Do Too Much? 1975 to 1996

"Some people think that the government in Washington is trying to do too many things that should be left to individuals and private businesses. Others disagree and think that the government should do even more to solve our country's problems. Still others have opinions somewhere in between. Where would you place yourself on a scale of 1 to 5 or haven't you made up your mind on this?"

(percent responding by sex, race, age, and education, 1975–96)

	government should do more (1 and 2)			agree with both (3)			government is doing too much (4 and 5)		
	1996	*1986*	*1975*	*1996*	*1986*	*1975*	*1996*	*1986*	*1975*
Total	**24%**	**25%**	**36%**	**38%**	**41%**	**29%**	**33%**	**29%**	**28%**
Men	24	24	34	33	35	25	39	36	35
Women	24	26	37	41	45	32	28	23	23
Black	39	49	61	40	34	21	11	10	9
White	21	20	32	37	42	30	37	32	31
Aged 18 to 29	25	31	46	43	39	29	28	24	21
Aged 30 to 39	29	29	34	37	41	31	31	25	28
Aged 40 to 49	23	22	30	35	41	31	36	35	32
Aged 50 to 59	22	24	33	35	40	29	38	30	33
Aged 60 to 69	22	19	34	35	40	29	38	35	31
Aged 70 or older	21	17	27	39	45	24	28	27	29
Not high school grad.	33	29	44	36	41	26	21	21	18
High school graduate	25	24	31	38	42	31	32	29	33
Bachelor's degree	17	19	27	39	40	38	41	39	33
Graduate degree	25	23	30	27	34	28	41	40	38

Note: Numbers may not add to 100 because "don't know" and no answer are not included.
Source: General Social Surveys, National Opinion Research Center, University of Chicago

Should Government Cut Spending?

Most people favor cutting government spending to help the economy.

Asked if government should cut spending to help the economy, the overwhelming majority (81 percent) of people say yes. But the public doesn't favor cuts in many of the services provided by government. Asked if they'd prefer to spend more on social programs such as health care and Social Security or pay less in taxes, Americans choose more spending.

The biggest difference of opinion on government spending is found by race. Fully 84 percent of whites favor cuts in government spending. Among blacks, a much lower 67 percent agree. But the gap was even wider in 1985 when 82 percent of whites, but only 47 percent of blacks, favored cuts in government spending.

More men than women favor cutting government spending (84 percent compared with 78 percent of women). Women have moved a little closer to men's position, however, since 1985.

Young adults (under age 30) are less likely than older Americans to favor cuts in government spending. But the proportion of 18-to-29-year-olds who favor spending cuts has grown since 1985 so that the gap in opinions by age has shrunk.

Should Government Cut Spending? 1996

"Here are some things the government might do for the economy.
Are you in favor or against it—cuts in government spending."

(percent responding by sex, race, age, and education, 1996)

	strongly in favor of	in favor of	neither	against	strongly against	in favor of, total	against, total
Total	**40%**	**41%**	**10%**	**4%**	**2%**	**81%**	**6%**
Men	43	41	9	3	2	84	5
Women	38	40	12	5	2	78	7
Black	29	38	16	8	5	67	13
White	42	42	9	3	1	84	4
Aged 18 to 29	32	41	15	6	3	73	9
Aged 30 to 39	39	45	12	2	1	84	3
Aged 40 to 49	41	43	8	4	1	84	5
Aged 50 to 59	44	36	10	4	2	80	6
Aged 60 to 69	48	38	4	3	4	86	7
Aged 70 or older	44	35	8	5	2	79	7
Not high school grad.	39	33	14	5	5	72	10
High school graduate	41	41	11	4	1	82	5
Bachelor's degree	45	46	7	0	1	91	1
Graduate degree	35	39	11	7	1	74	8

Note: Numbers may not add to 100 because "don't know" and no answer are not included.
Source: General Social Survey, National Opinion Research Center, University of Chicago

Should Government Cut Spending? 1985 to 1996

"Here are some things the government might do for the economy.
Are you in favor or against it—cuts in government spending."

(percent responding by sex, race, age, and education, 1985–96)

	favor/ strongly favor		neither		against/ strongly against	
	1996	*1985*	*1996*	*1985*	*1996*	*1985*
Total	**81%**	**79%**	**10%**	**11%**	**6%**	**8%**
Men	84	84	9	7	5	7
Women	78	74	12	14	7	9
Black	67	47	16	14	13	27
White	84	82	9	11	4	6
Aged 18 to 29	73	67	15	23	9	8
Aged 30 to 39	84	81	12	10	3	8
Aged 40 to 49	84	90	8	5	5	5
Aged 50 to 59	80	79	10	11	6	11
Aged 60 to 69	86	81	4	6	7	6
Aged 70 or older	79	79	8	8	7	9
Not a high school graduate	72	74	14	9	10	15
High school graduate	82	80	11	12	5	6
Bachelor's degree	91	76	7	16	1	4
Graduate degree	74	86	11	7	8	9

Note: Numbers may not add to 100 because "don't know" and no answer are not included.
Source: General Social Surveys, National Opinion Research Center, University of Chicago

Who Should Help the Poor?

Most people think a combination of government and individual effort is the answer.

Politicians have succeeded in reducing government aid to the poor. But while Americans are less likely today than they were in 1975 to believe government is the answer, they haven't yet embraced an "every man for himself" philosophy.

A plurality (45 percent) of Americans believes responsibility for improving the lot of the poor lies with both government and the individual. Almost equal numbers believe that government should do everything possible to help the poor (25 percent) or that it is entirely up to individuals to take care of themselves (26 percent).

In 1996, Americans were less likely than in 1975 to look to government to help the poor and more likely to believe it should be a combined effort of government and individuals. The proportion of those who say government is the answer has fallen in all demographic groups.

The largest difference of opinion is by race. Forty-five percent of blacks feel government should be responsible for helping the poor, but only 21 percent of whites agree. Twenty-eight percent of whites say people should get along without government help compared with 13 percent of blacks.

Significant disagreement also exists by education. College graduates are far more likely than those with less education to believe people should take care of themselves (32 to 34 percent compared with 26 percent of high school graduates and 16 percent of those with less education). Those with the most and least education are most likely to support government assistance to the poor.

Who Should Help the Poor? 1996

"Some people think that the government in Washington should do everything
possible to improve the standard of living of all poor Americans;
they are at point 1. Other people think it is not the government's responsibility,
and that each person should take care of himself; they are at point 5.
Where would you place yourself on this scale?"

(percent responding by sex, race, age, and education, 1996)

	government (strongly agree)		agree with both		take care of self (strongly agree)
	1	2	3	4	5
Total	**13%**	**12%**	**45%**	**15%**	**11%**
Men	12	12	41	19	12
Women	14	12	49	12	9
Black	29	16	38	5	8
White	10	11	46	17	11
Aged 18 to 29	14	14	48	15	6
Aged 30 to 39	13	14	45	18	8
Aged 40 to 49	13	12	42	15	12
Aged 50 to 59	11	12	44	19	12
Aged 60 to 69	14	10	42	11	17
Aged 70 or older	12	4	50	12	14
Not a high school graduate	24	9	45	7	9
High school graduate	13	11	46	15	11
Bachelor's degree	5	13	46	23	11
Graduate degree	10	21	35	21	11

Note: Numbers may not add to 100 because "don't know" is not included.
Source: General Social Survey, National Opinion Research Center, University of Chicago

Who Should Help the Poor? 1975 to 1996

"Some people think that the government in Washington should do everything possible to improve the standard of living of all poor Americans; they are at point 1. Other people think it is not the government's responsibility, and that each person should take care of himself; they are at point 5. Where would you place yourself on this scale?"

(percent responding by sex, race, age, and education, 1975–96)

	government (1 and 2)			agree with both (3)			take care of self (4 and 5)		
	1996	**1986**	**1975**	**1996**	**1986**	**1975**	**1996**	**1986**	**1975**
Total	**25%**	**30%**	**39%**	**45%**	**45%**	**35%**	**26%**	**22%**	**23%**
Men	24	28	37	41	44	33	31	26	28
Women	26	32	41	49	45	36	21	20	20
Black	45	54	68	38	34	23	13	7	6
White	21	26	35	46	46	36	28	25	25
Aged 18 to 29	28	31	44	48	45	36	21	22	17
Aged 30 to 39	27	33	39	45	46	34	26	18	24
Aged 40 to 49	25	27	34	42	47	37	27	24	27
Aged 50 to 59	23	33	37	44	41	37	31	24	24
Aged 60 to 69	24	27	42	42	46	29	28	25	27
Aged 70 or older	16	29	33	50	41	34	26	26	27
Not high school grad.	33	37	49	45	41	31	16	19	15
High school graduate	24	30	34	46	47	36	26	22	28
Bachelor's degree	18	26	30	46	46	36	34	27	33
Graduate degree	31	19	28	35	46	48	32	30	24

Note: Numbers may not add to 100 because "don't know" and no answer are not included.
Source: General Social Surveys, National Opinion Research Center, University of Chicago

Should Government Provide Housing for the Poor?

Most people think the government should make sure the poor have decent housing.

The majority of Americans (64 percent) say it definitely or probably should be the government's responsibility to provide decent housing for those who can't afford it. But a substantial minority (31 percent) disagrees.

Women are more likely than men to believe government should house the poor (68 percent compared with 58 percent of men). The difference in opinion is greater by race, however. Fully 84 percent of blacks (who are disproportionately likely to be poor) believe it should be the government's responsibility to house those who can't afford it. A much smaller proportion of whites (60 percent) agree. Nearly half of blacks (47 percent) believe this is definitely a government responsibility compared with 13 percent of whites.

The proportion of people who believe housing the poor is definitely the government's responsibility declines with education. One-third of people who did not complete high school say government definitely should be responsible for housing the poor, but this share drops to 20 percent among high school graduates. Among college graduates, only 10 to 13 percent say that providing housing is definitely a government responsibility.

Should Government Provide Housing for the Poor? 1996

"On the whole, do you think it should or should not be the government's responsibility to provide decent housing for those who can't afford it?"

(percent responding by sex, race, age, and education, 1996)

	definitely should be	probably should be	probably should not be	definitely should not be	should be, total	should not be, total
Total	**19%**	**45%**	**23%**	**8%**	**64%**	**31%**
Men	14	44	27	10	58	37
Women	22	46	20	7	68	27
Black	47	37	8	2	84	10
White	13	47	26	10	60	36
Aged 18 to 29	21	47	18	8	68	26
Aged 30 to 39	17	45	25	9	62	34
Aged 40 to 49	15	44	29	7	59	36
Aged 50 to 59	19	43	23	10	62	33
Aged 60 to 69	17	50	21	9	67	30
Aged 70 or older	28	39	16	8	67	24
Not a high school graduate	32	42	15	4	74	19
High school graduate	20	44	22	9	64	31
Bachelor's degree	10	44	33	10	54	43
Graduate degree	13	49	27	9	62	36

Note: Numbers may not add to 100 because "don't know" is not included.
Source: General Social Survey, National Opinion Research Center, University of Chicago

Should Government Provide for the Elderly?

Americans want government to make sure the old have a decent standard of living.

Most Americans (86 percent) say it probably or definitely should be government's responsibility to make sure the elderly have a decent standard of living. Only 13 percent say it probably or definitely should not be government's responsibility. Americans have become somewhat less likely to say it is definitely government's responsibility to care for the elderly than they were in 1985 and a little more likely to say it probably is.

Women are more likely than men to say providing for the elderly definitely should be government's responsibility (42 percent compared with 33 percent of men). But the overwhelming majorities of both men and women believe it should at least probably be up to government to make sure the elderly live decently.

Baby boomers, who have been bombarded with messages about threats to Social Security, are least likely of all age groups to believe government definitely has an obligation to the elderly (35 to 36 percent). People aged 60 or older are most likely to believe this (42 to 43 percent).

College graduates are far less likely than those with less education to believe government definitely has a responsibility toward the elderly. Only 22 to 27 percent of college graduates believe government definitely should provide for the elderly compared with 41 percent of high school graduates and 49 percent of those with less education.

Should Government Provide for the Elderly? 1996

"On the whole, do you think it should or should not be the government's responsibility to provide a decent standard of living for the old?"

(percent responding by sex, race, age, and education, 1996)

	definitely should be	probably should be	probably should not be	definitely should not be	should be, total	should not be, total
Total	**38%**	**48%**	**10%**	**3%**	**86%**	**13%**
Men	33	50	11	5	83	16
Women	42	46	8	2	88	10
Black	68	25	5	0	93	5
White	32	51	11	4	83	15
Aged 18 to 29	39	48	9	3	87	12
Aged 30 to 39	36	53	9	2	89	11
Aged 40 to 49	35	48	14	2	83	16
Aged 50 to 59	38	48	6	7	86	13
Aged 60 to 69	42	42	9	6	84	15
Aged 70 or older	43	38	11	3	81	14
Not a high school graduate	49	40	6	1	89	7
High school graduate	41	46	9	3	87	12
Bachelor's degree	22	60	13	5	82	18
Graduate degree	27	48	17	5	75	22

Note: Numbers may not add to 100 because "can't choose" is not included.
Source: General Social Survey, National Opinion Research Center, University of Chicago

Should Government Provide for the Elderly? 1985 to 1996

"On the whole, do you think it should or should not be the government's responsibility to provide a decent standard of living for the old?"

(percent responding by sex, race, age, and education, 1985–96)

	definitely should be		probably should be		probably should not be		definitely should not be	
	1996	*1985*	*1996*	*1985*	*1996*	*1985*	*1996*	*1985*
Total	**38%**	**42%**	**48%**	**45%**	**10%**	**9%**	**3%**	**2%**
Men	33	34	50	50	11	12	5	3
Women	42	48	46	40	8	7	2	2
Black	68	70	25	19	5	2	0	7
White	32	39	51	47	11	10	4	2
Aged 18 to 29	39	42	48	50	9	6	3	1
Aged 30 to 39	36	40	53	46	9	11	2	3
Aged 40 to 49	35	34	48	48	14	12	2	5
Aged 50 to 59	38	44	48	40	6	9	7	3
Aged 60 to 69	42	43	42	45	9	6	6	1
Aged 70 or older	43	52	38	34	11	8	3	3
Not a high school graduate	49	64	40	28	6	5	1	1
High school graduate	41	36	46	52	9	10	3	1
Bachelor's degree	22	33	60	47	13	13	5	4
Graduate degree	27	19	48	52	17	12	5	10

Note: Numbers may not add to 100 because "can't choose" is not included.
Source: General Social Surveys, National Opinion Research Center, University of Chicago

Should Government Provide for the Unemployed?

Americans are divided on government's obligation to the unemployed.

Americans lean slightly toward saying government is not responsible for providing the unemployed with a decent standard of living. Forty-nine percent say this probably or definitely should not be government's responsibility while 45 percent say it should be.

Blacks are far more likely than any other demographic segment to say providing a decent standard of living for the unemployed should be the responsibility of government. Seventy-three percent of blacks say it is probably or definitely government's responsibility compared with 40 percent of whites. Only 8 percent of whites say it is definitely a government responsibility compared with fully 33 percent of blacks.

The more education people have, the more likely they are to say it is not government's responsibility to make sure the unemployed have a decent standard of living. One-third of people who did not complete high school say providing a decent living for the unemployed is not government's responsibility compared with 58 to 60 percent of college graduates. In contrast, only 36 to 37 percent of college graduates believe it is government's responsibility. That figure stands at 60 percent among people who did not complete high school.

Should Government Provide for the Unemployed? 1996

"On the whole, do you think it should or should not be the government's responsibility to provide a decent standard of living for the unemployed?"

(percent responding by sex, race, age, and education, 1996)

	definitely should be	probably should be	probably should not be	definitely should not be	should be, total	should not be, total
Total	**12%**	**33%**	**31%**	**18%**	**45%**	**49%**
Men	11	31	33	21	42	54
Women	13	34	29	16	47	45
Black	33	40	16	5	73	21
White	8	32	33	20	40	53
Aged 18 to 29	14	30	36	15	44	51
Aged 30 to 39	10	35	32	16	45	48
Aged 40 to 49	12	27	36	22	39	58
Aged 50 to 59	11	34	27	22	45	49
Aged 60 to 69	11	41	27	19	52	46
Aged 70 or older	16	37	16	15	53	31
Not a high school graduate	22	38	23	9	60	32
High school graduate	13	32	31	18	45	49
Bachelor's degree	6	30	36	24	36	60
Graduate degree	6	31	36	22	37	58

Note: Numbers may not add to 100 because "can't choose" is not included.
Source: General Social Survey, National Opinion Research Center, University of Chicago

Should Government Provide for the Unemployed? 1985 to 1996

"On the whole, do you think it should or should not be the government's responsibility to provide a decent standard of living for the unemployed?"

(percent responding by sex, race, age, and education, 1985–96)

	definitely should be		probably should be		probably should not be		definitely should not be	
	1996	1985	1996	1985	1996	1985	1996	1985
Total	**12%**	**15%**	**33%**	**33%**	**31%**	**30%**	**18%**	**15%**
Men	11	13	31	32	33	35	21	16
Women	13	16	34	34	29	27	16	14
Black	33	39	40	30	16	13	5	13
White	8	13	32	33	33	32	20	16
Aged 18 to 29	14	16	30	40	36	26	15	14
Aged 30 to 39	10	11	35	32	32	43	16	10
Aged 40 to 49	12	11	27	26	36	29	22	27
Aged 50 to 59	11	19	34	31	27	29	22	16
Aged 60 to 69	11	15	41	38	27	26	19	10
Aged 70 or older	16	19	37	29	16	21	15	19
Not a high school graduate	22	27	38	34	23	20	9	10
High school graduate	13	11	32	31	31	34	18	18
Bachelor's degree	6	10	30	37	36	31	24	13
Graduate degree	6	5	31	33	36	36	22	21

Note: Numbers may not add to 100 because "can't choose" is not included.
Source: General Social Surveys, National Opinion Research Center, University of Chicago

Should Government Help
Low-Income Students?

The vast majority of Americans say government should help.

Americans know that education is the ticket out of poverty and most want to make sure that poverty doesn't prevent people from getting an education. The vast majority of Americans say it definitely or probably should be government's responsibility to give financial assistance to low-income college students. One-third say assisting students definitely should be government's responsibility.

The majority of blacks (58 percent) believe providing assistance to low-income students definitely should be government's responsibility compared with 29 percent of whites. Sixteen percent of whites, but only 5 percent of blacks, say it should not be government's responsibility.

Younger adults, who are most likely to be college students, are more likely than their elders to believe it definitely or probably should be government's responsibility to give financial aid to students. While 86 to 87 percent of people under age 40 say this, the proportion of those who agree drops to 75 percent among Americans aged 70 or older.

Surprisingly, only 25 to 28 percent of college graduates say it is definitely government's responsibility to provide financial aid to low-income students. In contrast, a larger 34 percent of high school graduates and 41 percent of those without a high school diploma believe government definitely should assist low-income students.

Should Government Help Low-Income Students? 1996

"On the whole, do you think it should or should not be the government's responsibility to give financial assistance to college students from low-income families?"

(percent responding by sex, race, age, and education, 1996)

	definitely should be	probably should be	probably should not be	definitely should not be	should be, total	should not be, total
Total	**34%**	**49%**	**10%**	**4%**	**83%**	**14%**
Men	30	52	11	4	82	15
Women	37	46	10	3	83	13
Black	58	32	4	1	90	5
White	29	52	12	4	81	16
Aged 18 to 29	48	39	8	2	87	10
Aged 30 to 39	32	54	10	3	86	13
Aged 40 to 49	28	53	13	4	81	17
Aged 50 to 59	28	53	9	8	81	17
Aged 60 to 69	26	52	12	6	78	18
Aged 70 or older	35	40	12	2	75	14
Not a high school graduate	41	38	9	5	79	14
High school graduate	34	48	10	4	82	14
Bachelor's degree	25	61	11	3	86	14
Graduate degree	28	51	15	4	79	19

Note: Numbers may not add to 100 because "don't know" is not included.
Source: General Social Survey, National Opinion Research Center, University of Chicago

Whose Responsibility Are Health Care Costs?

Few Americans believe government should stay out of health care.

Almost half of Americans (48 percent) think government primarily should be responsible for making sure people can pay their health care bills. About one-third believe it is the combined responsibility of government and the individual. Only 17 percent believe that government has no role in paying for health care. In 1975 people were slightly more likely to say it should be left up to individuals.

A solid majority of blacks (61 percent) say government should take primary responsibility for making sure people can pay for health care. Whites are less likely to agree, although a plurality (46 percent) believes government should have primary responsibility.

Older Americans are less likely than younger people to believe government should be primarily responsible for making sure people can pay for health care. Over half of people under age 40 (51 to 55 percent) take this position, but the figure drops to 43 percent among people in their 60s. It is interesting to note that only 36 percent of people aged 70 or older (who are almost universally covered by the government's largest health care program, Medicare) say government should make sure people can pay for health care. In 1975, the majority of people aged 70 or older believed government should be primarily responsible for health care.

The proportion of people who feel strongly that health care is a government responsibility falls with education, from 39 percent of those who did not complete high school to 20 to 21 percent of college graduates.

Whose Responsibility Are Health Care Costs? 1996

"In general, some people think that it is the responsibility of the government in Washington to see to it that people have help in paying for doctors and hospital bills. Others think that these matters are not the responsibility of the federal government and that people should take care of these things themselves. Where would you place yourself on a scale of 1 to 5 or haven't you made up your mind on this?"

(percent responding by sex, race, age, and education, 1996)

	govern- ment		agree with both		take care of self
	1	2	3	4	5
Total	**27%**	**21%**	**32%**	**10%**	**7%**
Men	25	21	30	13	8
Women	28	21	34	8	5
Black	44	17	29	2	4
White	24	22	33	12	7
Aged 18 to 29	28	27	30	10	3
Aged 30 to 39	27	24	30	11	6
Aged 40 to 49	27	22	31	10	7
Aged 50 to 59	28	18	33	11	7
Aged 60 to 69	30	13	37	9	7
Aged 70 or older	23	13	38	9	10
Not a high school graduate	39	15	30	4	6
High school graduate	27	20	33	10	7
Bachelor's degree	20	27	30	15	6
Graduate degree	21	29	28	13	7

Note: Numbers may not add to 100 because "don't know" and no answer are not included.
Source: General Social Survey, National Opinion Research Center, University of Chicago

Whose Responsibility Are Health Care Costs? 1975 to 1996

"In general, some people think that it is the responsibility of the government in Washington to see to it that people have help in paying for doctors and hospital bills. Others think that these matters are not the responsibility of the federal government and that people should take care of these things themselves. Where would you place yourself on a scale of 1 to 5 or haven't you made up your mind on this?"

(percent responding by sex, race, age, and education, 1975–96)

	government (1 and 2)			agree with both (3)			take care of self (4 and 5)		
	1996	*1986*	*1975*	*1996*	*1986*	*1975*	*1996*	*1986*	*1975*
Total	**48%**	**48%**	**49%**	**32%**	**31%**	**28%**	**17%**	**17%**	**21%**
Men	46	47	51	30	29	26	21	21	21
Women	49	49	46	34	33	30	13	15	21
Black	61	63	68	29	21	21	6	10	7
White	46	46	46	33	33	29	19	19	22
Aged 18 to 29	55	55	56	30	24	25	13	18	16
Aged 30 to 39	51	50	52	30	31	25	17	16	22
Aged 40 to 49	49	48	39	31	30	33	17	22	23
Aged 50 to 59	46	40	39	33	33	33	18	20	26
Aged 60 to 69	43	42	48	37	40	28	16	16	23
Aged 70 or older	36	46	52	38	36	29	19	15	16
Not high school grad.	54	55	53	30	29	28	10	12	15
High school graduate	47	45	44	33	33	29	17	19	25
Bachelor's degree	47	46	47	30	30	29	21	23	23
Graduate degree	50	40	52	28	34	20	20	24	24

Note: Numbers may not add to 100 because "don't know" and no answer are not included.
Source: General Social Surveys, National Opinion Research Center, University of Chicago

Should Government Provide Mental Health Care?

Most people believe government should provide care for the mentally ill.

It is a rare insurance policy that provides much coverage for mental illness. The failure of private insurers to pay for mental health care is undoubtedly a major reason why Americans believe government should take responsibility for insuring that the mentally ill receive the care they need. Almost three-quarters of Americans believe it definitely or probably should be government's responsibility to provide mental health care.

Men are more likely than women to feel that the government definitely or probably should not provide care for the mentally ill. Women are more likely than men to say they can't choose.

Eighty percent of blacks say providing mental health care should be government's responsibility compared with 71 percent of whites. Conversely, 21 percent of whites say it should not be government's responsibility compared with 10 percent of blacks.

Generation Xers (under age 30) are more likely than their elders to believe mental health care definitely or probably should be government's responsibility. Eighty percent of 18-to-29-year-olds say this compared with 69 to 73 percent of older adults.

The proportion of people who would assign responsibility for the mentally ill to the government drops with education. Fully 84 percent of people without a high school diploma believe providing mental health care should be government's responsibility, but this share drops to 62 percent among people with graduate degrees. While 24 to 26 percent of college graduates say mental health care should not be government's responsibility, only 13 to 19 percent of those with less education agree.

Should Government Provide Mental Health Care? 1996

"On the whole, do you think it should or should not be the government's responsibility to provide mental health care for persons with mental illnesses?"

(percent responding by sex, race, age, and education, 1996)

	definitely should be	probably should be	probably should not be	definitely should not be	should be, total	should not be, total
Total	**34%**	**39%**	**12%**	**7%**	**73%**	**19%**
Men	34	38	14	10	72	24
Women	34	39	11	5	73	16
Black	53	27	4	6	80	10
White	31	40	13	8	71	21
Aged 18 to 29	36	44	11	3	80	14
Aged 30 to 39	29	43	13	6	72	19
Aged 40 to 49	39	31	16	8	70	24
Aged 50 to 59	31	38	12	12	69	24
Aged 60 to 69	40	33	11	9	73	20
Aged 70 or older	34	37	5	12	71	17
Not a high school graduate	47	37	7	6	84	13
High school graduate	33	40	12	7	73	19
Bachelor's degree	33	40	14	10	73	24
Graduate degree	25	37	18	8	62	26

Note: Numbers may not add to 100 because "can't choose" and no answer are not included.
Source: General Social Survey, National Opinion Research Center, University of Chicago

Should Government Reduce Income Differences?

Americans increasingly favor government action to reduce income differences.

Americans are divided on whether or not it should be government's responsibility to reduce income differences between the rich and the poor. Forty-nine percent say it definitely or probably should not be government's responsibility to do this, while 45 percent say it definitely or probably should be. This is a big shift from 1985, when only 36 percent said government should reduce income differences. As the income disparity between rich and poor has grown, Americans clearly have become more concerned about it.

Two-thirds of blacks say it should be government's responsibility to reduce income differences, but only 41 percent of whites agree. Most whites (53 percent) say it should not be government's responsibility compared with only one-quarter of blacks.

Women and men also disagree on this issue. Almost half of women (49 percent) believe it should be government's responsibility to reduce income differences compared with 40 percent of men. Over half of men (56 percent), but only 43 percent of women, say government should not be responsible for reducing income differences.

Over half (52 percent) of people under age 30 say government should be responsible for reducing income disparities. People in their 40s are least likely to agree (36 percent) while other age groups fall in between (42 to 48 percent).

The solid majority of college graduates (62 to 66 percent) say government should not be responsible for reducing income disparities, but this share drops to 47 percent among high school graduates and to 29 percent among those who did not complete high school.

Should Government Reduce Income Differences? 1996

"On the whole, do you think it should or should not be the government's responsibility to reduce income differences between the rich and the poor?"

(percent responding by sex, race, age, and education, 1996)

	definitely should be	probably should be	probably should not be	definitely should not be	should be, total	should not be, total
Total	**16%**	**29%**	**25%**	**24%**	**45%**	**49%**
Men	14	26	26	30	40	56
Women	18	31	24	19	49	43
Black	33	34	16	9	67	25
White	13	28	26	27	41	53
Aged 18 to 29	17	35	24	18	52	42
Aged 30 to 39	16	31	27	22	47	49
Aged 40 to 49	13	23	29	29	36	58
Aged 50 to 59	15	27	23	27	42	50
Aged 60 to 69	19	29	18	31	48	49
Aged 70 or older	22	23	20	17	45	37
Not a high school graduate	25	33	19	10	58	29
High school graduate	18	29	24	23	47	47
Bachelor's degree	8	24	30	36	32	66
Graduate degree	7	29	30	32	36	62

Note: Numbers may not add to 100 because "can't choose" is not included.
Source: General Social Survey, National Opinion Research Center, University of Chicago

Should Government Reduce Income Differences? 1985 to 1996

"On the whole, do you think it should or should not be the government's responsibility to reduce income differences between the rich and the poor?"

(percent responding by sex, race, age, and education, 1985–96)

	definitely should be		probably should be		probably should not be		definitely should not be	
	1996	1985	1996	1985	1996	1985	1996	1985
Total	**16%**	**15%**	**29%**	**21%**	**25%**	**25%**	**24%**	**29%**
Men	14	14	26	19	26	24	30	36
Women	18	16	31	22	24	26	19	23
Black	33	35	34	22	16	24	9	6
White	13	13	28	20	26	26	27	31
Aged 18 to 29	17	9	35	27	24	28	18	23
Aged 30 to 39	16	14	31	21	27	37	22	23
Aged 40 to 49	13	9	23	17	29	21	29	44
Aged 50 to 59	15	24	27	14	23	19	27	31
Aged 60 to 69	19	15	29	23	18	18	31	34
Aged 70 or older	22	25	23	16	20	14	17	26
Not a high school graduate	25	24	33	23	19	19	10	17
High school graduate	18	16	29	21	24	24	23	31
Bachelor's degree	8	2	24	24	30	36	36	28
Graduate degree	7	2	29	14	30	19	32	62

Note: Numbers may not add to 100 because "can't choose" is not included.
Source: General Social Surveys, National Opinion Research Center, University of Chicago

Should Government Save Jobs?

College graduates say "no" while those with less education say "yes."

A plurality of Americans (47 percent) agrees that government should support declining industries to protect jobs. One-quarter say they are against the idea.

The more education people have, the less likely they are to favor government support of declining industries. Sixty-four percent of people who did not complete high school and 52 percent of high school graduates believe government should protect jobs, but only 22 to 30 percent of college graduates agree. Those with a high school diploma or less education have more at stake than college graduates, since the industries now in decline in the U.S. are the ones offering the less-educated a middle-class standard of living.

Over half of women, but only 41 percent of men, say government should support declining industries to protect jobs. One-third of men are opposed to this notion compared with only 18 percent of women.

Blacks and whites are miles apart on this issue. Fully 70 percent of blacks favor government support for industries to protect jobs, but only 43 percent of whites do.

The majority of people under age 30 (54 percent) and one-half of those aged 60 or older favor government support to protect jobs, but only 47 percent of baby boomers (aged 30 to 49) and 38 percent of people in their 50s agree.

Should Government Save Jobs? 1996

"Here are some things the government might do for the economy.
Are you in favor or against it—support declining industries to protect jobs."

(percent responding by sex, race, age, and education, 1996)

	strongly in favor of	in favor of	neither	against	strongly against	in favor of, total	against, total
Total	**13%**	**34%**	**24%**	**20%**	**5%**	**47%**	**25%**
Men	12	29	22	25	8	41	33
Women	14	38	27	15	3	52	18
Black	27	43	19	4	4	70	8
White	10	33	25	23	5	43	28
Aged 18 to 29	15	39	27	12	4	54	16
Aged 30 to 39	11	36	28	19	4	47	23
Aged 40 to 49	14	33	20	25	6	47	31
Aged 50 to 59	14	24	23	28	7	38	35
Aged 60 to 69	14	36	16	21	8	50	29
Aged 70 or older	13	37	30	12	2	50	14
Not high school grad.	21	43	23	7	2	64	9
High school graduate	14	38	25	16	4	52	20
Bachelor's degree	8	22	24	36	8	30	44
Graduate degree	7	15	25	33	12	22	45

Note: Numbers may not add to 100 because "don't know" and no answer are not included.
Source: General Social Survey, National Opinion Research Center, University of Chicago

Should Government Save Jobs? 1985 to 1996

"Here are some things the government might do for the economy. Are you in favor or against it—support declining industries to protect jobs."

(percent responding by sex, race, age, and education, 1985–96)

	favor/ strongly favor		neither		against/ strongly against	
	1996	1985	1996	1985	1996	1985
Total	**47%**	**50%**	**24%**	**23%**	**25%**	**25%**
Men	41	48	22	20	33	31
Women	52	52	27	27	18	20
Black	70	61	19	10	8	18
White	43	49	25	25	28	25
Aged 18 to 29	54	50	27	26	16	22
Aged 30 to 39	47	52	28	25	23	26
Aged 40 to 49	47	47	20	22	31	31
Aged 50 to 59	38	49	23	22	35	30
Aged 60 to 69	50	50	16	24	29	24
Aged 70 or older	50	56	30	23	14	17
Not a high school graduate	64	62	23	17	9	16
High school graduate	52	51	25	25	20	23
Bachelor's degree	30	39	24	26	44	32
Graduate degree	22	26	25	21	45	53

Note: Numbers may not add to 100 because "don't know" and no answer are not included.
Source: General Social Surveys, National Opinion Research Center, University of Chicago

Should Government Provide Jobs?

Most Americans don't believe government is responsible for providing jobs.

The majority of Americans (58 percent) say it is definitely or probably not the responsibility of the government to provide a job for everyone who wants one. A substantial minority (38 percent) disagrees, however.

Blacks are more than twice as likely as whites to believe government should provide jobs for everyone (69 percent compared with 32 percent of whites). The proportion of blacks favoring job provision by the government has increased from 62 percent since 1985, but the proportion of whites who agree remained essentially unchanged.

Half of people under age 30 believe government should be responsible for making sure everyone can get a job. This is up sharply from the 35 percent who felt this way in 1985. People in their 50s and 60s are least likely to say government definitely or probably should provide jobs (27 to 30 percent).

The proportion of people saying government should provide jobs declines sharply with education. Over half (55 percent) of people who did not complete high school are in favor of government providing jobs, but support drops to 24 percent among people with graduate degrees.

Should Government Provide Jobs? 1996

"On the whole, do you think it should or should not be the government's responsibility to provide a job for everyone who wants one?"

(percent responding by sex, race, age, and education, 1996)

	definitely should be	probably should be	probably should not be	definitely should not be	should be, total	should not be, total
Total	**13%**	**25%**	**31%**	**27%**	**38%**	**58%**
Men	11	24	32	31	35	63
Women	14	26	31	24	40	55
Black	31	38	13	11	69	24
White	9	23	35	30	32	65
Aged 18 to 29	19	31	29	15	50	44
Aged 30 to 39	13	26	35	24	39	59
Aged 40 to 49	12	21	33	31	33	64
Aged 50 to 59	7	20	31	38	27	69
Aged 60 to 69	10	20	28	39	30	67
Aged 70 or older	13	27	28	26	40	54
Not a high school graduate	24	31	21	18	55	39
High school graduate	13	26	32	25	39	57
Bachelor's degree	10	21	34	34	31	68
Graduate degree	8	16	36	38	24	74

Note: Numbers may not add to 100 because "can't choose" is not included.
Source: General Social Survey, National Opinion Research Center, University of Chicago

Should Government Provide Jobs? 1985 to 1996

"On the whole, do you think it should or should not be the government's responsibility to provide a job for everyone who wants one?"

(percent responding by sex, race, age, and education, 1985–96)

	definitely should be		probably should be		probably should not be		definitely should not be	
	1996	1985	1996	1985	1996	1985	1996	1985
Total	**13%**	**13%**	**25%**	**20%**	**31%**	**33%**	**27%**	**28%**
Men	11	13	24	18	32	32	31	33
Women	14	13	26	22	31	34	24	24
Black	31	40	38	22	13	24	11	7
White	9	10	23	20	35	34	30	30
Aged 18 to 29	19	15	31	20	29	40	15	21
Aged 30 to 39	13	7	26	24	35	38	24	23
Aged 40 to 49	12	10	21	23	33	24	31	39
Aged 50 to 59	7	14	20	20	31	27	38	35
Aged 60 to 69	10	15	20	18	28	34	39	29
Aged 70 or older	13	21	27	15	28	28	26	28
Not a high school graduate	24	23	31	25	21	29	18	15
High school graduate	13	12	26	19	32	34	25	33
Bachelor's degree	10	5	21	15	34	42	34	22
Graduate degree	8	2	16	12	36	29	38	57

Note: Numbers may not add to 100 because "can't choose" is not included.
Source: General Social Surveys, National Opinion Research Center, University of Chicago

Should Government Help Create New Jobs?

Americans favor government financing of projects to create new jobs.

Most people don't believe government is obligated to provide jobs for everyone who wants one, but they do think government should play a role in creating new jobs. Seventy-one percent favor government financing of projects to create new jobs. Only 10 percent are opposed.

Women are more likely than men to believe government should provide financing for new job creation (74 percent compared with 69 percent of men). Fourteen percent of men are against it, compared with 8 percent of women.

Blacks are much more likely than whites to want government to help create new jobs. Fully 82 percent of blacks say they want government involved in job creation compared with 70 percent of whites.

People under age 40 and those in their 60s are more likely than members of other age groups to believe government should help create new jobs. Seventy-two to 78 percent of Americans in these age groups favor government job creation compared with 62 to 67 percent of people aged 40 to 59 or aged 70 or older.

People with a high school diploma or less education have faced declining job opportunities during the past decade. This group is more likely than college graduates to believe government should help create new jobs. Three-quarters of people with a high school diploma or less education favor this, but the proportion drops to two-thirds among people with a bachelor's degree and to 58 percent among those with graduate degrees.

Should Government Help Create New Jobs? 1996

"Here are some things the government might do for the economy. Are you in favor or against it—government financing of projects to create new jobs."

(percent responding by sex, race, age, and education, 1996)

	strongly in favor of	in favor of	neither	against	strongly against	in favor of, total	against, total
Total	**26%**	**45%**	**15%**	**8%**	**2%**	**71%**	**10%**
Men	26	43	14	11	3	69	14
Women	27	47	15	6	2	74	8
Black	44	38	12	2	2	82	4
White	23	47	15	10	3	70	13
Aged 18 to 29	31	47	14	3	2	78	5
Aged 30 to 39	27	50	13	7	1	77	8
Aged 40 to 49	24	42	16	12	2	66	14
Aged 50 to 59	25	37	17	13	4	62	17
Aged 60 to 69	22	50	14	5	4	72	9
Aged 70 or older	25	42	13	11	3	67	14
Not high school grad.	38	38	14	5	1	76	6
High school graduate	27	47	14	7	2	74	9
Bachelor's degree	19	48	14	15	3	67	18
Graduate degree	16	42	17	12	6	58	18

Note: Numbers may not add to 100 because "don't know" and no answer are not included.
Source: General Social Survey, National Opinion Research Center, University of Chicago

Should Government Help Create New Jobs? 1985 to 1996

"Here are some things the government might do for the economy. Are you in favor or against it—government financing of projects to create new jobs."

(percent responding by sex, race, age, and education, 1985–96)

	favor/ strongly favor		neither		against/ strongly against	
	1996	**1985**	**1996**	**1985**	**1996**	**1985**
Total	**71%**	**68%**	**15%**	**16%**	**10%**	**14%**
Men	69	66	14	16	14	17
Women	74	71	15	16	8	12
Black	82	72	12	7	4	9
White	70	67	15	17	13	15
Aged 18 to 29	78	81	14	11	5	6
Aged 30 to 39	77	69	13	17	8	13
Aged 40 to 49	66	60	16	17	14	24
Aged 50 to 59	62	61	17	19	17	20
Aged 60 to 69	72	63	14	15	9	18
Aged 70 or older	67	69	13	17	14	12
Not a high school graduate	76	76	14	13	6	8
High school graduate	74	67	14	16	9	16
Bachelor's degree	67	67	14	18	18	12
Graduate degree	58	43	17	21	18	35

Note: Numbers may not add to 100 because "don't know" and no answer are not included.
Source: General Social Surveys, National Opinion Research Center, University of Chicago

Should Government Control Wages?

A plurality of Americans oppose government control of wages.

Forty-eight percent of Americans oppose government control of wages, while 27 percent favor it. The public was slightly more likely in 1996 than in 1985 to favor government control of wages.

Men are more likely than women to say they are against government control of wages (54 percent compared with 43 percent of women). Both men and women were slightly less likely to favor wage control in 1996 than they were in 1985.

Blacks are most likely to support government control of wages in order to help the economy. Forty-two percent of blacks support this notion compared with 24 percent of whites. Fully 18 percent of blacks strongly support government control of wages compared with only 6 percent of whites.

People under age 30 are divided on whether or not government should control wages to help the economy, with slightly more than one-third each in favor and opposed. A majority of people aged 40 to 69 (55 to 59 percent) opposes government control of wages as do pluralities of people in their 30s and aged 60 or older (46 percent).

A solid majority of college graduates (53 to 62 percent) opposes legislating wages, but opposition is lower among those with less education. Forty-seven percent of high school graduates oppose government control of wages and this share drops further to 37 percent among those with less education.

Should Government Control Wages? 1996

"Here are some things the government might do for the economy. Are you in favor or against it—control of wages by legislation."

(percent responding by sex, race, age, and education, 1996)

	strongly in favor of	in favor of	neither	against	strongly against	in favor of, total	against, total
Total	**8%**	**19%**	**21%**	**32%**	**16%**	**27%**	**48%**
Men	7	17	17	33	21	24	54
Women	9	20	23	31	12	29	43
Black	18	24	21	20	12	42	32
White	6	18	20	34	17	24	51
Aged 18 to 29	8	26	30	25	10	34	35
Aged 30 to 39	9	22	21	31	15	31	46
Aged 40 to 49	7	14	19	36	21	21	57
Aged 50 to 59	9	13	18	32	23	22	55
Aged 60 to 69	8	17	10	40	19	25	59
Aged 70 or older	7	19	18	35	11	26	46
Not high school grad.	13	22	21	27	10	35	37
High school graduate	8	19	22	31	16	27	47
Bachelor's degree	5	17	14	44	18	22	62
Graduate degree	6	14	18	27	26	20	53

Note: Numbers may not add to 100 because "don't know" and no answer are not included.
Source: General Social Survey, National Opinion Research Center, University of Chicago

Should Government Control Wages? 1985 to 1996

"Here are some things the government might do for the economy. Are you in favor or against it—control of wages by legislation."

(percent responding by sex, race, age, and education, 1985–96)

	favor/ strongly favor		neither		against/ strongly against	
	1996	*1985*	*1996*	*1985*	*1996*	*1985*
Total	**27%**	**22%**	**21%**	**22%**	**48%**	**52%**
Men	24	22	17	18	54	59
Women	29	22	23	26	43	48
Black	42	44	21	15	32	29
White	24	20	20	23	51	56
Aged 18 to 29	34	23	30	28	35	46
Aged 30 to 39	31	18	21	27	46	57
Aged 40 to 49	21	24	19	14	57	62
Aged 50 to 59	22	21	18	22	55	57
Aged 60 to 69	25	22	10	19	59	52
Aged 70 or older	26	31	18	19	46	44
Not a high school graduate	35	37	21	17	37	41
High school graduate	27	20	22	23	47	54
Bachelor's degree	22	12	14	33	62	52
Graduate degree	20	0	18	14	53	88

Note: Numbers may not add to 100 because "don't know" and no answer are not included.
Source: General Social Surveys, National Opinion Research Center, University of Chicago

Should Government Keep Prices Under Control?

College graduates are least likely to say government should keep prices in check.

Two-thirds of Americans say it definitely or probably should be government's responsibility to keep prices under control. This share is lower than it was in 1985, when three-quarters favored government controls. Years of low inflation are probably behind the decline. If inflation returned to the levels it reached during the 1970s, the proportion of those who say government should keep prices under control would probably rise again.

Women, who still do most of the family shopping, are more likely than men to say government should be responsible for controlling prices (71 percent compared with 62 percent of men).

Fully 88 percent of blacks believe controlling prices definitely or probably should be government's responsibility compared with 62 percent of whites. Blacks were just as likely in 1996 as in 1985 to say government should be responsible for controlling prices, but the proportion of whites supporting government control declined.

The oldest and youngest adults are more likely than other age groups to believe government should bear responsibility for keeping prices in check. More than three-quarters of people under age 30 and aged 70 or older favor price control compared with 63 to 68 percent of people in their 30s or aged 50 to 69. Only 56 percent of people in their 40s agree.

The proportion of people saying government should be responsible for keeping prices under control declines with education. Fewer than half of college graduates support government price controls compared with 71 percent of high school graduates and 84 percent of those who did not complete high school.

Should Government Keep Prices Under Control? 1996

"On the whole, do you think it should or should not be the government's responsibility to keep prices under control?"

(percent responding by sex, race, age, and education, 1996)

	definitely should be	*probably should be*	*probably should not be*	*definitely should not be*	*should be, total*	*should not be, total*
Total	**24%**	**43%**	**19%**	**11%**	**67%**	**30%**
Men	22	40	20	16	62	36
Women	25	46	18	7	71	25
Black	47	41	8	2	88	10
White	18	44	21	13	62	34
Aged 18 to 29	28	48	17	5	76	22
Aged 30 to 39	23	44	21	10	67	31
Aged 40 to 49	20	36	26	14	56	40
Aged 50 to 59	21	42	16	18	63	34
Aged 60 to 69	19	49	16	14	68	30
Aged 70 or older	34	43	9	9	77	18
Not a high school graduate	41	43	6	7	84	13
High school graduate	25	46	18	8	71	26
Bachelor's degree	12	36	29	21	48	50
Graduate degree	10	35	30	23	45	53

Note: Numbers may not add to 100 because "can't choose" is not included.
Source: General Social Survey, National Opinion Research Center, University of Chicago

Should Government Keep Prices Under Control? 1985 to 1996

"On the whole, do you think it should or should not be the government's responsibility to keep prices under control?"

(percent responding by sex, race, age, and education, 1985–96)

	definitely should be		probably should be		probably should not be		definitely should not be	
	1996	*1985*	*1996*	*1985*	*1996*	*1985*	*1996*	*1985*
Total	**24%**	**30%**	**43%**	**45%**	**19%**	**14%**	**11%**	**8%**
Men	22	25	40	46	20	18	16	9
Women	25	35	46	44	18	11	7	6
Black	47	62	41	26	8	4	2	6
White	18	27	44	46	21	16	13	8
Aged 18 to 29	28	29	48	52	17	15	5	3
Aged 30 to 39	23	23	44	52	21	17	10	6
Aged 40 to 49	20	24	36	39	26	23	14	12
Aged 50 to 59	21	35	42	34	16	14	18	11
Aged 60 to 69	19	34	49	47	16	6	14	11
Aged 70 or older	34	46	43	33	9	7	9	8
Not a high school graduate	41	50	43	38	6	4	7	4
High school graduate	25	29	46	49	18	15	8	5
Bachelor's degree	12	10	36	50	29	23	21	9
Graduate degree	10	12	35	21	30	29	23	38

Note: Numbers may not add to 100 because "can't choose" is not included.
Source: General Social Surveys, National Opinion Research Center, University of Chicago

Should Government Regulate Business Less?

Men are more likely than women to favor less regulation of business.

Almost half of Americans (48 percent) favor less government regulation of business. Thirty-one percent neither favor nor oppose less regulation, and 17 percent say they are against less regulation of business.

Well over half of men (59 percent) favor less regulation while 23 percent are neutral on this issue. Women are almost evenly divided between those who favor less regulation (40 percent) and those who say they neither favor nor oppose it (38 percent).

Like women, blacks are divided between those who favor less regulation (41 percent) and those who are neutral (40 percent). Whites, on the other hand, are solidly behind less regulation (50 percent). Only 29 percent of whites say they are neutral on this issue.

There is some variation by age on this question. People under age 40 are less supportive of reducing government regulation of business (41 to 43 percent compared with 51 to 54 percent of people aged 40 to 59 and aged 70 or older). People in their 60s are most likely to favor less government regulation of business (60 percent).

Should Government Regulate Business Less? 1996

"Here are some things the government might do for the economy. Are you in favor or against it—less government regulation of business."

(percent responding by sex, race, age, and education, 1996)

	strongly in favor of	in favor of	neither	against	strongly against	in favor of, total	against, total
Total	**15%**	**33%**	**31%**	**14%**	**3%**	**48%**	**17%**
Men	21	38	23	12	3	59	15
Women	10	30	38	16	3	40	19
Black	10	31	40	11	3	41	14
White	16	34	29	14	3	50	17
Aged 18 to 29	11	30	44	10	3	41	13
Aged 30 to 39	11	32	33	17	5	43	22
Aged 40 to 49	20	34	29	13	3	54	16
Aged 50 to 59	21	30	24	18	1	51	19
Aged 60 to 69	17	43	15	15	4	60	19
Aged 70 or older	13	38	27	12	3	51	15
Not high school grad.	14	29	36	12	4	43	16
High school graduate	14	35	32	14	2	49	16
Bachelor's degree	18	39	26	14	3	57	17
Graduate degree	20	20	22	24	6	40	30

Note: Numbers may not add to 100 because "don't know" and no answer are not included.
Source: General Social Survey, National Opinion Research Center, University of Chicago

Should Government Regulate Business Less? 1985 to 1996

"Here are some things the government might do for the economy. Are you in favor or against it—less government regulation of business."

(percent responding by sex, race, age, and education, 1985–96)

	favor/ strongly favor		neither		against/ strongly against	
	1996	*1985*	*1996*	*1985*	*1996*	*1985*
Total	**48%**	**48%**	**31%**	**32%**	**17%**	**19%**
Men	59	57	23	25	15	16
Women	40	40	38	37	19	20
Black	41	32	40	25	14	28
White	50	49	29	32	17	18
Aged 18 to 29	41	36	44	40	13	21
Aged 30 to 39	43	47	33	38	22	14
Aged 40 to 49	54	55	29	26	16	19
Aged 50 to 59	51	48	24	29	19	22
Aged 60 to 69	60	51	15	27	19	18
Aged 70 or older	51	58	27	19	15	18
Not a high school graduate	43	44	36	26	16	25
High school graduate	49	47	32	34	16	19
Bachelor's degree	57	45	26	45	17	7
Graduate degree	40	73	22	17	30	10

Note: Numbers may not add to 100 because "don't know" and no answer are not included.
Source: General Social Surveys, National Opinion Research Center, University of Chicago

Should Government Impose Environmental Laws on Industry?

Americans are united when it comes to protecting the environment.

Americans believe in protecting the environment. Eighty-six percent say it should definitely or probably be the responsibility of the government to impose strict laws on industry to protect the environment. Fully 45 percent say it should definitely be a government responsibility to protect the environment.

There is little disagreement among different demographic segments on this issue. Blacks are more likely than whites to say it should definitely be government's responsibility to protect the environment. Half of blacks want the government to do so compared with 44 percent of whites.

People with bachelor's degrees are less likely than both those with more and those with less education to say it definitely should be government's responsibility to impose environmental laws on industry (36 percent compared with 45 to 48 percent of those with more or less education).

Should Government Impose Environmental Laws on Industry? 1996

"On the whole, do you think it should or should not be the government's responsibility to impose strict laws to make industry do less damage to the environment?"

(percent responding by sex, race, age, and education, 1996)

	definitely should be	probably should be	probably should not be	definitely should not be	should be, total	should not be, total
Total	**45%**	**41%**	**8%**	**3%**	**86%**	**11%**
Men	45	41	9	3	86	12
Women	45	41	7	2	86	9
Black	50	38	4	3	88	7
White	44	42	9	3	86	12
Aged 18 to 29	44	43	7	2	87	9
Aged 30 to 39	48	40	8	2	88	10
Aged 40 to 49	41	43	11	3	84	14
Aged 50 to 59	49	39	5	2	88	7
Aged 60 to 69	44	39	8	7	83	15
Aged 70 or older	42	38	8	4	80	12
Not a high school graduate	47	37	5	5	84	10
High school graduate	45	41	9	2	86	11
Bachelor's degree	36	46	11	4	82	15
Graduate degree	48	40	8	3	88	11

Note: Numbers may not add to 100 because "can't choose" is not included.
Source: General Social Survey, National Opinion Research Center, University of Chicago

Consumer Information

Americans want government to make sure they have consumer information.

Over one-third of Americans strongly agree that it is the responsibility of government to require businesses to provide consumers with the information they need to make informed choices. The majority (59 percent) agree at least somewhat. Only 36 percent disagree.

Women are more likely to agree than men. Sixty-two percent of women agree that the government should require businesses to provide consumer information compared with 55 percent of men. Only one-third of women disagree compared with 41 percent of men.

Among people aged 18 to 49, 61 to 62 percent agree that the government should require businesses to provide information consumers need to make informed choices. Only 56 percent of people in their 60s agree. Among those aged 70 or older, only 49 percent agree.

The proportion of people who agree that the government should require businesses to provide consumer information increases with education. Among people who did not complete high school, 54 percent agree; among college graduates, 60 to 62 percent do.

Consumer Information, 1996

"Do you agree or disagree with this statement: It is the responsibility
of government to require businesses to provide consumers with
the information they need to make informed choices?"

(percent responding by sex, race, age, and education, 1996)

	strongly agree	somewhat agree	somewhat disagree	strongly disagree	don't know	agree, total	disagree, total
Total	**36%**	**23%**	**16%**	**20%**	**4%**	**59%**	**36%**
Men	33	22	18	23	3	55	41
Women	38	24	14	19	5	62	33
Black	39	22	12	20	6	61	32
White	35	23	17	21	4	58	38
Aged 18 to 29	37	24	16	19	3	61	35
Aged 30 to 39	39	22	18	19	1	61	37
Aged 40 to 49	35	27	13	20	4	62	33
Aged 50 to 59	41	18	16	22	4	59	38
Aged 60 to 69	33	23	19	21	5	56	40
Aged 70 or older	27	22	14	24	12	49	38
Not high school grad.	33	21	14	19	12	54	33
High school graduate	37	21	18	20	3	58	38
Bachelor's degree	34	26	16	22	2	60	38
Graduate degree	37	25	11	24	4	62	35

Note: Numbers may not add to 100 because "don't know" and no answer are not included.
Source: General Social Survey, National Opinion Research Center, University of Chicago

Should Government Run Banks?

Younger people are more likely to believe government should run banks.

Two-thirds of Americans believe banks should be privately run. Only 19 percent feel the government should run banks. But there are large differences of opinion by demographic characteristic.

Men are more likely than women to believe the private sector (73 percent compared with 64 percent of women) should run banks. Women are only slightly more likely than men to say the government should run banks, however. Thirteen percent of women say they can't choose.

Only 41 percent of blacks believe banks should be privately run, while 36 percent feel government should run banks. In contrast, whites are solidly on the side of private ownership. Fully 72 percent say the private sector should run banks, while only 16 percent would like to see government run them.

Support for private ownership increases with age. Only 57 percent of people under age 30 think the private sector should run banks, but this share rises to 80 percent among people in their 60s. (People aged 70 or older are less likely to say banks should be privately run, but a substantial proportion of this age group says it can't choose.)

Support for private ownership also rises with education, from 57 percent of those who did not complete high school to 77 percent of people with graduate degrees. People with less education are more likely to say they can't choose between the private sector and government.

Should Government Run Banks? 1996

"Do you think banks should mainly be run by private organizations
or companies, or by the government?"

(percent responding by sex, race, age, and education, 1996)

	privately run	government run	can't choose
Total	**68%**	**19%**	**10%**
Men	73	18	7
Women	64	21	13
Black	41	36	18
White	72	16	9
Aged 18 to 29	57	30	11
Aged 30 to 39	67	22	8
Aged 40 to 49	71	16	9
Aged 50 to 59	71	16	10
Aged 60 to 69	80	7	7
Aged 70 or older	69	12	15
Not a high school graduate	57	22	17
High school graduate	65	22	10
Bachelor's degree	69	20	8
Graduate degree	77	12	7

Note: Numbers may not add to 100 because no answer is not included.
Source: General Social Survey, National Opinion Research Center, University of Chicago

Should Government Run Hospitals?

Most people think hospitals should be run by the private sector.

Fewer than one-quarter of Americans think the government should run hospitals, while 64 percent think private organizations or companies should do it. Ten percent say they can't choose between government and the private sector.

A plurality of blacks (44 percent) thinks the government should run hospitals. Only 31 percent of blacks believe hospitals should be privately run. In contrast, whites solidly support private sector ownership. Seventy-one percent of whites say hospitals should be privately run while 18 percent believe they should be controlled by the government.

Barely half of 18-to-29-year-olds think hospitals should be privately run compared with 63 percent of people in their 30s and 67 to 69 percent of those aged 40 to 59 or 70 or older. Fully 76 percent of people in their 60s think hospitals should be privately run. The older people are, the less likely they are to support government control of hospitals. Thirty-five percent of people under age 30 think government should run hospitals, but this share drops to 10 percent among people aged 70 or older.

About one-quarter of people with a high school diploma or less education think government should run hospitals compared with a smaller 19 percent of college graduates. Seventy-two percent of college graduates believe the private sector should run hospitals compared with 63 percent of high school graduates and 55 percent of those without a high school diploma.

Should Government Run Hospitals? 1996

"Do you think hospitals should mainly be run by private organizations or companies, or by the government?"

(percent responding by sex, race, age, and education, 1996)

	privately run	government run	can't choose
Total	**64%**	**23%**	**10%**
Men	66	25	7
Women	62	21	13
Black	31	44	22
White	71	18	9
Aged 18 to 29	51	35	13
Aged 30 to 39	63	26	8
Aged 40 to 49	67	21	9
Aged 50 to 59	68	17	12
Aged 60 to 69	76	14	5
Aged 70 or older	69	10	15
Not a high school graduate	55	26	16
High school graduate	63	24	11
Bachelor's degree	72	19	7
Graduate degree	72	19	4

Note: Numbers may not add to 100 because no answer is not included.
Source: General Social Survey, National Opinion Research Center, University of Chicago

Should Government Run
the Electric Power Industry?

Most people believe private companies should own power plants.

Seven in 10 Americans believe electric power should be run by private companies rather than by government. Only 18 percent think power generation should be the province of government.

Men are more likely than women to believe electric power should be provided by private companies (73 percent compared with 68 percent of women). Women are more likely to say they can't choose between private and government ownership.

Three-quarters of whites, but only 46 percent of blacks, believe private companies should run the electric power industry. Only 15 percent of whites believe government should run electric power companies compared with 29 percent of blacks.

Younger generations are more likely than their elders to believe government should run the electric power industry. One-quarter of people under age 30 favor government ownership, as do 22 percent of people in their 30s. This share drops to 10 percent among people aged 70 or older. But majorities of all ages think electric power should be run by the private sector.

Only 60 percent of people who did not graduate from high school believe the electric power industry should be privately run. The figures rise to 73 to 78 percent among college graduates.

Should Government Run the Electric Power Industry? 1996

"Do you think electric power should mainly be run by private organizations or companies, or by the government?"

(percent responding by sex, race, age, and education, 1996)

	privately run	government run	can't choose
Total	**70%**	**18%**	**10%**
Men	73	18	7
Women	68	18	12
Black	46	29	23
White	75	15	8
Aged 18 to 29	63	24	11
Aged 30 to 39	70	22	7
Aged 40 to 49	71	16	10
Aged 50 to 59	75	11	10
Aged 60 to 69	73	14	9
Aged 70 or older	71	10	13
Not a high school graduate	60	18	18
High school graduate	69	19	10
Bachelor's degree	78	15	5
Graduate degree	73	19	4

Note: Numbers may not add to 100 because no answer is not included.
Source: General Social Survey, National Opinion Research Center, University of Chicago

Should Government Support
New Technology Development?

The majority of Americans believe government should support new technologies.

Americans don't just love new technologies, they believe the future depends on them. Three-quarters favor government support to help industry develop new products and technologies, up from two-thirds who felt this way in 1985. Only 6 percent say they are against government support for new technology development.

Only small differences exist by demographic characteristics in the proportions supporting government help in technology development. In 1985, however, differences were considerable. Since then, those who were less likely to favor support for development have changed their minds.

Only 48 percent of blacks favored government support for developing new technologies in 1985 compared with 71 percent of whites. By 1996, however 71 percent of blacks and 76 percent of whites favored it. In fact, blacks are now more likely than whites to say they strongly favor government support for technological development (27 percent compared with 23 percent of whites).

Should Government Support New Technology Development? 1996

"Here are some things the government might do for the economy. Are you in favor or against it—support for industry to develop new products and technology."

(percent responding by sex, race, age, and education, 1996)

	strongly in favor of	in favor of	neither	against	strongly against	in favor of, total	against, total
Total	**24%**	**51%**	**15%**	**5%**	**1%**	**75%**	**6%**
Men	28	48	12	6	2	76	8
Women	21	53	18	4	1	74	5
Black	27	44	21	3	1	71	4
White	23	53	14	5	1	76	6
Aged 18 to 29	24	50	20	3	1	74	4
Aged 30 to 39	23	54	15	5	1	77	6
Aged 40 to 49	26	51	15	5	1	77	6
Aged 50 to 59	28	44	13	9	2	72	11
Aged 60 to 69	23	54	11	4	4	77	8
Aged 70 or older	21	51	13	6	1	72	7
Not high school grad.	27	47	18	3	1	74	4
High school graduate	22	51	17	6	1	73	7
Bachelor's degree	29	53	10	5	1	82	6
Graduate degree	28	46	8	7	3	74	10

Note: Numbers may not add to 100 because "don't know" and no answer are not included.
Source: General Social Survey, National Opinion Research Center, University of Chicago

Should Government Support
New Technology Development? 1985 to 1996

"Here are some things the government might do for the economy. Are you in favor or against it—support for industry to develop new products and technology."

(percent responding by sex, race, age, and education, 1985–96)

	favor/ strongly favor		neither		against/ strongly against	
	1996	*1985*	*1996*	*1985*	*1996*	*1985*
Total	**75%**	**68%**	**15%**	**19%**	**6%**	**9%**
Men	76	74	12	15	8	11
Women	74	65	18	23	5	9
Black	71	48	21	20	4	17
White	76	71	14	19	6	9
Aged 18 to 29	74	63	20	23	4	11
Aged 30 to 39	77	74	15	19	6	7
Aged 40 to 49	77	76	15	12	6	10
Aged 50 to 59	72	66	13	20	11	14
Aged 60 to 69	77	64	11	21	8	11
Aged 70 or older	72	68	13	17	7	9
Not a high school graduate	74	66	18	17	4	12
High school graduate	73	67	17	22	7	10
Bachelor's degree	82	72	10	19	6	6
Graduate degree	74	76	8	14	10	10

Note: Numbers may not add to 100 because "don't know" and no answer are not included.
Source: General Social Surveys, National Opinion Research Center, University of Chicago

Chapter 3

Race and Immigration

On racial issues, we are a nation divided—not just by race, but by sex, age, and educational attainment. While people's attitudes about racial issues have changed substantially over the last two decades, gaps between groups remain.

Solid majorities of Americans support fair housing laws, would vote for a black presidential candidate, and don't believe interracial marriage should be illegal. But people are divided on the reasons for the lower socioeconomic status of blacks, with similar percentages attributing it to a lack of education and a lack of motivation.

Although overt racism is now relatively rare, stereotypes persist. More people say blacks are lazy than say whites are lazy. A larger proportion of Americans say most whites are intelligent than say most blacks are intelligent.

Although most Americans are descendants of immigrants, the majority would like to see fewer immigrants admitted to the U.S. One reason for the hostility toward immigrants is economic insecurity. Although most people believe immigrants make America more open to new ideas, almost half feel they take jobs away from the native-born workforce.

Blacks and whites have different opinions about racial issues, although they are united in their thoughts about immigration. On some questions, blacks and whites are miles apart. Whites are far more likely than blacks to attribute the lower socioeconomic status of blacks to lack of motivation. They are also more likely to think conditions for blacks have improved. Blacks are far more likely than whites to support affirmative action, fair housing laws, and busing. They are almost twice as likely as whites to say discrimination is the primary cause of the lower socioeconomic status of blacks.

Women tend to be more liberal than men on many issues, including race and immigration. Women are more supportive of fair housing laws and affirmative action for blacks. They are more likely than men to believe discrimination is the primary cause of the lower socioeconomic status of blacks. Men are more likely to attribute it to a lack of motivation.

Men are more likely than women to say immigrants increase crime and take jobs away from natives. But men are also more likely to believe immigrants encourage new ideas.

On many questions of race, the generations disagree at least as strongly as blacks and whites do. It is important to remember when examining attitudes by age that each successive age group is more racially diverse. Fully 85 percent of people aged 65 or older are white, compared with only about 70 percent of people in their 20s. Consequently, within younger generations, whites do not have as large a statistical dominance as they do among older generations. In addition, the attitudes of young whites are influenced by the greater racial diversity of their peer group.

On many questions, people under age 60 have distinctly different opinions from older people's. People under age 60 are more likely to support fair housing laws and are less likely to believe interracial marriage should be outlawed. A majority of people aged 60 or older say "blacks shouldn't push where they aren't wanted," compared with fewer than one-third of people under age 50.

The older people are, the less likely they are to say they would vote for a black presidential candidate and the more likely they are to believe conditions for blacks have improved in the past few years.

Education has a strong influence on attitudes toward race and immigration. There is, however, considerable overlap between age and education because younger generations are better educated than older ones. Because of this overlap, it is not always clear whether education or age has the greater influence on attitudes.

On many questions, people with college degrees stand apart from those with less education. College graduates are much more likely to believe a lack of education is the primary cause of the lower socioeconomic status of blacks, while those with less education are more likely to attribute their status to lack of motivation. College graduates are also more likely to believe it is better for the nation if different racial and ethnic groups maintain distinct customs rather than blend in.

People who did not graduate from high school are more likely than those with at least a high school diploma to oppose busing and to say marriage between blacks and whites should be outlawed. They are considerably more likely than those with more education to say blacks' lower socioeconomic status is caused by "less inborn ability to learn."

Changes in Conditions for Blacks

Whites are almost twice as likely as blacks to believe conditions for blacks have improved.

Over half of Americans say conditions for blacks have improved in the past few years. Only 9 percent believe things have gotten worse.

Blacks and whites disagree sharply on this question. Only 35 percent of blacks say conditions have improved compared with 62 percent of whites. Only 7 percent of whites say things have gotten worse compared with 21 percent of blacks.

The older people are, the more they believe conditions have improved for blacks. Among baby boomers (aged 30 to 49) and Generation Xers (under age 30), 53 percent say conditions for blacks have improved. But a larger 62 to 67 percent of people aged 50 to 69 believe things have gotten better. Fully 71 percent of people aged 70 or older believe conditions have improved. Although the question specifically asked about changes in conditions in the past few years, it is possible that many older people are comparing conditions today with conditions from many years ago.

The percentage of those who say conditions have improved for blacks declines with education. While 61 percent of people who did not complete high school feel blacks are better off now than they were a few years ago, this share drops to only 48 percent among people with graduate degrees.

Changes in Conditions for Blacks, 1996

"In the past few years, do you think conditions for black people have improved, gotten worse, or stayed about the same?"

(percent responding by sex, race, age, and education, 1996)

	improved	stayed the same	gotten worse
Total	**58%**	**29%**	**9%**
Men	60	27	9
Women	55	31	10
Black	35	43	21
White	62	26	7
Aged 18 to 29	53	33	11
Aged 30 to 39	53	34	9
Aged 40 to 49	53	31	11
Aged 50 to 59	62	25	10
Aged 60 to 69	67	26	5
Aged 70 or older	71	20	5
Not a high school graduate	61	26	9
High school graduate	59	29	8
Bachelor's degree	54	32	10
Graduate degree	48	31	16

Note: Numbers may not add to 100 because "don't know" and no answer are not included.
Source: General Social Survey, National Opinion Research, University of Chicago

Should Blacks "Push Where They Are Not Wanted"?

The young and old disagree on this question.

Few Americans today would publicly state that blacks should not push themselves where they are not wanted, but many whites (and some blacks) frequently made this argument during the 1960s. While growing racial sensitivity has made Americans more careful of what they say, it hasn't completely changed attitudes. Even today, 39 percent of Americans agree at least slightly with this statement.

Forty percent of whites agree strongly or slightly that blacks should not push themselves where they are not wanted, but the real surprise is that 33 percent of blacks also agree. This is a big change from 1976, however, when 70 percent of whites agreed. Blacks were also more likely to agree in the past. In 1985 (blacks were not asked the question before 1978), 47 percent of blacks agreed that blacks should not push where they are not wanted.

Men are slightly more likely than women to feel blacks should not push where they are not wanted. People with different educational levels, however, are worlds apart on this question. Only 20 to 22 percent of college graduates say blacks should not push, compared with fully 56 percent of people who did not graduate from high school.

Agreement with this statement fell in every demographic segment between 1976 and 1996. The strongest sign of continuing decline is the large proportion of younger people who disagree. Among people under aged 50, 62 to 68 percent disagree with the idea that blacks shouldn't push, compared with 56 percent of people in their 50s and a mere 33 to 36 percent of those aged 60 or older.

Should Blacks "Push Where They Are Not Wanted"? 1996

"Here is an opinion other people have expressed in connection with black–white relations: 'Blacks shouldn't push themselves where they're not wanted.' How do you feel about this statement?"

(percent responding by sex, race, age, and education, 1996)

	agree strongly	agree slightly	disagree slightly	disagree strongly	agree, total	disagree, total
Total	**16%**	**23%**	**24%**	**33%**	**39%**	**57%**
Men	17	24	24	30	41	54
Women	15	21	24	35	36	59
Black	19	14	11	49	33	60
White	16	24	26	30	40	56
Aged 18 to 29	12	19	27	41	31	68
Aged 30 to 39	14	18	25	39	32	64
Aged 40 to 49	11	22	26	36	33	62
Aged 50 to 59	17	21	20	36	38	56
Aged 60 to 69	27	34	22	14	61	36
Aged 70 or older	27	32	20	13	59	33
Not a high school graduate	28	28	19	19	56	38
High school graduate	19	24	25	29	43	54
Bachelor's degree	6	14	28	48	20	76
Graduate degree	3	19	19	54	22	73

Note: Numbers may not add to 100 because "no opinion" and no answer are not included.
Source: General Social Survey, National Opinion Research Center, University of Chicago

Should Blacks Push Where They're Not Wanted? 1976 to 1996

"Here is an opinion other people have expressed in connection with black–white relations: 'Blacks shouldn't push themselves where they're not wanted.' How do you feel about this statement?"

(percent responding by sex, race, age, and education, 1976–96)

	agree strongly or slightly			disagree strongly or slightly		
	1996	*1985*	*1976*	*1996*	*1985*	*1976*
Total	**39%**	**57%**	**70%**	**57%**	**41%**	**28%**
Men	41	60	71	54	38	27
Women	36	55	68	59	43	30
Black	33	47	*	60	48	*
White	40	58	70	56	39	28
Aged 18 to 29	31	43	55	68	56	43
Aged 30 to 39	32	48	66	64	50	33
Aged 40 to 49	33	65	68	62	31	29
Aged 50 to 59	38	69	78	56	30	21
Aged 60 to 69	61	69	80	36	28	16
Aged 70 or older	59	63	85	33	33	13
Not a high school graduate	56	71	81	38	26	15
High school graduate	43	58	69	54	38	29
Bachelor's degree	20	39	49	76	58	48
Graduate degree	22	36	36	73	61	62

* Question not asked of blacks in 1976.
Note: Numbers may not add to 100 because "no opinion" and no answer are not included.
Source: General Social Surveys, National Opinion Research Center, University of Chicago

Fair Housing Laws

Support for fair housing laws has grown in all demographic segments.

In 1976, 62 percent of Americans believed a homeowner should have the right to refuse to sell a house to someone because of his or her race. By 1996, only 29 percent still felt this way. While this proportion is still substantial, it is likely to decline further in the years ahead.

On this issue, people are as strongly divided by age as they are by race. As older generations die and are replaced by younger ones, the proportion of the total population that supports fair housing laws will rise. Forty-one percent of people aged 60 or older think a homeowner should have the right to refuse to sell on the basis of race, compared with only one-quarter of people under age 50.

Men are more likely than women to disagree with fair housing laws, although both sexes are more likely to support them than they were two decades ago. People with more education are more likely to favor fair housing laws. Support rises from 61 percent among people who did not complete high school to 74 percent of those with graduate degrees.

Blacks are more supportive of fair housing laws than whites. In 1976, a strong majority of whites (62 percent) felt it should be the owner's decision (blacks were not asked this question in that year). The proportion has fallen steadily over the years to just 31 percent in 1996. Only 20 percent of blacks favored leaving it up to the home-owner in 1986, a proportion that had fallen to 16 percent by 1996.

Fair Housing Laws, 1996

"Suppose there is a community-wide vote on the general housing issue. There are two possible laws to vote on. Which law would you vote for? 1) One law says that a homeowner can decide for himself whom to sell his house to, even if he prefers not to sell to blacks; 2) the second law says that a homeowner cannot refuse to sell to someone because of their race or color."

(percent responding by sex, race, age, and education, 1996)

	up to owner	can't refuse
Total	**29%**	**67%**
Men	33	61
Women	25	71
Black	16	75
White	31	65
Aged 18 to 29	25	69
Aged 30 to 39	25	70
Aged 40 to 49	24	73
Aged 50 to 59	28	68
Aged 60 to 69	41	55
Aged 70 or older	41	51
Not a high school graduate	31	61
High school graduate	30	65
Bachelor's degree	28	70
Graduate degree	23	74

Note: Numbers may not add to 100 because "don't know" and no answer are not included.
Source: General Social Survey, National Opinion Research Center, University of Chicago

Fair Housing Laws, 1976 to 1996

"Suppose there is a community-wide vote on the general housing issue. There are two possible laws to vote on. Which law would you vote for? 1) One law says that a homeowner can decide for himself whom to sell his house to, even if he prefers not to sell to blacks; 2) the second law says that a homeowner cannot refuse to sell to someone because of their race or color."

(percent responding by sex, race, age, and education, 1976–96)

	up to owner			can't refuse		
	1996	*1986*	*1976*	*1996*	*1986*	*1976*
Total	**29%**	**47%**	**62%**	**67%**	**51%**	**34%**
Men	33	48	63	61	49	34
Women	25	45	62	71	52	35
Black	16	20	*	75	76	*
White	31	51	62	65	47	34
Aged 18 to 29	25	36	48	69	61	49
Aged 30 to 39	25	36	59	70	61	39
Aged 40 to 49	24	45	66	73	52	30
Aged 50 to 59	28	50	68	68	48	29
Aged 60 to 69	41	65	71	55	32	24
Aged 70 or older	41	64	75	51	32	19
Not a high school graduate	31	52	70	61	43	26
High school graduate	30	49	61	65	48	36
Bachelor's degree	28	38	53	70	61	42
Graduate degree	23	26	48	74	71	52

* Question not asked of blacks prior to 1978.
Note: Numbers may not add to 100 because "don't know," "neither," and no answer are not included.
Source: General Social Surveys, National Opinion Research Center, University of Chicago

Busing

Busing is still a contentious issue among Americans.

Busing children between school districts to achieve racial balance has been controversial since it began. Throughout the years of the General Social Survey, a majority of the public has been opposed to busing. While opposition is down sharply from 1976, the majority is still against busing.

Women are more likely than men to approve of busing (39 percent compared with 30 percent of men). People who did not complete high school are more likely than those with more education to favor busing. Fully 45 percent of the least educated favor busing compared with 30 to 35 percent of people with a high school diploma or more education.

There is a large gap in the opinions of whites and blacks. The majority of blacks (57 percent) favor busing. Among whites, support for busing has grown over the years, from 12 percent in 1976 to 31 percent in 1996. But this is still 26 percentage points lower than the percentage of blacks who favor busing.

A big difference is also found by age. Interestingly, younger people are more likely than older people to favor busing. People in their 20s and 30s, unlike their elders, actually experienced busing. Judging by their response, they did not find it an overwhelmingly negative experience. While 47 percent of people under age 30 oppose busing, almost as many (45 percent) support it. Among people aged 30 to 39, about half oppose busing while a sizable minority (41 percent) favors it. Support is lowest among people in their 50s and 60s (20 to 28 percent).

Busing, 1996

"In general, do you favor or oppose the busing of black and white school children from one district to another?"

(percent responding by sex, race, age, and education, 1996)

	favor	*oppose*
Total	**35%**	**58%**
Men	30	62
Women	39	55
Black	57	39
White	31	62
Aged 18 to 29	45	47
Aged 30 to 39	41	51
Aged 40 to 49	32	63
Aged 50 to 59	28	68
Aged 60 to 69	20	73
Aged 70 or older	34	57
Not a high school graduate	45	49
High school graduate	34	58
Bachelor's degree	30	65
Graduate degree	35	58

Note: Numbers may not add to 100 because "don't know" and no answer are not included.
Source: General Social Survey, National Opinion Research Center, University of Chicago

Busing, 1976 to 1996

"In general, do you favor or oppose the busing of black and white
school children from one district to another?"

(percent responding by sex, race, age, and education, 1976–96)

	favor			oppose		
	1996	*1986*	*1976*	*1996*	*1986*	*1976*
Total	**35%**	**29%**	**16%**	**58%**	**68%**	**82%**
Men	30	26	16	62	71	83
Women	39	32	16	55	65	81
Black	57	59	50	39	36	47
White	31	25	12	62	72	85
Aged 18 to 29	45	40	19	47	56	78
Aged 30 to 39	41	33	14	51	66	85
Aged 40 to 49	32	27	15	63	71	84
Aged 50 to 59	28	23	15	68	76	84
Aged 60 to 69	20	19	14	73	77	83
Aged 70 or older	34	24	15	57	70	78
Not a high school graduate	45	32	19	49	63	78
High school graduate	34	28	13	58	70	84
Bachelor's degree	30	26	12	65	70	87
Graduate degree	35	31	33	58	66	67

Note: Numbers may not add to 100 because "don't know" and no answer are no included.
Source: General Social Surveys, National Opinion Research Center, University of Chicago

Black Presidential Candidate

Age and education make the biggest difference on this issue.

Nine in 10 Americans say they would vote for a black presidential candidate. Only 7 percent say they would not. As many candidates have discovered, what people say is not necessarily what they will do in the privacy of the voting booth. But judging by the strength of public support when General Colin Powell was considering a run for the presidency, Americans are ready to set aside racial differences if the right candidate comes along.

Virtually all blacks would vote for a black presidential candidate. Although whites are slightly less likely to say they would vote for a black, the gap between blacks and whites is considerably smaller than it was in 1974. Women and men are near agreement on this issue, as they have been for the past 20 years.

Younger generations are more accepting of the idea of a black president than older ones. Among people aged 60 or older 11 to 12 percent would not vote for a black candidate, compared with 7 percent or fewer people under age 60. In 1974, about one-quarter of people then aged 60 or older said they would not vote for their party's nominee if the candidate was black.

People who did not complete high school are least likely to say they would vote for a black candidate. Only 80 percent say they would vote for a black compared with 89 percent of high school graduates and 95 percent of college graduates.

Black Presidential Candidate, 1996

"If your party nominated a black for president, would you
vote for him if he were qualified for the job?"

(percent responding by sex, race, age, and education, 1996)

	yes	*no*
Total	**90%**	**7%**
Men	88	9
Women	91	5
Black	95	2
White	89	8
Aged 18 to 29	91	6
Aged 30 to 39	94	5
Aged 40 to 49	93	4
Aged 50 to 59	89	7
Aged 60 to 69	84	12
Aged 70 or older	81	11
Not a high school graduate	80	14
High school graduate	89	8
Bachelor's degree	95	2
Graduate degree	95	1

Note: Numbers may not add to 100 because "don't know" and no answer are not included.
Source: General Social Survey, National Opinion Research Center, University of Chicago

Black Presidential Candidate, 1974 to 1996

"If your party nominated a black for president, would you
vote for him if he were qualified for the job?"

(percent responding by sex, race, age, and education, 1974–96)

	yes			no		
	1996	**1986**	**1974**	**1996**	**1986**	**1974**
Total	**90%**	**85%**	**80%**	**7%**	**12%**	**16%**
Men	88	85	78	9	13	18
Women	91	84	81	5	12	15
Black	95	95	92	2	3	3
White	89	83	78	8	14	18
Aged 18 to 29	91	87	84	6	10	12
Aged 30 to 39	94	88	84	5	9	14
Aged 40 to 49	93	91	88	4	7	9
Aged 50 to 59	89	85	74	7	13	22
Aged 60 to 69	84	83	71	12	15	24
Aged 70 or older	81	71	67	11	24	26
Not a high school graduate	80	77	72	14	19	23
High school graduate	89	86	82	8	12	13
Bachelor's degree	95	91	89	2	7	9
Graduate degree	95	93	89	1	0	11

Note: Numbers may not add to 100 because "don't know" and no answer are not included.
Source: General Social Surveys, National Opinion Research Center, University of Chicago

Interracial Marriage

Changing times are reflected in the views of young and old.

Regardless of whether they personally approve of interracial marriage, few Americans believe it should be illegal. As on other racial issues, opinions on interracial marriage have changed substantially in the past two decades. By 1996, only 11 percent of the public still supported laws against interracial marriage.

Women are slightly more likely than men to favor laws against marriage between blacks and whites. Both men and women are far less likely to support such laws now than they were 20 years ago, however.

Only 4 percent of blacks, but 13 percent of whites, believe interracial marriage should be illegal. Differences are much larger by age, and older Americans are much more likely than younger people to want interracial marriage outlawed. Only 5 to 8 percent of people under age 50 favor laws against marriage between blacks and whites compared with 22 to 29 percent of people aged 60 or older.

The less educated are much more likely than those with more education to believe interracial marriage should be illegal. Only 2 to 4 percent of college graduates want to outlaw marriages between blacks and whites compared with 27 percent of people without a high school diploma.

Interracial Marriage, 1996

"Do you think there should be laws against marriages between blacks and whites?"

(percent responding by sex, race, age, and education, 1996)

	yes	*no*
Total	**11%**	**87%**
Men	9	89
Women	13	85
Black	4	93
White	13	85
Aged 18 to 29	5	95
Aged 30 to 39	6	92
Aged 40 to 49	8	90
Aged 50 to 59	12	85
Aged 60 to 69	22	75
Aged 70 or older	29	66
Not a high school graduate	27	69
High school graduate	11	87
Bachelor's degree	4	95
Graduate degree	2	98

Note: Numbers may not add to 100 because "don't know" and no answer are not included.
Source: General Social Survey, National Opinion Research Center, University of Chicago

Interracial Marriage, 1976 to 1996

"Do you think there should be laws against marriages between blacks and whites?"

(percent responding by sex, race, age, and education, 1976–96)

	yes			no		
	1996	*1985*	*1976*	*1996*	*1985*	*1976*
Total	**11%**	**26%**	**32%**	**87%**	**71%**	**65%**
Men	9	25	28	89	73	69
Women	13	26	34	85	70	62
Black	4	7	*	93	88	*
White	13	28	32	85	69	65
Aged 18 to 29	5	14	13	95	83	86
Aged 30 to 39	6	16	24	92	83	75
Aged 40 to 49	8	19	27	90	80	70
Aged 50 to 59	12	33	44	85	63	52
Aged 60 to 69	22	38	43	75	57	52
Aged 70 or older	29	49	58	66	44	35
Not a high school graduate	27	44	54	69	50	42
High school graduate	11	23	24	87	74	74
Bachelor's degree	4	11	10	95	88	88
Graduate degree	2	7	7	98	93	93

* Question not asked of blacks prior to 1980.
Note: Numbers may not add to 100 because "don't know" and no answer are not included.
Source: General Social Surveys, National Opinion Research Center, University of Chicago

Intelligence of Blacks and Whites

Stereotypes persist about the relative intelligence of blacks and whites.

Few Americans are overtly racist these days, but negative stereotypes about blacks persist. When asked to rate the intelligence of blacks and whites on a scale from 1 (most are unintelligent) to 7 (most are intelligent), fully 42 percent rate whites a 5 or higher, but only 27 percent rate blacks a 5 or higher. One-half of the public rates blacks in the middle of the scale compared with 41 percent who put whites in the middle.

Not surprisingly, blacks and whites differ widely in their responses to this question. Forty-three percent of whites rate the occurrence of intelligence among whites a 5 or higher, but only 25 percent of whites make the same assessment of blacks. Forty-two percent of blacks rate blacks a 5 or higher while a smaller 36 percent of blacks rate whites this high.

Women show a greater disparity than men in their ratings of the occurrence of intelligence among blacks and whites. Forty-four percent of women rate the occurrence of intelligence among whites a 5 or higher, but only 29 percent rate blacks this high. Among men 38 percent rate whites a 5 or higher while 25 percent rate blacks that high.

Every age group rates the occurrence of intelligence among whites higher than among blacks. The oldest age group (aged 70 or older) is least likely to place blacks at a 5 or higher on the intelligence scale.

People who graduated from college are more likely than those with less education to make similar assessments of the intelligence of blacks and whites. Twenty-seven percent of people with bachelor's degrees rate whites a 5 or higher and 22 percent rate blacks this high. But among people with only a high school diploma, 50 percent rate whites a 5 or higher, whereas only 30 percent do so for blacks.

Intelligence of Blacks and Whites, 1996

"A score of 1 means you think almost all of the people in that group are unintelligent. A score of 7 means that you think almost all the people in the group are intelligent. How would you rate whites and blacks?"

(percent responding by sex, race, age, and education, 1996)

	whites					blacks				
	1 or 2 4%	*3* 8%	*4* 41%	*5* 24%	*6 or 7* 18%	*1 or 2* 4%	*3* 12%	*4* 50%	*5* 19%	*6 or 7* 8%
Total	4%	8%	41%	24%	18%	4%	12%	50%	19%	8%
Men	4	9	43	21	17	6	12	51	18	7
Women	3	7	39	25	19	2	12	50	20	9
Black	8	7	41	21	15	1	9	40	23	19
White	3	8	41	25	18	4	14	52	19	6
Aged 18 to 29	3	6	42	25	19	5	8	52	23	7
Aged 30 to 39	2	6	41	28	20	2	9	56	20	8
Aged 40 to 49	5	10	45	22	15	5	12	52	17	9
Aged 50 to 59	6	13	39	19	18	3	16	42	23	8
Aged 60 to 69	1	9	44	22	20	2	16	49	16	10
Aged 70 or older	7	7	28	21	24	5	20	41	11	8
Not a high school graduate	6	5	37	22	21	5	10	43	22	8
High school graduate	4	8	34	28	22	4	15	46	21	9
Bachelor's degree	2	9	55	14	13	1	9	62	12	10
Graduate degree	0	10	65	13	7	5	11	63	11	3

Note: Numbers may not add to 100 because "don't know" and no answer are not included.
Source: General Social Survey, National Opinion Research, University of Chicago

Work Habits of Blacks and Whites

Whites are more likely than blacks to be considered hard working.

On a scale of 1 (almost all are hard working) to 7 (almost all are lazy), Americans are more likely to say whites are hard working and blacks lazy. Despite a decline in overt racism, substantial numbers of people still cling to racial stereotypes.

Similar percentages of the public put blacks and whites in the middle of the hard working scale. Forty-three percent of people place whites in the middle and 44 percent place blacks in the middle. The differences are at the extremes.

Blacks make similar assessments of the work habits of blacks and whites, but whites do not. Fully 40 percent of whites rate whites from 1 to 3 on the hard working scale, but only 14 percent make the same assessment of blacks. In contrast, 36 percent of whites rate blacks a 5 or higher, but only 13 percent rate whites at that level.

The oldest Americans are most likely to consider blacks lazy and whites hard working. Fully 43 percent of those aged 70 or older place blacks at the lazy end of the scale, rating them a 5 to 7. Only 14 percent of this age group makes the same assessment of whites. Among the youngest Americans, a much smaller 28 percent give blacks a rating of 5 to 7. Nevertheless, even the youngest adults rate whites better than blacks, with only 17 percent giving whites a rating of 5 to 7 on the hard working scale.

Education also plays a role in the degree to which people stereotype blacks and whites. Thirty-four to 37 percent of people with no more than a high school diploma place blacks at 5 to 7 on the scale, but only 21 to 27 percent of college graduates do.

Work Habits of Blacks and Whites, 1996

"A score of 1 means you think almost all of the people in that group are hard-working. A score of 7 means that you think almost all the people in the group are lazy. How would you rate whites and blacks?"

(percent responding by sex, race, age, and education, 1996)

	whites					blacks				
	1 or 2	3	4	5	6 or 7	1 or 2	3	4	5	6 or 7
Total	**15%**	**24%**	**43%**	**11%**	**3%**	**7%**	**10%**	**44%**	**22%**	**13%**
Men	12	26	43	13	3	8	10	43	21	14
Women	17	22	42	10	4	7	10	44	22	11
Black	15	19	39	14	7	20	16	43	12	5
White	15	25	43	11	2	5	9	45	23	13
Aged 18 to 29	15	27	37	16	1	11	12	45	19	9
Aged 30 to 39	14	21	47	12	4	5	9	46	23	12
Aged 40 to 49	14	21	49	10	2	8	10	48	19	11
Aged 50 to 59	9	29	43	10	5	6	11	37	27	13
Aged 60 to 69	21	25	43	5	2	6	7	47	17	17
Aged 70 or older	23	23	30	10	4	6	9	32	25	18
Not a high school graduate	19	19	34	13	7	10	11	36	21	13
High school graduate	18	25	40	13	2	8	9	42	23	14
Bachelor's degree	6	22	53	9	2	4	10	50	19	8
Graduate degree	5	25	61	4	1	2	15	58	14	7

Note: Numbers may not add to 100 because "don't know" and no answer are not included.
Source: General Social Survey, National Opinion Research, University of Chicago

Causes of Socioeconomic Differences

Americans are divided on the cause of socioeconomic differences between blacks and whites.

Most Americans are aware that, on average, blacks have worse jobs, income, and housing than white people. But the public is divided on the reasons for those differences. Is it due to discrimination, a lack of educational opportunity, a lack of will or motivation, or because blacks have less ability to learn?

Overall, people are most likely to cite lack of education or lack of motivation as causes for the lower socioeconomic status of blacks. Women, baby boomers (aged 30 to 49) and people in their 50s are about equally likely to cite lack of education or lack of motivation as reasons. The college educated are most likely to cite lack of education as the cause of socioeconomic differences. Men, older Americans, and people without a college degree are most likely to believe a lack of motivation is behind the difference. Blacks are the only demographic segment that cites discrimination as the primary cause.

Discrimination

A minority of adults (38 percent) believe the lower socioeconomic status of blacks is due to discrimination. While 42 percent of women think discrimination is the main reason, only 32 percent of men agree. Far more striking is the racial difference. Fully 60 percent of blacks, but only 33 percent of whites, believe discrimination is behind the differences in socioeconomic status between blacks and whites.

People who did not complete high school and the oldest Americans (aged 70 or older) are most likely to think discrimination is the cause of socioeconomic differences. Both groups have grown more likely to cite discrimination since 1977. Conversely, people under age 40 and college graduates have become less likely to blame discrimination than they were in 1977.

Lack of Education

Forty-five percent of adults say lack of educational opportunity is to blame for differences between blacks and whites in jobs, income, and housing. A majority of blacks

(53 percent) believe lack of education is the primary cause, as do a majority of people with college degrees. In fact, there is a bigger difference of opinion by education than by race. Only 40 percent of people without a college degree believe lack of education is behind the difference in socioeconomic status. In contrast, 58 to 66 percent of college graduates believe education is the key.

Lack of Will or Motivation

Americans are nearly evenly split on whether a lack of will or motivation is the cause of differences in the socioeconomic status of blacks and whites. While 47 percent believe this is the main cause, 46 percent say it is not.

Only 39 percent of blacks, compared with 49 percent of whites, consider lack of motivation a cause of blacks' lower socioeconomic status. By age, younger respondents are less likely than older ones to believe blacks lack motivation.

The largest difference is found by educational attainment. Most of the least educated Americans believe blacks lack the will or motivation to succeed. But this opinion is less common among the college educated. Only 30 to 34 percent of people with college degrees agree.

Americans are much less likely today to believe that blacks lack will or motivation than they were in 1977. Whether examined by sex, race, age, or education, the percentages of those who hold this belief were lower in 1996 than in 1977.

Less Ability to Learn

Only 10 percent of Americans believe blacks are innately less able to learn than whites. Even in 1977, only one-quarter of whites believed this was a reason for blacks' lower socioeconomic status.

Older Americans and those with less education (two groups with considerable overlap) are most likely to believe blacks lack the ability to learn. Only 5 to 8 percent of people under age 50 agree, as do 11 percent of those in their 50s, 18 percent of those in their 60s, and 20 percent of those aged 70 or older.

A college education also strongly shapes opinions on this issue. Twenty-one percent of people who did not complete high school believe blacks have less inborn ability to learn as do 10 percent of high school graduates. In contrast, only 3 to 4 percent of college graduates agree.

Causes of Socioeconomic Differences, 1996

"On the average blacks have worse jobs, income, and housing than white people. What do you think these differences are mainly due to?"

(percent responding by sex, race, age, and education, 1996)

	discrimination		lacking chance for education		lack of will or motivation		less ability to learn	
	yes	no	yes	no	yes	no	yes	no
Total	**38%**	**57%**	**45%**	**52%**	**47%**	**46%**	**10%**	**87%**
Men	32	63	41	55	48	45	9	88
Women	42	52	48	49	47	47	11	86
Black	60	34	53	46	39	56	10	88
White	33	62	43	54	49	45	10	87
Aged 18 to 29	37	59	42	56	46	49	7	92
Aged 30 to 39	33	62	43	54	43	50	5	93
Aged 40 to 49	39	55	46	50	44	51	8	88
Aged 50 to 59	38	56	44	53	46	47	11	87
Aged 60 to 69	35	61	43	53	56	35	18	77
Aged 70 or older	47	44	52	42	59	31	20	69
Not a high school graduate	45	47	40	53	60	32	21	71
High school graduate	36	59	40	57	51	42	10	86
Bachelor's degree	37	57	58	40	34	62	4	95
Graduate degree	39	56	66	33	30	65	3	97

Note: Responses may not add to 100 because "don't know" and no answer are not included.
Source: General Social Survey, National Opinion Research Center, University of Chicago

Causes of Socioeconomic Differences:
Discrimination, 1977 to 1996

"On the average blacks have worse jobs, income, and housing than white people.
Do you think these differences are mainly due to discrimination?"

(percent of respondents by sex, race, age, and education, 1977–96)

	yes			no		
	1996	*1986*	*1977*	*1996*	*1986*	*1977*
Total	**38%**	**43%**	**39%**	**57%**	**53%**	**56%**
Men	32	44	36	52	54	60
Women	42	43	41	63	53	53
Black	60	70	*	34	24	*
White	33	39	39	62	58	56
Aged 18 to 29	37	47	49	59	50	48
Aged 30 to 39	33	46	43	62	52	55
Aged 40 to 49	39	41	31	55	56	63
Aged 50 to 59	38	37	31	56	60	63
Aged 60 to 69	35	39	35	61	58	61
Aged 70 or older	47	44	40	44	49	47
Not a high school graduate	45	47	36	47	47	55
High school graduate	36	41	38	59	56	59
Bachelor's degree	37	43	50	57	57	47
Graduate degree	39	45	44	56	51	54

* Question not asked of blacks prior to 1985.
Note: Numbers may not add to 100 because "don't know" and no answer are not included.
Source: General Social Surveys, National Opinion Research Center, University of Chicago

Cause of Socioeconomic Differences:
Lack of Education, 1977 to 1996

"On the average blacks have worse jobs, income, and housing than white people. Do you think these differences are because most blacks don't have the chance to education that it takes to rise out of poverty?"

(percent responding by sex, race, age, and education, 1977–96)

	yes			no		
	1996	1986	1977	1996	1986	1977
Total	**45%**	**52%**	**48%**	**52%**	**46%**	**47%**
Men	41	53	46	55	44	50
Women	48	50	50	49	47	45
Black	53	61	*	46	34	*
White	43	50	49	54	48	47
Aged 18 to 29	42	55	53	56	43	45
Aged 30 to 39	43	55	51	54	43	48
Aged 40 to 49	46	49	43	50	47	51
Aged 50 to 59	44	48	45	53	49	51
Aged 60 to 69	43	46	53	53	52	42
Aged 70 or older	52	53	45	42	45	47
Not a high school graduate	40	43	42	53	54	53
High school graduate	40	49	47	57	49	49
Bachelor's degree	58	73	69	40	26	27
Graduate degree	66	73	61	33	26	35

* Question not asked of blacks prior to 1985.
Note: Numbers may not add to 100 because "don't know" and no answer are not included.
Source: General Social Surveys, National Opinion Research Center, University of Chicago

Causes of Socioeconomic Differences:
Lack of Motivation, 1977 to 1996

"On the average blacks have worse jobs, income, and housing than white people. Do you think these differences are because most blacks just don't have the motivation or will power to pull themselves up out of poverty?"

(percent responding by sex, race, age, and education, 1977–96)

	yes			no		
	1996	*1986*	*1977*	*1996*	*1986*	*1977*
Total	**47%**	**58%**	**62%**	**46%**	**37%**	**32%**
Men	48	58	65	45	37	30
Women	47	58	59	47	37	34
Black	39	36	*	56	58	*
White	49	62	62	45	34	32
Aged 18 to 29	46	53	52	49	42	43
Aged 30 to 39	43	54	60	50	44	37
Aged 40 to 49	44	56	65	51	40	26
Aged 50 to 59	46	62	63	47	31	29
Aged 60 to 69	56	67	69	35	28	25
Aged 70 or older	59	67	72	31	27	20
High school dropout	60	64	69	32	29	24
High school graduate	51	60	63	42	36	32
Bachelor's degree	34	48	47	62	48	49
Graduate degree	30	34	35	65	63	53

* Question not asked of blacks prior to 1985.
Note: Numbers may not add to 100 because "don't know" and no answer are not included.
Source: General Social Surveys, National Opinion Research Center, University of Chicago

Causes of Socioeconomic Differences:
Less Innate Ability, 1977 to 1996

"On the average blacks have worse jobs, income, and housing than white people. Do you think these differences are because most blacks have less inborn ability to learn?"

(percent of respondents by sex, race, age, and education, 1977–96)

	yes			no		
	1996	*1986*	*1977*	*1996*	*1986*	*1977*
Total	**10%**	**20%**	**25%**	**87%**	**76%**	**70%**
Men	9	21	28	88	76	68
Women	11	19	22	86	77	72
Black	10	18	*	88	79	*
White	10	20	24	87	76	70
Aged 18 to 29	7	13	12	92	86	85
Aged 30 to 39	5	10	14	93	87	82
Aged 40 to 49	8	16	25	88	81	68
Aged 50 to 59	11	28	27	87	67	68
Aged 60 to 69	18	28	46	77	66	45
Aged 70 or older	20	38	43	69	53	48
High school dropout	21	34	38	71	60	54
High school graduate	10	19	21	86	78	75
Bachelor's degree	4	5	11	95	93	87
Graduate degree	3	4	10	97	96	82

* Question not asked of blacks prior to 1985.
Note: Numbers may not add to 100 because "don't know" and no answer are not included.
Source: General Social Surveys, National Opinion Research Center, University of Chicago

Affirmative Action for Blacks

Blacks and whites are sharply divided on preferential hiring.

Three-quarters of Americans are opposed to the preferential hiring and promotion of blacks. One-half are strongly opposed. But blacks and whites are miles apart on this issue.

An overwhelming percentage of whites are opposed to the preferential hiring and promotion of blacks. Fully 83 percent oppose affirmative action, with 58 percent saying they are strongly opposed. In contrast, only 46 percent of blacks are opposed to affirmative action, and only 26 percent are strongly opposed. Blacks are just as likely to favor affirmative action as they are to oppose it. Forty-seven percent support preferential hiring, with 35 percent strongly in favor.

Men are somewhat more likely than women to oppose affirmative action. There is some variation in opinions by age. Those in their 30s are most opposed to affirmative action (82 percent) while those aged 70 or older are least likely to be against it (71 percent).

People who did not complete high school are least likely to oppose affirmative action. Sixty-one percent of those without a high school degree are against it compared with 77 to 85 percent of those with more education.

Affirmative Action for Blacks, 1996

"Some people say that because of past discrimination, blacks should be given preference in hiring and promotion. Others say that such preference is wrong because it discriminates against whites. Are you for or against preferential hiring and promotion of blacks?"

(percent responding by sex, race, age, and education, 1996)

	strongly favor	not strongly favor	not strongly oppose	strongly oppose	favor, total	oppose, total
Total	**9%**	**6%**	**25%**	**52%**	**15%**	**77%**
Men	8	5	25	55	13	80
Women	10	8	24	50	18	74
Black	35	12	20	26	47	46
White	5	5	25	58	10	83
Aged 18 to 29	11	7	24	51	18	75
Aged 30 to 39	7	6	27	55	13	82
Aged 40 to 49	9	7	26	51	16	77
Aged 50 to 59	12	6	23	53	18	76
Aged 60 to 69	10	4	22	56	14	78
Aged 70 or older	10	7	23	48	17	71
Not a high school graduate	16	8	27	34	24	61
High school graduate	9	5	23	56	14	79
Bachelor's degree	6	7	29	56	13	85
Graduate degree	10	11	27	50	21	77

Note: Numbers may not add to 100 because "don't know" and no answer are not included.
Source: General Social Survey, National Opinion Research, University of Chicago

Discrimination against Whites?

Most people think it is at least somewhat likely that a white person will lose a job or promotion to an equally or less qualified black person.

There is little support for affirmative action these days. One reason for this is fear among whites of losing a job or promotion solely on the basis of race. Most Americans believe it is at least somewhat likely that a white person won't get a job or promotion while an equally or less qualified black person gets one.

People who did not complete high school or have only a high school diploma are more inclined than college graduates to believe a white person is very likely to be passed over for a job or promotion in favor of an equally or less qualified black. (Responses by demographic categories other than race tend to reflect the majority white opinion.) Only 13 to 15 percent of college graduates believe it is very likely that a white person will lose a job or promotion to a black person. But among those without college degrees, 23 to 28 percent feel it is very likely. Historically, blacks have primarily competed for jobs with less educated whites, so it is not surprising that this group would feel more vulnerable in the face of affirmative action.

Blacks and whites disagree on this issue; 48 percent of blacks, but only 23 percent of whites, say it is not very likely that a white person will be passed over for an equally or less qualified black person. One-quarter of whites, but only 18 percent of blacks, say it is very likely.

Discrimination against Whites? 1996

"What do you think the chances are these days that a white person won't get a job or promotion while an equally or less qualified black person gets one instead?"

(percent responding by sex, race, age, and education, 1996)

	very likely	somewhat likely	not very likely
Total	**24%**	**44%**	**28%**
Men	22	42	31
Women	26	44	25
Black	18	30	48
White	25	47	23
Aged 18 to 29	26	47	24
Aged 30 to 39	23	43	30
Aged 40 to 49	19	46	31
Aged 50 to 59	34	40	23
Aged 60 to 69	22	44	28
Aged 70 or older	25	39	29
Not a high school graduate	23	36	30
High school graduate	28	44	25
Bachelor's degree	15	46	34
Graduate degree	13	51	32

Note: Numbers may not add to 100 because "don't know" and no answer are not included.
Source: General Social Survey, National Opinion Research, University of Chicago

Immigration

Over half of Americans want to reduce the number of immigrants to the U.S.

Ours may be a nation of immigrants, but in the current political climate we are a nation hostile to immigrants. Few Americans want to increase the number of immigrants to the U.S., and most would like to see it reduced.

While 26 percent of Americans would decrease immigration "a little," 30 percent would reduce it "a lot." Those most likely to say it should be reduced a lot are people aged 50 or older and the less educated.

Over half of whites (59 percent) would reduce the number of immigrants to the U.S. compared with 45 percent of blacks. One-quarter of blacks say they can't choose between changing immigration levels or leaving them the same.

Generation Xers (under age 30) are less interested than older people in reducing the number of immigrants (49 percent). Fully two-thirds of people in their 60s want the number of immigrants reduced.

There is also disagreement by education. People with graduate degrees are least supportive of reducing immigration—only 33 percent compared with 50 to 61 percent of people with less education.

Immigration, 1996

"Do you think the number of immigrants to America nowadays should be
increased a lot, increased a little, left the same as it is now,
decreased a little, or decreased a lot?"

(percent responding by sex, race, age, and education, 1996)

	increase a lot	increase a little	leave the same	decrease a little	decrease a lot	can't choose	increase, total	decrease, total
Total	**3%**	**5%**	**24%**	**26%**	**30%**	**13%**	**8%**	**56%**
Men	3	6	26	28	29	9	9	57
Women	2	4	22	24	31	16	6	55
Black	5	4	21	20	25	25	9	45
White	1	5	23	27	32	11	6	59
Aged 18 to 29	3	5	33	25	24	10	8	49
Aged 30 to 39	3	5	19	28	30	15	8	58
Aged 40 to 49	3	5	25	25	27	15	8	52
Aged 50 to 59	2	5	22	21	33	17	7	54
Aged 60 to 69	1	5	16	31	37	9	6	68
Aged 70 or older	2	5	23	24	39	8	7	63
Not high school grad.	6	6	17	16	36	18	12	52
High school graduate	2	3	21	27	34	13	5	61
Bachelor's degree	1	8	31	30	20	11	9	50
Graduate degree	4	8	41	19	14	13	12	33

Note: Numbers may not add to 100 because of rounding.
Source: General Social Survey, National Opinion Research Center, University of Chicago

Effects of Immigrants

Most people believe immigrants make the nation more open to new ideas.

The public is divided on whether immigrants increase crime or are good for the economy. Forty-seven percent of Americans believe immigrants take jobs away from natives. Sixty percent believe, however, that immigrants make America more open to new ideas and cultures.

Men are more likely than women to believe immigrants are good for the economy and encourage new ideas, but they are also more likely to believe immigrants increase crime rates. Blacks are more likely than whites to believe immigrants take jobs away. Whites see immigrants more positively, with 62 percent, compared with only 43 percent of blacks, saying immigrants encourage new ideas.

People aged 60 or older have a more negative view of immigrants than do younger people. They are more likely to believe immigrants bring more crime and take away jobs and they are less likely to think immigrants make the nation more open to new ideas. Most likely to believe immigrants encourage new ideas are people in their 40s and 50s.

By far the sharpest difference of opinion is by education. Fully 49 percent of people who did not complete high school and 35 percent of those with high school diplomas say immigrants increase crime rates. Only 10 to 19 percent of college graduates agree. Over half of people without college degrees believe immigrants take jobs away from people born in the U.S. compared with just 24 to 34 percent of college graduates.

College graduates are much more likely to see immigrants in positive terms. From 41 to 53 percent say immigrants are good for the economy, but only 26 to 28 percent of those with less education agree. The proportion of those who say immigrants encourage new ideas rises sharply with education, from only 39 percent among people who did not complete high school to fully 86 percent of people with graduate degrees.

Effects of Immigrants, 1996

"Do you agree or disagree with these statements: immigrants increase crime rates; immigrants are generally good for America's economy; immigrants take jobs away from people who were born in America; immigrants make America more open to new ideas and cultures."

(percent responding by sex, race, age, and education, 1996)

	increase crime			good for economy			take jobs away			encourage new ideas		
	agree	neither	disagree	agree	neither	disagree	agree	neither	disagree	agree	neither	disagree
Total	32%	28%	37%	33%	32%	32%	47%	23%	28%	60%	21%	16%
Men	36	27	35	39	25	33	46	21	31	63	18	16
Women	29	29	37	27	36	31	48	24	26	57	23	15
Black	31	29	33	28	34	30	56	25	16	43	30	18
White	33	29	35	31	32	33	48	23	28	62	20	15
Aged 18 to 29	32	32	34	28	41	28	45	27	28	56	28	14
Aged 30 to 39	30	32	36	28	32	37	48	21	29	61	23	14
Aged 40 to 49	30	27	31	37	29	29	44	22	32	64	19	14
Aged 50 to 59	22	24	47	38	29	27	41	25	32	65	16	14
Aged 60 to 69	41	26	28	33	25	34	52	22	23	59	18	21
Aged 70 or older	48	21	25	35	25	33	64	17	17	52	17	23
Not a high school graduate	49	21	22	26	22	43	61	17	15	39	23	28
High school graduate	35	29	33	28	31	35	51	22	25	55	24	17
Bachelor's degree	19	33	46	41	35	21	34	27	39	77	14	8
Graduate degree	10	26	63	53	32	13	24	20	53	86	7	7

Note: Numbers may not add to 100 because "can't choose" is not included.
Source: General Social Survey, National Opinion Research, University of Chicago

Maintain Distinct Customs or Blend In?

Americans are unsure about the best approach for a multicultural nation.

Forty-three percent of Americans believe it is better for the nation if different racial and ethnic groups blend into the larger society. A substantial minority (31 percent) say it's better if they maintain their distinct customs and traditions. Almost as many (27 percent) say they don't know which is best.

Whites are more likely than blacks to believe different racial and ethnic groups should blend into the larger society (45 percent compared with 36 percent of blacks). Blacks are more likely to say they don't know. Women are much more likely than men to say they don't know (31 percent compared with 21 percent of men).

The percentage of those who say different groups should try to blend in rises with age. Only 35 percent of people under age 30 think it's best if the nation is a melting pot with different groups blending in, but the figure rises to 57 percent among people aged 70 or older.

There is a distinct difference by education as well. Among those with college degrees 34 to 38 percent believe different groups should maintain their customs. Only 27 to 29 percent of those with less education agree. People who did not complete high school are also less likely than those with more education to say different groups should blend in. Over one-third of this group says they don't know.

Maintain Customs or Blend In? 1996

"Some people say that it is better for a country if different racial and ethnic groups maintain their distinct customs and traditions. Others say that it is better if these groups adapt and blend into the larger society. Which of these views comes closer to your own?"

(percent responding by sex, race, age, and education, 1996)

	maintain distinct customs	blend in	don't know
Total	**31%**	**43%**	**27%**
Men	34	45	21
Women	28	41	31
Black	33	36	31
White	29	45	25
Aged 18 to 29	36	35	29
Aged 30 to 39	32	36	32
Aged 40 to 49	32	44	24
Aged 50 to 59	29	49	22
Aged 60 to 69	25	51	24
Aged 70 or older	21	57	22
Not a high school graduate	27	38	35
High school graduate	29	43	28
Bachelor's degree	34	45	22
Graduate degree	38	44	18

Note: Numbers may not add to 100 because of rounding.
Source: General Social Survey, National Opinion Research, University of Chicago

Chapter 4

Religion

Most Americans are religious, but there is a great deal of diversity in religious opinion and practice. And religious diversity is on the rise. The proportions of the public identifying themselves as Protestant, Catholic, or Jewish have been stable or declined slightly during the past two decades, while the share of those saying they observe other religions or have no religious preference rose.

A solid majority (73 percent) of Americans believe in life after death. Most people pray at least once a day (58 percent). But fewer than half of Americans attend religious services at least once a month. Only one-quarter of adults have a great deal of confidence in religious leaders.

Women are slightly more religious than men. They are less likely than men to say they have no religious preference and more likely to pray daily and attend religious services regularly. Women are also more likely to believe in a literal interpretation of the Bible and to disapprove of the Supreme Court ruling that declared school prayer unconstitutional.

Religion plays a larger role in the lives of blacks than of whites. Blacks are most likely to pray at least once a day and to attend religious services regularly. They are far more likely than whites to view the Bible as the literal word of God. A higher proportion of blacks than whites say they have a great deal of confidence in the leaders of organized religion.

Distinct differences exist in religious beliefs and practices by age. Among older generations of Americans, Protestants are the solid majority. But in the younger age groups, diversity is the rule. People under age 50 are less likely than their elders to be Protestant and more likely to be Catholic, to adhere to some other religion (such as Muslim), or to have no religious preference. Younger generations are considerably less likely to attend religious services regularly or to pray every day. They are more likely than older people to approve of the Supreme Court ruling on school prayer.

Some of the largest differences of opinion regarding religion are by education. People with college degrees are less likely to be Protestant than are those with less education. But the well-educated are more likely than those without college degrees to attend religious services regularly. The college educated are far less likely to believe in a literal interpretation of the Bible. They are about twice as likely as those with less education to approve of the Supreme Court ruling on school prayer.

Religious Preference

Religious diversity is increasing.

A 57 percent majority of Americans are Protestant, while one-quarter are Catholic. People of other religions, such as Muslims, Hindus, or Buddhists, make up 5 percent of the population, while Jews represent 2 percent. Fully 12 percent of Americans have no religious preference.

The religious makeup of America has been changing for decades. There are fewer Protestants today than there were in 1976. The proportion of those without a religious preference has risen 4 percentage points from its 8 percent in 1976.

Religious composition will change even more as younger generations replace older ones. Among people aged 50 or older, nearly 7 in 10 are Protestant, but among people under age 30, fewer than half are Protestant. Fully 7 percent of the youngest adults are of "other" religions (primarily Islam) and 20 percent say they have no religious preference. Some of these young people will begin to identify with a particular religion as they grow older, but many will continue to seek spiritual fulfillment outside of organized religion. Among people in their 40s, 14 percent say they have no religious preference.

The religious preferences of men and women differ only slightly. Women are more likely to be Protestant and men are more likely to have no religious preference.

There are sharp differences between blacks and whites in religious preference. Fully 81 percent of blacks are Protestant compared with only 55 percent of whites. While 25 percent of whites are Catholic, among blacks the proportion is only 8 percent. Twelve percent of whites, but only 8 percent of blacks, have no religious preference.

Religious Preference, 1996

"What is your religious preference? Is it Protestant, Catholic, Jewish, some other religion, or no religion?"

(percent responding by sex, race, age, and education, 1996)

	Protestant	*Catholic*	*Jewish*	*other*	*none*
Total	**57%**	**24%**	**2%**	**5%**	**12%**
Men	52	26	2	5	15
Women	62	21	3	5	9
Black	81	8	0	2	8
White	55	25	3	4	12
Aged 18 to 29	47	25	2	7	20
Aged 30 to 39	54	26	2	7	11
Aged 40 to 49	53	24	3	6	14
Aged 50 to 59	69	19	3	3	7
Aged 60 to 69	68	24	0	1	5
Aged 70 or older	69	20	5	2	5
Not a high school graduate	63	20	1	4	12
High school graduate	60	24	1	4	11
Bachelor's degree	51	24	6	5	13
Graduate degree	47	26	6	10	11

Note: Numbers may not add to 100 because "don't know" and no answer are not included.
Source: General Social Survey, National Opinion Research Center, University of Chicago

Religious Preference, 1976 to 1996

"What is your religious preference? Is it Protestant, Catholic, Jewish, some other religion, or no religion?"

(percent responding by sex, race, age, and education, 1976–96)

	Protestant			Catholic			Jewish			other			none		
	1996	1986	1976	1996	1986	1976	1996	1986	1976	1996	1986	1976	1996	1986	1976
Total	**57%**	**63%**	**63%**	**24%**	**26%**	**26%**	**2%**	**3%**	**2%**	**5%**	**2%**	**1%**	**12%**	**7%**	**8%**
Men	52	57	61	26	27	25	2	3	2	5	3	2	15	10	10
Women	62	67	65	21	25	27	3	2	2	5	2	0	9	4	6
Black	81	85	84	8	5	12	0	1	0	2	3	0	8	5	5
White	55	60	62	25	28	27	3	3	2	4	1	1	12	7	8
Aged 18 to 29	47	60	53	25	26	28	2	1	1	7	2	2	20	10	15
Aged 30 to 39	54	55	63	26	31	25	2	2	1	7	3	1	11	8	9
Aged 40 to 49	53	59	61	24	25	31	3	3	1	6	4	2	14	9	5
Aged 50 to 59	69	70	71	19	20	25	3	5	2	3	0	0	7	4	2
Aged 60 to 69	68	67	73	24	26	21	0	3	2	1	1	0	5	3	3
Aged 70 or older	69	73	70	20	21	23	5	3	4	2	1	0	5	2	3
Not high school grad.	63	70	68	20	20	27	1	2	1	4	1	0	12	7	4
High school graduate	60	63	61	24	28	27	1	2	2	4	1	1	11	6	8
Bachelor's degree	51	53	58	24	28	26	6	6	1	5	6	3	13	7	13
Graduate degree	47	49	61	26	23	16	6	10	5	10	6	3	11	13	15

Note: Numbers may not add to 100 because "don't know" and no answer are not included.
Source: General Social Surveys, National Opinion Research Center, University of Chicago

Religious Background

Americans are less likely to be raised as Protestants than in years past.

The majority (60 percent) of Americans were raised as Protestants, while a substantial minority (29 percent) were raised as Catholics. Two percent were raised Jewish, while 6 percent were raised in another religion. Three percent were raised with no religion.

Blacks are more likely than whites to have been raised as Protestants (83 percent versus 58 percent). They are considerably less likely to have been raised as Catholics. This was also true in 1976.

Younger generations are more likely to have been raised as Catholics and less likely to be raised as Protestants, in part because of the immigration of Hispanics to the United States. Fewer than one-quarter of people aged 50 or older were raised in the Catholic religion compared with 31 to 34 percent of people under age 50. While 71 percent of the oldest Americans were raised as Protestants, only 51 percent of the youngest adults were.

People with college degrees are more likely than those with less education to have been raised Jewish. They are also more likely to have been raised in some other religion, reflecting the relatively large share of Hindu and Muslim immigrants among the best-educated Americans.

Religious Background, 1996

"In what religion were you raised?"

(percent responding by sex, race, age, and education, 1996)

	Protestant	Catholic	Jewish	other	none
Total	**60%**	**29%**	**2%**	**3%**	**6%**
Men	56	32	2	3	7
Women	63	26	3	3	5
Black	83	9	0	1	5
White	58	31	3	2	6
Aged 18 to 29	51	31	1	5	11
Aged 30 to 39	55	33	2	4	6
Aged 40 to 49	56	34	3	4	4
Aged 50 to 59	71	21	3	2	4
Aged 60 to 69	69	23	1	2	5
Aged 70 or older	71	19	5	1	3
Not a high school graduate	65	23	1	3	8
High school graduate	61	29	1	2	6
Bachelor's degree	56	29	6	4	4
Graduate degree	48	36	6	6	4

Note: Numbers may not add to 100 because "don't know" and no answer are not included.
Source: General Social Survey, National Opinion Research Center, University of Chicago

Religious Background, 1976 to 1996

"In what religion were you raised?"

(percent responding by sex, race, age, and education, 1976–96)

	Protestant			Catholic			Jewish			other			none		
	1996	1986	1976	1996	1986	1976	1996	1986	1976	1996	1986	1976	1996	1986	1976
Total	**60%**	**65%**	**65%**	**29%**	**28%**	**29%**	**2%**	**2%**	**2%**	**3%**	**2%**	**1%**	**6%**	**3%**	**3%**
Men	56	62	64	32	29	29	2	3	2	3	2	2	7	4	3
Women	63	67	65	26	27	29	3	2	2	3	2	1	5	2	3
Black	83	91	88	9	8	10	0	1	0	1	0	0	5	1	2
White	58	62	63	31	31	30	3	3	2	2	1	1	6	3	3
Aged 18 to 29	51	62	59	31	31	34	1	1	2	5	2	1	11	5	4
Aged 30 to 39	55	58	65	33	36	29	2	2	1	4	2	1	6	2	4
Aged 40 to 49	56	64	57	34	27	35	3	2	1	4	3	3	4	3	4
Aged 50 to 59	71	70	69	21	22	25	3	5	2	2	1	2	4	1	1
Aged 60 to 69	69	66	72	23	25	22	1	3	3	2	2	0	5	4	3
Aged 70 or older	71	76	72	19	18	22	5	3	4	1	2	1	3	2	2
Not high school grad.	65	71	68	23	22	27	1	1	1	3	1	1	8	5	2
High school graduate	61	65	63	29	30	30	1	2	2	2	1	1	6	3	4
Bachelor's degree	56	57	63	29	31	29	6	5	2	4	5	3	4	2	4
Graduate degree	48	49	69	36	31	21	6	8	8	6	9	2	4	4	0

Note: Numbers may not add to 100 because "don't know" and no answer are not included.
Source: General Social Surveys, National Opinion Research Center, University of Chicago

Religious Attendance

Fewer than half of Americans attend religious services regularly.

In a busy world, it is not surprising that the majority of Americans do not attend religious services on a weekly basis. Only 29 percent say they attend at least once a week, and only 45 percent attend once a month or more. In 1976, a larger 35 percent attended services at least weekly while 49 percent attended at least monthly.

Thirty-four percent of women, but only 24 percent of men, attend services at least once a week. Blacks are slightly more likely than whites to attend services weekly.

Many religious institutions have noticed a drop in attendance among younger generations. While 45 percent of people aged 70 or older say they attend religious services at least weekly, only 27 to 29 percent of people aged 30 to 49 do so. Regular attendance is lowest among young adults, with only 19 percent of people under age 30 attending at least weekly.

People who did not complete high school are most likely to say they never attend church (23 percent). This is higher than it was for the same group in 1976, when 13 percent said they never attend. One explanation for this is the older age of those with little education. Many of the oldest Americans are too frail to leave their homes to attend religious services.

Religious Attendance, 1996

"How often do you attend religious services?"

(percent responding by sex, race, age, and education, 1996)

	weekly or more	1 to 3 times a month	up to several times a year	never
Total	**29%**	**16%**	**37%**	**15%**
Men	24	14	41	18
Women	34	17	33	13
Black	32	26	30	8
White	29	14	38	16
Aged 18 to 29	19	18	42	19
Aged 30 to 39	27	17	40	14
Aged 40 to 49	29	15	38	15
Aged 50 to 59	32	17	35	14
Aged 60 to 69	38	15	31	11
Aged 70 or older	45	11	25	16
Not a high school graduate	29	12	32	23
High school graduate	29	16	38	14
Bachelor's degree	31	16	38	13
Graduate degree	33	17	36	11

Note: Numbers may not add to 100 because "don't know" and no answer are not included.
Source: General Social Survey, National Opinion Research Center, University of Chicago

Religious Attendance, 1976 to 1996

"How often do you attend religious services?"

(percent responding by sex, race, age, and education, 1976–96)

	weekly or more			1 to 3 times a month			up to several times a month			never		
	1996	*1986*	*1976*	*1996*	*1986*	*1976*	*1996*	*1986*	*1976*	*1996*	*1986*	*1976*
Total	**29%**	**36%**	**35%**	**16%**	**18%**	**14%**	**37%**	**31%**	**38%**	**15%**	**14%**	**13%**
Men	24	28	28	14	18	15	41	37	43	18	17	13
Women	34	42	40	17	18	12	33	27	34	13	12	13
Black	32	35	37	26	30	25	30	26	33	8	9	5
White	29	37	35	14	16	13	38	32	38	16	15	14
Aged 18 to 29	19	24	24	18	21	15	42	40	40	19	15	21
Aged 30 to 39	27	32	30	17	18	17	40	34	38	14	16	14
Aged 40 to 49	29	35	36	15	20	15	38	33	41	15	12	8
Aged 50 to 59	32	44	44	17	13	10	35	29	38	14	12	8
Aged 60 to 69	38	44	42	15	19	11	31	24	38	11	13	8
Aged 70 or older	45	52	44	11	15	13	25	19	30	16	14	12
Not a high school graduate	29	34	36	12	17	14	32	30	37	23	19	13
High school graduate	29	36	34	16	19	13	38	33	39	14	12	13
Bachelor's degree	31	41	38	16	18	13	38	27	38	13	14	11
Graduate degree	33	39	34	17	16	20	36	33	31	11	13	15

Note: Numbers may not add to 100 because "don't know" and no answer are not included.
Source: General Social Surveys, National Opinion Research Center, University of Chicago

Prayer

Most Americans say a daily prayer.

The majority of Americans say they pray at least once a day (58 percent), a proportion that hasn't changed much since 1985.

Women are much more likely to pray than men. Two-thirds of women say a prayer at least daily compared with only 45 percent of men. One-quarter of men pray less often than once a week compared with only 12 percent of women.

Blacks are more likely than whites to pray daily (73 percent of blacks compared with 55 percent of whites). Twenty percent of whites, but only 7 percent of blacks, pray less often than once a week.

Not surprisingly, the proportion of people who pray at least daily rises with age, from just 42 percent of people under age 30 to 76 percent of people aged 70 or older.

Frequent prayer is also more likely among the less educated—who are also disproportionately older. While 67 percent of people without a high school diploma pray at least once a day, only 53 to 54 percent of those with college degrees join in.

Prayer, 1996

"About how often do you pray?"

(percent responding by sex, race, age, and education, 1996)

	several times a day	once a day	several times a week	once a week	less than once a week	never
Total	**26%**	**32%**	**14%**	**8%**	**18%**	**3%**
Men	20	25	16	10	25	3
Women	30	36	12	7	12	2
Black	41	32	15	4	7	0
White	24	31	13	9	20	3
Aged 18 to 29	13	29	15	10	28	4
Aged 30 to 39	21	29	20	8	17	3
Aged 40 to 49	27	35	10	10	17	2
Aged 50 to 59	33	27	13	5	19	3
Aged 60 to 69	41	31	10	7	10	0
Aged 70 or older	35	41	8	6	7	2
Not a high school graduate	37	30	7	7	15	3
High school graduate	24	34	15	9	17	2
Bachelor's degree	24	30	14	9	18	5
Graduate degree	22	31	11	2	28	5

Note: Numbers may not add to 100 because "don't know" and no answer are not included.
Source: General Social Survey, National Opinion Research Center, University of Chicago

Prayer, 1985 to 1996

"About how often do you pray?"

(percent responding by sex, race, age, and education, 1985–96)

	daily or more		once to several times a week		less than once a week		never	
	1996	1985	1996	1985	1996	1985	1996	1985
Total	**58%**	**57%**	**22%**	**20%**	**18%**	**20%**	**3%**	**1%**
Men	45	46	26	24	25	28	3	2
Women	66	67	19	17	12	14	2	1
Black	73	75	19	13	7	9	0	1
White	55	55	22	21	20	21	3	1
Aged 18 to 29	42	40	25	29	28	29	4	1
Aged 30 to 39	50	49	28	25	17	25	3	1
Aged 40 to 49	62	56	20	26	17	17	2	1
Aged 50 to 59	60	66	18	11	19	20	3	1
Aged 60 to 69	72	74	17	12	10	10	0	1
Aged 70 or older	76	80	14	8	7	9	2	1
Not a high school graduate	67	68	14	13	15	16	3	1
High school graduate	58	55	24	21	17	20	2	1
Bachelor's degree	54	50	23	26	18	22	5	1
Graduate degree	53	42	13	28	28	26	5	2

Note: Numbers may not add to 100 because "don't know" and no answer are not included.
Source: General Social Surveys, National Opinion Research Center, University of Chicago

Life after Death

Most people believe in life after death.

Most Americans take comfort in their belief in an afterlife. Almost three-quarters (73 percent) say they believe in life after death, a proportion that has not changed in the past 20 years.

There is little disagreement on this issue by sex, race, age, and educational attainment. Blacks, however, are slightly less likely than whites (66 percent compared with 74 percent) to believe in life after death.

Interestingly, the oldest Americans are slightly less likely than younger people to believe in an afterlife. While 77 percent of people in their 40s say they believe in life after death, only 65 percent of those aged 70 or older agree. People who did not complete high school are less likely than those with more education to believe in an afterlife. Older Americans make up a large percentage of those without a high school diploma, however, which helps explain the differences in opinion by education.

Life After Death, 1996

"Do you believe there is a life after death?"

(percent responding by sex, race, age, and education, 1996)

	yes	no	undecided
Total	**73%**	**16%**	**10%**
Men	72	16	10
Women	74	15	10
Black	66	19	12
White	74	15	9
Aged 18 to 29	72	16	10
Aged 30 to 39	76	14	9
Aged 40 to 49	77	12	10
Aged 50 to 59	71	17	10
Aged 60 to 69	72	17	8
Aged 70 or older	65	22	11
Not a high school graduate	62	22	15
High school graduate	75	14	10
Bachelor's degree	73	18	6
Graduate degree	72	17	10

Note: Numbers may not add to 100 because no answer is not included.
Source: General Social Survey, National Opinion Research Center, University of Chicago

Life After Death, 1976 to 1996

"Do you believe there is a life after death?"

(percent responding by sex, race, age, and education, 1976–96)

	yes			no			undecided		
	1996	**1986**	**1976**	**1996**	**1986**	**1976**	**1996**	**1986**	**1976**
Total	**73%**	**76%**	**72%**	**16%**	**17%**	**20%**	**10%**	**7%**	**8%**
Men	72	72	71	16	20	22	10	7	7
Women	74	79	72	15	14	18	10	7	10
Black	66	76	67	19	15	25	12	10	8
White	74	76	72	15	17	19	9	7	8
Aged 18 to 29	72	79	68	16	15	24	10	6	9
Aged 30 to 39	76	75	75	14	19	17	9	6	8
Aged 40 to 49	77	78	71	12	15	21	10	7	8
Aged 50 to 59	71	77	70	17	17	20	10	6	10
Aged 60 to 69	72	73	70	17	19	22	8	7	8
Aged 70 or older	65	72	79	22	15	13	11	12	8
Not high school grad.	62	71	71	22	21	21	15	7	8
High school graduate	75	79	72	14	14	20	10	7	8
Bachelor's degree	73	77	72	18	16	19	6	7	9
Graduate degree	72	66	59	17	24	25	10	9	16

Note: Numbers may not add to 100 because no answer is not included.
Source: General Social Surveys, National Opinion Research Center, University of Chicago

What Is the Bible?

Most say it is inspired by God, but not to be taken literally.

Nearly half of Americans view the Bible as "the inspired word of God," not to be taken literally. Only 30 percent say it should be taken literally. Seventeen percent believe it is an ancient book of fables "recorded by men." Since 1985, the proportion accepting a literal interpretation has fallen in most demographic segments, while the proportion saying it is inspired by God or simply a book written by humans has grown.

Disagreements on how the Bible should be interpreted are found within every demographic segment. Women are more likely than men to say the Bible is the actual word of God, although women now are less likely to believe this than they were in 1985. Men are more likely to believe the Bible is simply an ancient book.

Blacks and whites disagree more sharply. Fully 54 percent of blacks, but only 27 percent of whites, believe the Bible is the actual word of God. Whites are considerably more likely to say the Bible is inspired by God or simply an ancient book. Both blacks and whites were less likely to support a literal interpretation in 1996 than they were in 1985.

Generational differences of opinion are less pronounced, but are still apparent. Least likely to believe the Bible should be taken literally are people under age 30 (24 percent), while people aged 60 to 69 are most likely to believe in literal interpretation (41 percent).

The widest gaps are found by education. Nearly half of people who did not complete high school believe the Bible should be taken literally, but only 11 percent of those with graduate degrees agree. College graduates are most likely to say the Bible is a book of ancient fables (27 percent compared with 14 to 15 percent of those with less education.)

What Is the Bible? 1996

"Which of these statements comes closest to describing your feelings about the Bible? a) The Bible is the actual word of God and is to be taken literally, word for word; b) The Bible is the inspired word of God but not everything in it should be taken literally, word for word; or c) The Bible is an ancient book of fables, legends, history, and moral precepts recorded by men."

(percent responding by sex, race, age, and education, 1996)

	actual word	inspired word	ancient book
Total	**30%**	**49%**	**17%**
Men	26	49	22
Women	34	50	13
Black	54	30	13
White	27	53	18
Aged 18 to 29	24	54	19
Aged 30 to 39	30	51	15
Aged 40 to 49	28	52	18
Aged 50 to 59	32	45	20
Aged 60 to 69	41	46	12
Aged 70 or older	36	42	16
Not a high school graduate	48	31	15
High school graduate	33	50	14
Bachelor's degree	14	57	27
Graduate degree	11	57	27

Note: Numbers may not add to 100 because "don't know" and no answer are not included.
Source: General Social Survey, National Opinion Research Center, University of Chicago

What Is the Bible? 1985 to 1996

"Which of these statements comes closest to describing your feelings about the Bible? a) The Bible is the actual word of God and is to be taken literally, word for word; b) The Bible is the inspired word of God but not everything in it should be taken literally, word for word; or c) The Bible is an ancient book of fables, legends, history, and moral precepts recorded by men."

(percent responding by sex, race, age, and education, 1985–96)

	actual word		inspired word		ancient book	
	1996	*1985*	*1996*	*1985*	*1996*	*1985*
Total	**30%**	**38%**	**49%**	**48%**	**17%**	**12%**
Men	26	31	49	51	22	14
Women	34	43	50	45	13	10
Black	54	68	30	24	13	8
White	27	34	53	51	18	12
Aged 18 to 29	24	32	54	49	19	16
Aged 30 to 39	30	32	51	55	15	10
Aged 40 to 49	28	31	52	52	18	16
Aged 50 to 59	32	46	45	43	20	9
Aged 60 to 69	41	46	46	43	12	8
Aged 70 or older	36	49	42	39	16	7
Not a high school graduate	48	64	31	26	15	8
High school graduate	33	34	50	53	14	11
Bachelor's degree	14	18	57	59	27	19
Graduate degree	11	7	57	68	27	23

Note: Numbers may not add to 100 because "don't know" and no answer are not included.
Source: General Social Surveys, National Opinion Research Center, University of Chicago

Confidence in the Leaders of Organized Religion

Only one-quarter of Americans have a great deal of confidence in religious leaders.

The leaders of organized religion do not inspire the confidence they undoubtedly wish to. Only one-quarter of Americans say they have a great deal of confidence in the leaders of organized religion, down from 30 percent in 1976. About one-half say they have "only some" confidence. Nineteen percent say they have hardly any confidence in religious leaders.

Men and women are in agreement on this issue. Blacks, however, are slightly more likely than whites to have a great deal of confidence in religious leaders (33 percent versus 24 percent). Since 1976, confidence in religious leaders has increased slightly among blacks but dropped among whites.

Confidence in religious leaders is highest among the oldest Americans. Thirty-six percent of people aged 70 or older have a great deal of confidence in religious leaders compared with 21 percent of those aged 30 to 49. Among people under age 30, however, 28 percent have a great deal of confidence in religious leaders.

Confidence falls with increasing education. Among people who did not complete high school, 31 percent have a great deal of confidence in religious leaders. But among those with graduate degrees, only 18 percent have a great deal of confidence.

Confidence in the Leaders of Organized Religion, 1996

"As far as the people running organized religion are concerned, would you say you have a great deal of confidence, only some confidence, or hardly any confidence at all in them?"

(percent responding by sex, race, age, and education, 1996)

	a great deal	only some	hardly any
Total	**25%**	**51%**	**19%**
Men	25	50	20
Women	25	52	18
Black	33	46	16
White	24	53	19
Aged 18 to 29	28	46	21
Aged 30 to 39	21	58	17
Aged 40 to 49	21	53	21
Aged 50 to 59	24	49	24
Aged 60 to 69	24	58	13
Aged 70 or older	36	39	15
Not a high school graduate	31	43	17
High school graduate	26	51	18
Bachelor's degree	20	56	21
Graduate degree	18	58	19

Note: Numbers may not add to 100 because "don't know" and no answer are not included.
Source: General Social Survey, National Opinion Research Center, University of Chicago

Confidence in the Leaders of Organized Religion, 1976 to 1996

"As far as the people running organized religion are concerned,
would you say you have a great deal of confidence, only some confidence,
or hardly any confidence at all in them?"

(percent responding by sex, race, age, and education, 1976–96)

	a great deal			only some			hardly any		
	1996	*1986*	*1976*	*1996*	*1986*	*1976*	*1996*	*1986*	*1976*
Total	**25%**	**25%**	**30%**	**51%**	**50%**	**44%**	**19%**	**21%**	**18%**
Men	25	24	31	50	52	43	20	21	19
Women	25	26	30	52	49	46	18	21	18
Black	33	29	28	46	48	45	16	17	17
White	24	25	31	53	51	44	19	21	18
Aged 18 to 29	28	24	30	46	52	46	21	21	20
Aged 30 to 39	21	20	25	58	56	45	17	22	22
Aged 40 to 49	21	19	32	53	55	45	21	24	17
Aged 50 to 59	24	29	27	49	45	48	24	22	21
Aged 60 to 69	24	30	30	58	44	42	13	18	16
Aged 70 or older	36	35	43	39	42	39	15	18	9
Not high school grad.	31	28	30	43	42	41	17	24	19
High school graduate	26	26	31	51	51	46	18	19	18
Bachelor's degree	20	18	30	56	60	48	21	20	17
Graduate degree	18	18	36	58	55	44	19	23	15

Note: Numbers may not add to 100 because "don't know" and no answer are not included.
Source: General Social Surveys, National Opinion Research Center, University of Chicago

School Prayer

Most people disapprove of the Supreme Court ruling on prayer in the schools.

A majority (56 percent) of Americans say they disapprove of the Supreme Court ruling that declared school prayer unconstitutional. Forty percent say they approve of the decision. There has been a slight shift in opinions since 1975, however, with more people approving of the ruling today than two decades ago.

There are large differences of opinion on this issue among different demographic segments. Men and women disagree slightly; men are more likely to approve of the ruling. Blacks and whites show a larger split. Fully 42 percent of whites, but only 28 percent of blacks, approve of the ruling.

Generational differences are striking on this issue. Only 28 percent of people aged 70 or older approve of the ruling. This rises to one-third among those aged 50 to 69 and to 41 percent among those aged 30 to 49. A majority of people under age 30 (51 percent) approve of the ruling.

The largest difference in opinion is by education. Fully 61 to 65 percent of people with college degrees approve of the ruling. This compares with only 25 to 34 percent of those with less education.

School Prayer, 1996

"The United States Supreme Court has ruled that no state or local government
may require the reading of the Lord's Prayer or Bible verses in public schools.
Do you approve or disapprove of the court ruling?"

(percent responding by sex, race, age, and education, 1996)

	approve	disapprove
Total	**40%**	**56%**
Men	42	53
Women	38	58
Black	28	67
White	42	55
Aged 18 to 29	51	44
Aged 30 to 39	41	55
Aged 40 to 49	41	56
Aged 50 to 59	33	64
Aged 60 to 69	33	63
Aged 70 or older	28	64
Not a high school graduate	25	67
High school graduate	34	62
Bachelor's degree	61	35
Graduate degree	65	34

Note: Numbers may not add to 100 because "no opinion" and no answer are not included.
Source: General Social Survey, National Opinion Research Center, University of Chicago

School Prayer, 1975 to 1996

"The United States Supreme Court has ruled that no state or local government may require the reading of the Lord's Prayer or Bible verses in public schools. Do you approve or disapprove of the court ruling?"

(percent responding by sex, race, age, and education, 1975–96)

	approve			disapprove		
	1996	*1986*	*1975*	*1996*	*1986*	*1975*
Total	**40%**	**37%**	**35%**	**56%**	**61%**	**62%**
Men	42	40	36	53	58	60
Women	38	35	34	58	62	63
Black	28	24	25	67	72	69
White	42	40	37	55	58	61
Aged 18 to 29	51	46	47	44	51	48
Aged 30 to 39	41	45	36	55	54	60
Aged 40 to 49	41	41	30	56	59	69
Aged 50 to 59	33	25	33	64	69	65
Aged 60 to 69	33	25	25	63	72	73
Aged 70 or older	28	26	29	64	70	68
Not a high school graduate	25	24	28	67	71	70
High school graduate	34	36	35	62	62	61
Bachelor's degree	61	58	55	35	41	41
Graduate degree	65	69	58	34	31	40

Note: Numbers may not add to 100 because "no opinion" and no answer are not included.
Source: General Social Surveys, National Opinion Research Center, University of Chicago

Chapter 5

Work and Money

Americans are satisfied with their work and relatively content with their financial situations. Most still believe our country allows the average family an opportunity to improve its standard of living, although the share of those who do not agree climbed to one in four between 1987 and 1996.

Most people believe they enjoy a better standard of living than their parents did at the same age, but barely half believe their children will have a better standard of living when they grow up. Women are a little more optimistic than men about their children's future. Most women, but slightly less than half of men, think their children will have a better standard of living as adults.

Most people say they would continue to work even if they didn't need the money. The overwhelming majority of workers believe they are at least somewhat successful in their jobs. They do not attribute their success solely to luck, either. Seven in 10 say hard work rather than luck enables people to get ahead.

Americans would like employers to be more family friendly. Majorities say employers should offer paid time off to new parents and give workers more flexible working hours to handle family responsibilities.

Historically, blacks have had lower incomes than whites and this is behind some of the differences of opinion on financial issues. Blacks are more likely than whites to say they are not satisfied with their financial situation. But blacks are more hopeful than whites that their children will enjoy a better standard of living as adults.

Blacks are less likely than whites to be satisfied with their jobs and to feel very successful at work. They are twice as likely to think they will lose their jobs within 12 months. So it is no surprise that they would be more likely to quit work if they had enough money to live comfortably for the rest of their lives.

On many financial issues, differences in attitudes are strongly associated with age. Behind this association is life stage. Young adults are in entry-level jobs and generally have low incomes. The middle-aged are at the peak of their careers and earnings. Most older Americans are retired and dependent on pensions and Social Security.

Young workers are least satisfied with their jobs and financial situation. They are most likely to feel they are not very successful in their work lives. But low-level jobs have at least one benefit. Younger people are more confident than their elders that they could easily find another job with the same pay and benefits.

Satisfaction with job and financial situation rises with age. But so does the desire to retire. Barely half of workers in their 50s would continue working if they didn't need the money. But three-quarters of workers under age 30 would keep reporting to work even if they won the lottery.

Older workers are less likely than younger workers to believe they could be laid off in the near future, but they also realize it would be difficult to find another job with equivalent pay and benefits.

As a rule, the higher their educational level, the more money people make. This accounts for the greater financial satisfaction found among the college educated. The college educated are more likely than those without college degrees to feel successful at work. Interestingly, they are less likely to attribute their success to hard work and more likely to believe luck plays an equal role in getting ahead.

Satisfaction with Financial Situation

Americans are neither satisfied nor dissatisfied with their finances.

Most Americans don't say that their financial situation is bad, but most don't consider it really good either. Only 28 percent of adults say they are pretty well satisfied with their finances. The same share says they are not at all satisfied. The most common response is the middle ground, with 44 percent saying they are more or less satisfied. This percentage does not vary much by demographic characteristic, but several groups are more likely than average to say they are pretty well or not at all satisfied.

Thirty-seven percent of blacks say they are not at all satisfied with their finances, versus only 26 percent of whites. But the proportion of blacks who are pretty well satisfied with their finances was much higher in 1996 than in 1976, 20 versus 11 percent.

The percentage of people who are most satisfied with their finances rises with age. This is not surprising since younger workers tend to work in lower-wage jobs. One-third of people under age 30 say they are not at all satisfied with their finances, but the proportion drops with age to just 15 percent among people aged 70 or older.

The oldest Americans are most likely to be pretty well satisfied with their finances—47 percent compared with 21 to 39 percent of younger people. This generation has been more successful than any previous generation in building a financially secure retirement—thanks in large measure to gains in home equity, Social Security benefits, and generous pensions. Future generations of retirees may have less reason to be so sanguine.

Education boosts earnings. This relationship is reflected in the fact that the more education people have, the more likely they are to be pretty well satisfied with their financial situation.

Satisfaction with Financial Situation, 1996

"So far as you and your family are concerned, would you say that you are pretty well satisfied with your present financial situation, more or less satisfied, or not satisfied at all?"

(percent responding by sex, race, age, and education, 1996)

	pretty well satisfied	more or less satisfied	not at all satisfied
Total	**28%**	**44%**	**28%**
Men	28	48	25
Women	28	42	30
Black	20	43	37
White	29	45	26
Aged 18 to 29	21	45	33
Aged 30 to 39	21	49	29
Aged 40 to 49	25	45	30
Aged 50 to 59	28	43	29
Aged 60 to 69	39	38	22
Aged 70 or older	47	38	15
Not a high school graduate	25	40	34
High school graduate	26	45	29
Bachelor's degree	32	46	21
Graduate degree	40	41	18

Note: Numbers may not add to 100 because "don't know" and no answer are not included.
Source: General Social Survey, National Opinion Research Center, University of Chicago

Satisfaction with Financial Situation, 1976 to 1996

"So far as you and your family are concerned, would you say that
you are pretty well satisfied with your present financial situation,
more or less satisfied, or not satisfied at all?"

(percent responding by sex, race, age, and education, 1976–96)

	pretty well satisfied			more or less satisfied			not at all satisfied		
	1996	*1986*	*1976*	*1996*	*1986*	*1976*	*1996*	*1986*	*1976*
Total	**28%**	**30%**	**31%**	**44%**	**43%**	**46%**	**28%**	**27%**	**23%**
Men	28	30	31	48	43	44	25	26	25
Women	28	30	30	42	42	47	30	27	22
Black	20	20	11	43	39	47	37	40	42
White	29	32	32	45	43	46	26	25	22
Aged 18 to 29	21	23	26	45	44	43	33	33	31
Aged 30 to 39	21	22	24	49	47	52	29	31	24
Aged 40 to 49	25	28	24	45	42	50	30	29	26
Aged 50 to 59	28	33	33	43	39	50	29	28	15
Aged 60 to 69	39	40	37	38	39	41	22	20	21
Aged 70 or older	47	47	48	38	40	39	15	13	13
Not high school grad.	25	31	28	40	40	46	34	30	26
High school graduate	26	27	32	45	42	44	29	31	23
Bachelor's degree	32	41	34	46	46	47	21	14	20
Graduate degree	40	39	41	41	48	52	18	14	7

Note: Numbers may not add to 100 because "don't know" and no answer are not included.
Source: General Social Surveys, National Opinion Research Center, University of Chicago

Changes in Financial Situation

Americans are split between those who have fared better and those who have fared worse.

Almost equal percentages of Americans say their financial situation has gotten better (39 percent) and gotten worse (40 percent) during the past few years. Only 21 percent say their situation has not changed. Overall, Americans' current assessment of short-term changes in their financial situation is similar to that of 1976.

More men than women say their financial situation has improved—43 percent of men compared with 35 percent of women. Women are more likely than men to say their situation has gotten worse—42 versus 38 percent.

Blacks and whites are equally likely to say their financial situation has improved. But blacks are more likely than whites to say their situation has gotten worse (44 percent of blacks compared with 39 percent of whites).

The attitudes of young and old are far apart on this issue. The proportion of those saying their financial situation has improved drops with age, while the proportion of those saying their situation has deteriorated rises with age. Some of this difference is due to the rising incomes of younger adults as they gain job experience. Most people over age 60, on the other hand, have fixed incomes that, at best, rise at the rate of inflation.

People who did not complete high school are more likely than those with more education to say their financial situation has gotten worse in the past few years. Changes in the economy have reduced the wages of less-educated workers, leaving many of those without a high school diploma in a difficult financial situation.

Changes in Financial Situation, 1996

"During the last few years, has your financial situation been getting better, worse, or has it stayed the same?"

(percent responding by sex, race, age, and education, 1996)

	gotten better	stayed the same	gotten worse
Total	**39%**	**21%**	**40%**
Men	43	19	38
Women	35	22	42
Black	39	16	44
White	39	22	39
Aged 18 to 29	51	16	32
Aged 30 to 39	48	17	35
Aged 40 to 49	35	26	39
Aged 50 to 59	32	28	40
Aged 60 to 69	28	27	44
Aged 70 or older	17	18	64
Not a high school graduate	23	25	52
High school graduate	39	22	39
Bachelor's degree	46	18	35
Graduate degree	49	17	34

Note: Numbers may not add to 100 because "don't know" and no answer are not included.
Source: General Social Survey, University of Chicago, National Opinion Research Center

Changes in Financial Situation, 1976 to 1996

"During the last few years, has your financial situation been getting better, worse, or has it stayed the same?"

(percent responding by sex, race, age, and education, 1976–96)

| | gotten better | | | stayed the same | | | gotten worse | | |
	1996	1986	1976	1996	1986	1976	1996	1986	1976
Total	**39%**	**40%**	**36%**	**21%**	**21%**	**23%**	**40%**	**38%**	**41%**
Men	43	46	39	19	19	22	38	34	39
Women	35	36	34	22	23	24	42	41	42
Black	39	35	21	16	23	36	44	41	43
White	39	41	37	22	21	22	39	37	41
Aged 18 to 29	51	51	46	16	19	22	32	30	32
Aged 30 to 39	48	48	45	17	19	23	35	33	32
Aged 40 to 49	35	48	37	26	19	26	39	32	38
Aged 50 to 59	32	27	32	28	31	22	40	41	45
Aged 60 to 69	28	26	21	27	23	26	44	50	53
Aged 70 or older	17	25	19	18	22	19	64	52	61
Not high school grad.	23	22	21	25	26	29	52	51	50
High school graduate	39	40	41	22	23	21	39	37	38
Bachelor's degree	46	67	54	18	9	16	35	24	30
Graduate degree	49	67	48	17	13	18	34	26	34

Note: Numbers may not add to 100 because "don't know" and no answer are not included.
Source: General Social Surveys, National Opinion Research Center, University of Chicago

Standard of Living Relative to That of Parents

Most people believe they are better off than their parents were at the same age.

Most adults believe their current standard of living is better than what their parents experienced at the same age. A 61 percent majority say they have a better standard of living than their parents, and 32 percent say it is much better.

Blacks are more likely than whites to say their standard of living is higher than that of their parents. Seventy percent of blacks, compared with 60 percent of whites, feel they are better off.

Substantial differences exist among generations. About three-quarters of people aged 60 or older say they are better off than their parents were at their age. Today's elderly have been spared the extreme poverty experienced by many of the elderly in the past, thanks in large part to Social Security. Current retirees have also benefited from unique economic circumstances such as the rapid rise in home values during the 1970s and 1980s as the baby-boom generation bid up the price of homes. This has left today's older Americans better off in retirement than any previous generation.

Younger Americans, on the other hand, have been struggling since the early 1970s with stagnating or declining wages. Only 5 percent of people aged 70 or older say they are worse off than their parents were at that age, compared with fully 22 percent of people in their 30s and 18 percent of those in their 40s.

Standard of Living Relative to That of Parents, 1996

"Compared to your parents when they were the age you are now,
do you think your own standard of living now is much better, somewhat better,
about the same, somewhat worse, or much worse than theirs was?"

(percent responding by sex, race, age, and education, 1996)

	much better	somewhat better	about the same	somewhat worse	much worse	better, total	worse, total
Total	**32%**	**29%**	**21%**	**12%**	**4%**	**61%**	**16%**
Men	36	27	20	12	3	63	15
Women	29	31	21	12	4	60	16
Black	35	35	14	11	2	70	13
White	31	29	22	12	4	60	16
Aged 18 to 29	30	33	22	12	3	63	15
Aged 30 to 39	23	28	25	18	4	51	22
Aged 40 to 49	29	30	22	12	6	59	18
Aged 50 to 59	36	26	21	10	5	62	15
Aged 60 to 69	45	27	14	7	3	72	10
Aged 70 or older	46	30	15	5	0	76	5
Not high school grad.	38	30	16	9	5	68	14
High school graduate	32	28	22	12	4	60	16
Bachelor's degree	27	33	23	14	3	60	17
Graduate degree	33	26	25	10	2	59	12

Note: Numbers may not add to 100 because "don't know" and no answer are not included.
Source: General Social Survey, National Opinion Research Center, University of Chicago

Children's Future Standard of Living

A bare majority believe their children will do better than they are now.

All parents want their children to have a life that is at least as good as theirs. But barely half of Americans believe their children will live better than they themselves do today. Nearly one-quarter (23 percent) believe their children's standard of living will be somewhat or much worse.

The percentage who say their children will do better differs by demographic segment. Among Americans who now have a below-average standard of living, a relatively large percentage expect a better life for their children. Blacks, for example, have the greatest expectations for their children's future. Fully 62 percent believe their children's standard of living will be at least somewhat better than their own. Only 49 percent of whites feel this way.

People with graduate degrees, who command above-average salaries, are least likely to believe their children's standard of living will be better than their own. Only 34 percent of people with graduate degrees expect their children to improve on their own standard of living compared with over half of people with a high school diploma or less education.

Children's Future Standard of Living, 1996

"When your children are at the age you are now, do you think their standard of living will be much better, somewhat better, about the same, somewhat worse, or much worse than yours is now?"

(percent responding by sex, race, age, and education, 1996)

	much better	somewhat better	about the same	somewhat worse	much worse	better, total	worse, total
Total	**21%**	**30%**	**21%**	**18%**	**5%**	**51%**	**23%**
Men	20	27	23	20	6	47	26
Women	23	32	19	17	5	55	22
Black	29	33	10	19	5	62	24
White	20	29	23	18	5	49	23
Aged 18 to 29	26	33	18	15	5	59	20
Aged 30 to 39	17	32	23	16	6	49	22
Aged 40 to 49	22	27	20	22	6	49	28
Aged 50 to 59	16	30	24	23	4	46	27
Aged 60 to 69	21	27	21	20	7	48	27
Aged 70 or older	28	26	19	14	2	54	16
Not high school grad.	22	32	15	18	6	54	24
High school graduate	25	30	18	17	6	55	23
Bachelor's degree	13	31	28	21	3	44	24
Graduate degree	14	20	34	26	3	34	29

Note: Numbers may not add to 100 because "don't know" and no answer are not included.
Source: General Social Survey, National Opinion Research Center, University of Chicago

Would You Work If You Were Rich?

Money isn't the only thing that motivates workers.

About one-third of working Americans would log off their computers or hang up their hammers if they had enough money to live comfortably for the rest of their lives. But two-thirds say they would go on working even if they didn't need the money. Money may be a major reason for working, but it is clearly not the only one.

Men are slightly more likely than women to say they would go on working, although the gap is smaller than it was in 1976, when 71 percent of men but only 64 percent of women said they would continue working. Whites are more likely than blacks to say they would continue working—68 versus 61 percent. The opposite was true in 1976.

Opinions vary the most by age. Three-quarters of young adults, with the enthusiasm of those just entering the work force, say they would keep on working. Among those in their 40s, who have been in the work force for two decades, the proportion drops to 66 percent. Only 54 percent of workers in their 50s, the age at which many people begin to think about retirement, would continue to work if they didn't need the money. Those in their 60s, the age at which most people do retire, are least likely to want to continue working. But the proportion rises again among workers aged 70 or older. Most of these older workers are working only because they want to. Although the actual percentages change from year to year, this pattern was also evident in surveys conducted in 1985 and 1976.

Would You Work If You Were Rich? 1996

"If you were to get enough money to live as comfortably as you would like for the rest of your life, would you continue to work or would you stop working?"

(percent responding by sex, race, age, and education, 1996)

	continue to work	stop working
Total	**67%**	**32%**
Men	69	30
Women	65	33
Black	61	37
White	68	31
Aged 18 to 29	75	24
Aged 30 to 39	72	28
Aged 40 to 49	66	32
Aged 50 to 59	54	43
Aged 60 to 69	48	49
Aged 70 or older	67	24
Not a high school graduate	67	29
High school graduate	64	35
Bachelor's degree	72	27
Graduate degree	67	30

Note: Asked of people who were currently working or temporarily out of work at the time of the survey. Numbers may not add to 100 because "don't know" is not included.
Source: General Social Survey, National Opinion Research Center, University of Chicago

Would You Work if You Were Rich? 1976 to 1996

"If you were to get enough money to live as comfortably as you would like for the rest of your life, would you continue to work or would you stop working?"

(percent responding by sex, race, age, and education, 1976–96)

	continue to work			stop working		
	1996	*1985*	*1976*	*1996*	*1985*	*1976*
Total	**67%**	**68%**	**68%**	**32%**	**30%**	**31%**
Men	69	69	71	30	30	28
Women	65	67	64	33	30	33
Black	61	53	78	37	44	21
White	68	70	67	31	28	31
Aged 18 to 29	75	78	76	24	22	22
Aged 30 to 39	72	75	72	28	23	26
Aged 40 to 49	66	66	69	32	31	30
Aged 50 to 59	54	55	59	43	42	41
Aged 60 to 69	48	46	43	49	51	57
Aged 70 or older	67	50	53	24	44	47
Not a high school graduate	67	57	63	29	42	36
High school graduate	64	66	66	35	31	33
Bachelor's degree	72	80	77	27	19	21
Graduate degree	67	81	81	30	16	19

Note: Asked of people who were currently working or temporarily out of work at the time of the survey. Numbers may not add to 100 because "don't know" is not included.
Source: General Social Surveys, National Opinion Research Center, University of Chicago

Hard Work or Luck?

Most people believe working hard is the key to getting ahead.

A majority of Americans believe it is hard work by which they get ahead. But a substantial minority (29 percent) believe lucky breaks are equally or more important.

Women are more likely than men to believe hard work is the way to get ahead. The oldest and the youngest Americans are more likely than other age groups to feel that hard work is more important than luck. Least likely to agree are people in their 50s. Only 64 percent of this age group view hard work as the most important factor compared with 74 percent of people under age 30.

Interestingly, people with higher levels of education are less likely to believe hard work is the key to success. Three-quarters of people with a high school diploma or less education believe hard work is the key to success. But only 59 to 63 percent of the college educated share this view.

The proportion of Americans saying hard work is more important than luck increased from 1976 to 1996 in every demographic segment. The biggest change was among blacks—in 1976 only 46 percent said hard work was most important, but the proportion rose to 66 percent by 1996.

Hard Work or Luck? 1996

"Some people say that people get ahead by their own hard work; others say that lucky breaks or help from other people are more important. Which do you think is most important?"

(percent responding by sex, race, age, and education, 1996)

	hard work	hard work, luck equally important	luck
Total	**69%**	**18%**	**11%**
Men	66	19	14
Women	72	17	10
Black	66	16	15
White	70	18	11
Aged 18 to 29	74	13	11
Aged 30 to 39	68	20	10
Aged 40 to 49	68	19	11
Aged 50 to 59	64	20	14
Aged 60 to 69	68	19	12
Aged 70 or older	71	15	13
Not a high school graduate	74	13	12
High school graduate	73	16	10
Bachelor's degree	59	26	14
Graduate degree	63	22	15

Note: Numbers may not add to 100 because "don't know" and no answer are not included.
Source: General Social Survey, National Opinion Research Center, University of Chicago

Hard Work or Luck? 1976 to 1996

"Some people say that people get ahead by their own hard work; others say that lucky breaks or help from other people are more important. Which do you think is most important?"

(percent responding by sex, race, age, and education, 1976–96)

	hard work			hard work, luck equally important			luck		
	1996	*1985*	*1976*	*1996*	*1985*	*1976*	*1996*	*1985*	*1976*
Total	**69%**	**66%**	**62%**	**18%**	**18%**	**24%**	**11%**	**14%**	**13%**
Men	66	64	57	19	18	25	14	16	17
Women	72	67	66	17	19	23	10	13	10
Black	66	54	46	16	19	33	15	22	21
White	70	67	64	18	19	23	11	13	12
Aged 18 to 29	74	69	60	13	18	23	11	13	16
Aged 30 to 39	68	70	63	20	15	25	10	14	11
Aged 40 to 49	68	61	64	19	26	23	11	13	12
Aged 50 to 59	64	60	59	20	19	28	14	18	12
Aged 60 to 69	68	69	58	19	16	26	12	14	15
Aged 70 or older	71	61	70	15	18	18	13	17	9
Not high school grad.	74	66	64	13	14	21	12	17	13
High school graduate	73	64	63	16	20	24	10	15	13
Bachelor's degree	59	70	56	26	16	31	14	12	13
Graduate degree	63	63	61	22	27	28	15	9	10

Note: Numbers may not add to 100 because "don't know" and no answer are not included.
Source: General Social Surveys, National Opinion Research Center, University of Chicago

Job Security

Most people do not believe they are in imminent danger of losing their jobs.

In spite of massive layoffs by large corporations around the country, most workers don't believe they will lose their jobs in the near future.

Blacks are less secure than whites about their jobs. While 89 percent of whites say they don't think their jobs are at risk, only 79 percent of blacks say this. In 1986 the gap was wider, however. In that year 89 percent of whites, but only 69 percent of blacks, felt their jobs were secure.

Except for workers aged 70 or older, job security rises with age. Among workers under age 30, 84 percent say they aren't likely to lose their jobs in the next 12 months, a proportion that rises to fully 96 percent among workers in their 60s.

People without college degrees feel more vulnerable than those with college degrees. Twelve percent of those without a bachelor's degree say they are likely to lose their jobs in the coming year compared with 7 to 9 percent of college graduates. Workers who did not complete high school were more secure in 1996 than they were a decade earlier, however. In 1996, 83 percent thought it unlikely they would lose their jobs, up from 77 percent in 1986.

Job Security, 1996

"Thinking about the next 12 months, how likely do you think it is that you will lose your job or be laid off?"

(percent responding by sex, race, age, and education, 1996)

	very likely	fairly likely	not too likely	not at all likely	likely, total	not likely, total
Total	**4%**	**7%**	**28%**	**59%**	**11%**	**87%**
Men	3	6	26	62	9	88
Women	5	7	29	56	12	85
Black	6	12	26	53	18	79
White	4	5	28	61	9	89
Aged 18 to 29	6	7	28	56	13	84
Aged 30 to 39	5	8	29	57	13	86
Aged 40 to 49	2	8	30	57	10	87
Aged 50 to 59	3	5	25	66	8	91
Aged 60 to 69	3	3	17	79	6	96
Aged 70 or older	14	4	18	57	18	75
Not a high school graduate	5	7	24	59	12	83
High school graduate	5	7	28	58	12	86
Bachelor's degree	4	5	27	62	9	89
Graduate degree	2	5	30	63	7	93

Note: Asked of people who were employed at the time of the survey. Numbers may not add to 100 because "don't know" and no answer are not included.
Source: General Social Survey, National Opinion Research, University of Chicago

Job Security, 1977 to 1996

"Thinking about the next 12 months, how likely do you think it is
that you will lose your job or be laid off?"

(percent responding by sex, race, age, and education, 1977–96)

	very/fairly likely			not too/not at all likely		
	1996	*1986*	*1977*	*1996*	*1986*	*1977*
Total	**11%**	**11%**	**10%**	**87%**	**87%**	**88%**
Men	9	10	10	88	87	88
Women	12	10	10	85	87	87
Black	18	23	9	79	69	84
White	9	8	10	89	89	87
Aged 18 to 29	13	9	13	84	90	82
Aged 30 to 39	13	12	12	86	86	87
Aged 40 to 49	10	7	10	87	87	89
Aged 50 to 59	8	13	6	91	81	92
Aged 60 to 69	6	11	5	96	87	92
Aged 70 or older	18	0	12	75	93	88
Not a high school graduate	12	17	13	83	77	83
High school graduate	12	11	10	86	86	87
Bachelor's degree	9	6	3	89	91	97
Graduate degree	7	2	7	93	99	93

Note: Asked of people who were employed at the time of the survey. Numbers may not add to 100 because "don't know" and no answer are not included.
Source: General Social Surveys, National Opinion Research, University of Chicago

Ease of Finding a New Job

Younger workers are least worried about replacing their current jobs.

It's fortunate that most workers don't feel in imminent danger of losing their jobs, since only 26 percent believe it would be very easy to find a new one with equivalent pay and benefits.

One-third of workers say it would be somewhat easy to replace their current job, but the largest proportion—39 percent—say it would not be easy at all. Some demographic segments would find it easier than others, however.

Younger people believe they could very easily find another job with about the same pay and benefits. Only 22 percent of workers under age 30 believe it would not be easy—probably because their jobs typically require little experience or specialized knowledge. As workers get older, however, finding an equivalent job becomes much more difficult. Forty-eight percent of workers in their 40s and 56 percent of those in their 50s say it would not be easy to replace their current pay and benefits.

Workers without a high school degree worry more than those with more education about getting another job with the same pay and benefits. Half say it would not be easy compared with 30 percent of workers with bachelor's degrees. A higher percentage of workers with graduate degrees—41 percent—say they would have difficulty finding an equivalent job. Many of these workers are in highly specialized occupations with a limited number of jobs requiring their particular skills and knowledge.

Ease of Finding a New Job, 1996

"About how easy would it be for you to find a job with another employer with approximately the same income and fringe benefits you have now?"

(percent responding by sex, race, age, and education, 1996)

	very easy	somewhat easy	not easy at all
Total	**26%**	**32%**	**39%**
Men	27	31	38
Women	26	32	39
Black	26	29	42
White	26	32	39
Aged 18 to 29	35	42	22
Aged 30 to 39	28	39	31
Aged 40 to 49	21	28	48
Aged 50 to 59	23	20	56
Aged 60 to 69	27	15	51
Aged 70 or older	18	14	54
Not a high school graduate	29	16	51
High school graduate	26	32	39
Bachelor's degree	28	39	30
Graduate degree	27	28	41

Note: Asked of people who were employed at the time of the survey. Numbers may not add to 100 because "don't know" and no answer are not included.
Source: General Social Survey, National Opinion Research, University of Chicago

Ease of Finding a New Job, 1977 to 1996

"About how easy would it be for you to find a job with another employer with approximately the same income and fringe benefits you have now?"

(percent responding by sex, race, age, and education, 1977–96)

	very easy			somewhat easy			not easy at all		
	1996	1986	1977	1996	1986	1977	1996	1986	1977
Total	**26%**	**27%**	**26%**	**32%**	**32%**	**29%**	**39%**	**38%**	**41%**
Men	27	26	27	31	32	28	38	40	41
Women	26	29	26	32	33	31	39	36	41
Black	26	19	19	29	39	28	42	39	47
White	26	28	27	32	31	29	39	38	40
Aged 18 to 29	35	29	27	42	39	41	22	31	30
Aged 30 to 39	28	28	31	39	38	27	31	33	39
Aged 40 to 49	21	30	23	28	26	28	48	40	45
Aged 50 to 59	23	24	23	20	20	24	56	50	50
Aged 60 to 69	27	13	24	15	22	10	51	62	59
Aged 70 or older	18	31	25	14	8	31	54	54	19
Not high school grad.	29	22	22	16	19	24	51	55	49
High school graduate	26	26	27	32	33	30	39	39	41
Bachelor's degree	28	35	31	39	36	31	30	26	35
Graduate degree	27	30	31	28	36	33	41	34	30

Note: Asked of people who were employed at the time of the survey. Numbers may not add to 100 because "don't know" and no answer are not included.
Source: General Social Surveys, National Opinion Research, University of Chicago

Job Satisfaction

Few people say they are dissatisfied with their jobs.

An overwhelming majority of workers (85 percent) say they are satisfied with the work they do. Forty-five percent say they are very satisfied. In every demographic segment, the percentage of those who say they are moderately or very satisfied with their work is substantially the same as in 1976.

Whites are more likely than blacks to say they are satisfied with the work they do. Eighty-six percent of whites, but only 79 percent of blacks, are satisfied with their jobs.

There is a great deal of variation by age in the percentage saying they are very satisfied with their jobs. Only 37 percent of people under age 30 are very satisfied. The figure rises to 66 percent among people in their 60s, and drops only slightly (to 59 percent) among people in their 70s who are still working. Besides the fact that most young people are in relatively low-paying jobs, young adults are often not sure of their career path. Many will change jobs several times before finding work with which they are happy.

There is little variation by education in the percentages saying they are very or moderately satisfied with their work. People with graduate degrees are more likely to say they are very satisfied, however.

Job Satisfaction, 1996

"On the whole, how satisfied are you with the work you do?"

(percent responding by sex, race, age, and education, 1996)

	very satisfied	moderately satisfied	a little dissatisfied	very dissatisfied	satisfied, total	dissatisfied, total
Total	45%	40%	11%	4%	85%	15%
Men	46	40	10	4	86	14
Women	44	39	12	4	83	16
Black	40	39	16	6	79	22
White	46	40	10	4	86	14
Aged 18 to 29	37	43	13	6	80	19
Aged 30 to 39	43	43	11	3	86	14
Aged 40 to 49	44	40	11	5	84	16
Aged 50 to 59	51	35	9	5	86	14
Aged 60 to 69	66	25	6	4	91	10
Aged 70 or older	59	25	11	5	84	16
Not a high school graduate	45	38	10	5	83	15
High school graduate	43	41	11	4	84	15
Bachelor's degree	46	38	12	4	84	16
Graduate degree	55	31	9	5	86	14

Note: Asked of people currently working at least 10 hours per week. Numbers may not add to 100 because "don't know" and no answer are not included.
Source: General Social Survey, National Opinion Research, University of Chicago

Job Satisfaction, 1986 to 1996

"On the whole, how satisfied are you with the work you do?"

(percent responding by sex, race, age, and education, 1986–96)

	very/moderately satisfied			a little/very dissatisfied		
	1996	*1986*	*1976*	*1996*	*1986*	*1976*
Total	**85%**	**88%**	**85%**	**15%**	**12%**	**13%**
Men	86	90	86	14	11	13
Women	83	87	84	16	12	14
Black	79	83	77	22	17	20
White	86	89	85	14	11	13
Aged 18 to 29	80	85	77	19	15	21
Aged 30 to 39	86	88	86	14	11	13
Aged 40 to 49	84	89	87	16	11	12
Aged 50 to 59	86	89	89	14	11	9
Aged 60 to 69	91	93	93	10	7	4
Aged 70 or older	84	93	82	16	8	12
Not a high school graduate	83	86	84	15	13	14
High school graduate	84	88	85	15	12	14
Bachelor's degree	84	92	88	16	8	10
Graduate degree	86	91	91	14	10	9

Note: Asked of people currently working at least 10 hours per week. Numbers may not add to 100 because "don't know" and no answer are not included.
Source: General Social Surveys, National Opinion Research, University of Chicago

Success in Work Life

Older workers are more likely to feel very successful in their work lives.

A plurality of workers (45 percent) say they are somewhat successful in their work lives. About the same percentage say they are very or completely successful.

Whites are far more likely than blacks to say they are very successful at work. Fully 40 percent of whites say this, compared with only 25 percent of blacks. Blacks are more likely to say they are somewhat successful.

The oldest workers are most likely to feel completely successful in their work. This feeling of success is undoubtedly why they are still working when the majority of their peers have retired. The youngest workers, those under age 30, are most likely to say they are not very successful. These Generation Xers are still in the early stages of their careers and haven't had much time to achieve success.

People with college degrees are more likely than those with less education to say they are successful in their work lives. Fifty-two percent of college graduates and 64 percent of people with graduate degrees say they are very or completely successful, compared with 39 percent of high school graduates and 47 percent of those who did not graduate from high school.

Success in Work Life, 1996

"How successful do you feel in your work life?"

(percent responding by sex, race, age, and education, 1996)

	completely successful	very successful	somewhat successful	not very successful	not at all successful
Total	**9%**	**37%**	**45%**	**7%**	**2%**
Men	10	35	47	7	1
Women	8	39	42	8	2
Black	8	25	54	6	5
White	9	40	43	7	1
Aged 18 to 29	8	30	47	13	1
Aged 30 to 39	7	35	48	7	1
Aged 40 to 49	9	41	42	4	2
Aged 50 to 59	11	39	44	6	1
Aged 60 to 69	14	48	32	5	2
Aged 70 or older	17	29	46	4	4
Not a high school graduate	19	28	43	8	0
High school graduate	9	30	49	9	1
Bachelor's degree	5	47	40	6	1
Graduate degree	8	56	31	4	1

Note: Asked of people who were employed at the time of the survey. Numbers may not add to 100 because "don't know" and no answer are not included.
Source: General Social Survey, National Opinion Research, University of Chicago

Social Class

Few people identify with the upper or lower classes.

Regardless of the definitions sociologists and economists use to classify people by economic class, few Americans see themselves as part of the upper or lower classes. Instead, most consider themselves as part of the working class (45 percent) or middle class (45 percent).

Forty-seven percent of whites consider themselves part of the middle class, compared with only one-third of blacks, who generally have lower incomes than whites. Over half of blacks say they are in the working class.

There is a decided shift from working class to middle class as people get older. Only 37 percent of people under age 30 feel they are part of the middle class, but this share rises to over half among people aged 60 or older. Conversely, 55 percent of the 18-to-29-year-olds say they are in the working class, compared with fewer than one-third of people aged 60 or older.

The most pronounced disparity is by education. The more educated people are, the higher their salaries. While 65 to 67 percent of college graduates say they are middle class, this is true of only 33 to 38 percent of people without college degrees.

Social Class, 1996

"If you were asked to use one of four names for your social class,
which would you say you belong in: the lower class, the working class,
the middle class, or the upper class?"

(percent responding by sex, race, age, and education, 1996)

	lower class	working class	middle class	upper class
Total	6%	45%	45%	4%
Men	4	46	45	4
Women	7	44	45	4
Black	9	55	33	2
White	5	43	47	4
Aged 18 to 29	6	55	37	2
Aged 30 to 39	5	50	42	2
Aged 40 to 49	4	46	44	5
Aged 50 to 59	6	40	46	7
Aged 60 to 69	5	33	56	4
Aged 70 or older	9	30	55	6
Not a high school graduate	13	51	33	2
High school graduate	6	53	38	2
Bachelor's degree	1	25	65	8
Graduate degree	1	16	67	13

Note: Numbers may not add to 100 because "don't know" and no answer are not included.
Source: General Social Survey, National Opinion Research, University of Chicago

Social Class, 1976 to 1996

"If you were asked to use one of four names for your social class, which would you say you belong in: the lower class, the working class, the middle class, or the upper class?"

(percent responding by sex, race, age, and education, 1976–96)

	lower class			working class			middle class			upper class		
	1996	1986	1976	1996	1986	1976	1996	1986	1976	1996	1986	1976
Total	6%	6%	4%	45%	43%	46%	45%	46%	47%	4%	3%	2%
Men	4	5	5	46	44	46	45	46	46	4	3	2
Women	7	7	4	44	42	46	45	47	48	4	3	1
Black	9	15	12	55	51	58	33	31	28	2	2	2
White	5	5	4	43	42	45	47	49	49	4	4	1
Aged 18 to 29	6	6	7	55	49	48	37	44	44	2	0	1
Aged 30 to 39	5	5	3	50	47	49	42	43	46	2	4	1
Aged 40 to 49	4	5	4	46	42	50	44	47	44	5	5	2
Aged 50 to 59	6	9	2	40	41	53	46	44	45	7	6	0
Aged 60 to 69	5	11	4	33	34	44	56	53	50	4	2	2
Aged 70 or older	9	5	5	30	37	29	55	51	62	6	5	3
Not a high school graduate	13	14	7	51	49	56	33	34	36	2	1	1
High school graduate	6	5	3	53	48	48	38	44	47	2	3	1
Bachelor's degree	1	2	1	25	22	19	65	68	78	8	8	2
Graduate degree	1	0	2	16	14	13	67	75	75	13	10	7

Note: Numbers may not add to 100 because "don't know" and no answer are not included.
Source: General Social Survey, National Opinion Research, University of Chicago

Comparing Incomes

Education is the biggest factor in income differences.

Americans have a fairly accurate assessment of their income relative to that of other Americans. Twenty-one percent say their income is above average, while 30 percent say it is below average, leaving half of Americans thinking their income is about average.

Blacks are more likely than whites to think their incomes are below average, but the difference has narrowed since 1976. In that year, half of blacks said their incomes were below or far below average compared with 27 percent of whites. In 1996, just 37 percent of blacks said they had below-average incomes, as did 29 percent of whites.

The oldest (aged 70 or older) and youngest (under age 30) Americans are least likely to say their incomes are above average. Only 14 percent of the elderly and 16 percent of young adults think their incomes are above or far above average. In contrast, 21 to 27 percent of people aged 30 to 69 say their incomes are higher than average. Most likely to say so are people in their 50s (27 percent). This is the age at which earnings peak for most people.

In today's economy, higher education translates into higher incomes. People without high school diplomas are most likely to say their incomes are below or far below average. This share has increased 7 percentage points since 1976. College graduates and those with graduate degrees are most likely to say they have incomes that are above or far above average, at 39 and 50 percent, respectively .

Comparing Incomes, 1996

"Compared with American families in general, would you say your family income is far below average, below average, average, above average, or far above average?"

(percent responding by sex, race, age, and education, 1996)

	far below average	below average	average	above average	far above average	below average, total	above average, total
Total	**6%**	**24%**	**48%**	**18%**	**3%**	**30%**	**21%**
Men	6	20	48	21	3	26	24
Women	6	27	48	16	2	33	18
Black	8	29	54	8	1	37	9
White	6	23	46	20	3	29	23
Aged 18 to 29	8	27	49	14	2	35	16
Aged 30 to 39	4	21	52	19	2	25	21
Aged 40 to 49	6	20	48	22	3	26	25
Aged 50 to 59	8	24	41	24	3	32	27
Aged 60 to 69	5	24	46	19	3	29	22
Aged 70 or older	5	34	45	12	2	39	14
Not high school grad.	11	33	44	8	2	44	10
High school graduate	6	26	51	14	1	32	15
Bachelor's degree	4	14	42	34	5	18	39
Graduate degree	3	11	32	44	6	14	50

Note: Numbers may not add to 100 because "don't know" and no answer are not included.
Source: General Social Survey, National Opinion Research, University of Chicago

Comparing Incomes, 1976 to 1996

"Compared with American families in general, would you say your family income is far below average, below average, average, above average, or far above average?"

(percent responding by sex, race, age, and education, 1971–96)

	far below/below average			average			above/far above average		
	1996	**1986**	**1976**	**1996**	**1986**	**1976**	**1996**	**1986**	**1976**
Total	**30%**	**30%**	**29%**	**48%**	**49%**	**55%**	**21%**	**20%**	**16%**
Men	26	26	30	48	48	48	24	26	21
Women	33	32	28	48	50	60	18	17	11
Black	37	45	50	54	42	43	9	11	5
White	29	27	27	46	50	56	23	22	17
Aged 18 to 29	35	37	32	49	48	53	16	15	14
Aged 30 to 39	25	24	26	52	53	53	21	22	20
Aged 40 to 49	26	25	23	48	45	53	25	30	24
Aged 50 to 59	32	28	24	41	49	59	27	22	16
Aged 60 to 69	29	31	36	46	51	52	22	18	11
Aged 70 or older	39	31	31	45	51	60	14	14	6
Not high school grad.	44	40	37	44	52	57	10	7	5
High school graduate	32	29	26	51	53	58	15	18	16
Bachelor's degree	18	21	19	42	40	39	39	39	40
Graduate degree	14	11	18	32	31	31	50	56	50

Note: Numbers may not add to 100 because "don't know" and no answer are not included.
Source: General Social Survey, National Opinion Research, University of Chicago

Flextime

Most people would like employers to offer flexible working hours.

Americans strongly support "flextime," a system that allows for flexible working hours. Fully 87 percent of adults believe employers should allow flextime for workers to handle family responsibilities.

Although many workplace issues generate disagreement among different segments of the population, this is not one of them. Only one age group stands out on this question. Among people in their 60s, only 79 percent believe employers should allow workers more flexibility in their working hours. Sixteen percent say they should not. In comparison, 85 to 89 percent of the other age groups favor flexible hours.

There are also differences by education in people's responses to this question. People with lower levels of education are less likely to support flextime. Only 84 percent of those without a high school diploma (many of whom are also older) and 86 percent of high school graduates want employers to offer flexible working hours. This share rises to 90 to 93 percent among those with college degrees.

Flextime, 1996

"It is becoming more common for employers to offer ways for people to combine work and being a parent. Please tell me whether or not you think that employers should allow workers more flexible working hours to handle family responsibilities."

(percent responding by sex, race, age, and education, 1996)

	yes	no
Total	**87%**	**10%**
Men	86	12
Women	89	8
Black	88	8
White	88	10
Aged 18 to 29	89	9
Aged 30 to 39	89	9
Aged 40 to 49	89	9
Aged 50 to 59	88	10
Aged 60 to 69	79	16
Aged 70 or older	85	9
Not a high school graduate	84	11
High school graduate	86	11
Bachelor's degree	90	7
Graduate degree	93	5

Note: Numbers may not add to 100 because "don't know" and no answer are not included.
Source: General Social Survey, National Opinion Research, University of Chicago

Parental Leave

Not surprisingly, those who need it most are the most supportive.

The solid majority of Americans (72 percent) believe employers should offer paid time off to new parents. Most likely to support this are people under age 40, who are also most likely to be having children. Fully 84 percent of people aged 18 to 29 and 80 percent of those in their 30s say employers should give parents some paid time off.

After age 40, support drops off considerably, although the majority still favors paid leave for new parents. The least support is found among people in their 60s, only 58 percent of whom believe employers should offer paid parental leave.

Women are stronger supporters than men, which is not surprising since women are most often the primary caregivers of children. Seventy-six percent of women would like to see employers offer paid time off for new parents compared with 68 percent of men.

Blacks are considerably more likely than whites to support parental leave (82 percent of blacks compared with 71 percent of whites). This may be because blacks generally have lower incomes than whites and taking unpaid time off can be a more severe financial hardship for low-wage earners.

Parental Leave, 1996

"It is becoming more common for employers to offer ways for people to combine work and being a parent. Please tell me whether or not you think that employers should offer paid time off to new parents."

(percent responding by sex, race, age, and education, 1996)

	yes	*no*
Total	**72%**	**23%**
Men	68	27
Women	76	20
Black	82	14
White	71	25
Aged 18 to 29	84	12
Aged 30 to 39	80	17
Aged 40 to 49	68	28
Aged 50 to 59	66	28
Aged 60 to 69	58	38
Aged 70 or older	66	26
Not a high school graduate	73	20
High school graduate	72	24
Bachelor's degree	72	24
Graduate degree	77	20

Note: Numbers may not add to 100 because "don't know" and no answer are not included.
Source: General Social Survey, National Opinion Research, University of Chicago

Achieving the Good Life

Americans are more skeptical of their ability to improve their standard of living than they were in 1987.

Most people still believe in the American dream of equal opportunity. Sixty-four percent say that, the way things are in America, people like themselves have a good chance of improving their standard of living. But about one-quarter disagree, up from only 10 percent in 1987. Pessimism is up in all demographic segments.

There is little disagreement between blacks and whites on this issue, but that was not the case in 1987. In that year, whites were considerably more optimistic about the average person's ability to improve his or her standard of living—71 percent compared with 63 percent of blacks. While the optimism of blacks has increased only 2 percentage points since 1987, that of whites has dropped sharply—falling from 71 percent in 1987 to 62 percent in 1996.

Adults under age 30 are more optimistic than their elders, in spite of stereotypes that portray that age group as alienated and pessimistic. Seventy percent say people like themselves have a chance for a better life, compared with only 61 percent of people in their 40s and 70s. Least likely to agree are those in their 60s (56 percent).

People who have at least a high school diploma are more optimistic about their chances than those who did not complete high school. While 64 to 68 percent of people with a high school diploma or more education believe it is possible for people like them to improve their standard of living, only 58 percent of those who did not complete high school agree. Considering the changes in the economy that make it difficult for those with little education to obtain jobs that pay well, they are probably right.

Achieving the Good Life, 1996

"The way things are in America, people like me and my family have a good chance of improving our standard of living. Do you agree or disagree?"

(percent responding by sex, race, age, and education, 1996)

	strongly agree	agree	neither	disagree	strongly disagree	agree, total	disagree, total
Total	**13%**	**51%**	**11%**	**20%**	**4%**	**64%**	**24%**
Men	16	51	10	18	4	67	22
Women	10	50	12	22	4	60	26
Black	11	54	10	22	1	65	23
White	13	49	11	20	4	62	24
Aged 18 to 29	15	55	13	15	2	70	17
Aged 30 to 39	14	51	11	19	4	65	23
Aged 40 to 49	13	48	10	22	4	61	26
Aged 50 to 59	12	51	12	22	4	63	26
Aged 60 to 69	10	46	7	29	6	56	35
Aged 70 or older	11	50	10	19	4	61	23
Not high school grad.	9	49	7	26	5	58	31
High school graduate	13	51	11	19	4	64	23
Bachelor's degree	15	51	11	20	3	66	23
Graduate degree	17	51	15	13	2	68	15

Note: Numbers may not add to 100 because "can't choose" and no answer are not included.
Source: General Social Survey, National Opinion Research, University of Chicago

Achieving the Good Life, 1987 to 1996

"The way things are in America, people like me and my family have a good chance of improving our standard of living. Do you agree or disagree?"

(percent responding by sex, race, age, and education, 1987–96)

	agree/ strongly agree		neither		disagree/ strongly disagree	
	1996	1987	1996	1987	1996	1987
Total	**64%**	**70%**	**11%**	**17%**	**24%**	**10%**
Men	67	73	10	14	22	10
Women	60	67	12	19	26	10
Black	65	63	10	18	23	12
White	62	71	11	17	24	10
Aged 18 to 29	70	65	13	23	17	9
Aged 30 to 39	65	65	11	18	23	15
Aged 40 to 49	61	74	10	13	26	9
Aged 50 to 59	63	74	12	14	26	9
Aged 60 to 69	56	79	7	10	35	7
Aged 70 or older	61	66	10	20	23	10
Not a high school graduate	58	67	7	17	31	12
High school graduate	64	70	11	18	23	11
Bachelor's degree	66	76	11	13	23	8
Graduate degree	68	68	15	24	15	8

Note: Numbers may not add to 100 because "can't choose" and no answer are not included.
Source: General Social Surveys, National Opinion Research, University of Chicago

Chapter 6

Marriage and Family

Americans may fret over the general state of marriage and family, but most of those who have tied the knot say they have happy marriages and successful family lives. A solid majority values the companionship of marriage over freedom and prefers to do things with their spouse rather than pursue separate interests.

The traditional division of labor in marriage—a male breadwinner and a female homemaker—is undesirable to most Americans, however. Younger generations are especially likely to feel spouses should share the responsibilities of money making and caring for home and family.

Although families are still extremely important to Americans, the era of the large family has passed. For most people, two children is the ideal number. Twenty years ago, in contrast, three, four, or even more children were favored by a substantial percentage of Americans—especially older people.

The big challenge today is balancing work and family responsibilities. While most people say they are at least somewhat successful at doing this, large percentages sometimes miss family occasions or neglect household chores because of work demands. And Americans are more likely to work extra hours, rather than cut back on their work responsibilities because of their families.

The public is concerned about the future of the family, however. Substantial numbers fear today's children will grow up to find family life worse than it is now. A larger percentage believes children's chances of happiness will be the same as they are today, however.

One fact bodes well for today's families: men and women are in agreement on most marriage and family issues. Work is a source of potential conflict between the sexes, however. Women are slightly more likely than men to believe family life suffers because men work to much. Bearing out these perceptions, men are more likely than women to say they sometimes miss family occasions or holidays because of work.

These differences may account for the slightly larger percentage of men who long for the good old days of traditional marriage.

Marriage rates among blacks have dropped sharply in the past few decades. Attitudinal differences by race reveal the ambivalence of blacks toward marriage. Blacks are considerably more likely than whites to believe personal freedom is more important than marriage, although the majority of blacks still choose marriage. Blacks are also far less likely to say they have very happy marriages and to feel they are very or completely successful in their family life. Blacks are less likely than whites to believe children will have the same chance at happy families as adults have now. They are more likely to think future families will find happiness even harder to come by.

Generational differences are most pronounced in questions about traditional roles. For many older people, the traditional gender-based division of labor is still preferable. But the attitudes of even the oldest Americans are changing on this issue, and the majority now say responsibilities should be shared. Boomers and Generation Xers are most likely to feel both husband and wife should contribute to household income, and more than half of older Americans agree.

Traditional relationships are also more likely to be favored by people with no more than a high school diploma. This group is also less likely to feel very or completely successful in their family life. Most likely to feel successful are those with college degrees. Perhaps that feeling of success comes from avoiding too much togetherness. The college educated are more likely than those with less education to say they prefer a relationship in which the partners pursue separate interests.

Marital Happiness

Fortysomethings are least likely to say their marriages are very happy.

Most married people describe their marriages as very happy (61 percent). Few say their marriages are not too happy. Since 1976, however, the incidence of very happy marriages has declined in some demographic groups. The steepest decline has been among the oldest Americans.

Men are slightly more likely than women to say their marriages are very happy. A much bigger difference is found by race. While 61 percent of whites say they have very happy marriages, only 49 percent of blacks do. Blacks are almost as likely to say their marriages are only pretty happy (43 percent).

People in their 20s and 60s are most likely to say they have very happy marriages. In 1976, the oldest Americans (aged 70 or older) were most likely to say their marriages were very happy, but the proportion saying this fell from 78 percent to only 63 percent in 1996. Behind this drop may be the increasing longevity of the chronically ill, burdening the spouse with home health care duties.

There was little difference in response to this question by education in 1996. Between 1976 and 1996, however, marital happiness has declined for most educational groups.

Marital Happiness, 1996

"Taking all things together, how would you describe your marriage? Would you say that your marriage is very happy, pretty happy, or not too happy?"

(percent of respondents by sex, race, age, and education, 1996)

	very happy	pretty happy	not too happy
Total	**61%**	**36%**	**2%**
Men	64	33	3
Women	59	38	2
Black	49	43	5
White	61	36	2
Aged 18 to 29	67	30	2
Aged 30 to 39	59	37	2
Aged 40 to 49	55	42	2
Aged 50 to 59	63	34	2
Aged 60 to 69	71	27	2
Aged 70 or older	63	35	1
Not a high school graduate	60	36	2
High school graduate	61	36	2
Bachelor's degree	64	33	2
Graduate degree	62	35	2

Note: Asked of people who were currently married at the time of the survey. Numbers may not add to 100 because "don't know" and no answer are not included.
Source: General Social Survey, National Opinion Research Center, University of Chicago

Marital Happiness, 1976 to 1996

"Taking all things together, how would you describe your marriage? Would you say that your marriage is very happy, pretty happy, or not too happy?"

(percent responding by sex, race, age, and education, 1976–96)

	very happy			pretty happy			not too happy		
	1996	1986	1976	1996	1986	1976	1996	1986	1976
Total	**61%**	**63%**	**67%**	**36%**	**33%**	**31%**	**2%**	**3%**	**2%**
Men	64	61	69	33	36	29	3	3	1
Women	59	64	64	38	31	32	2	4	3
Black	49	51	52	43	43	46	5	5	2
White	61	63	68	36	32	30	2	3	2
Aged 18 to 29	67	62	73	30	34	26	2	4	1
Aged 30 to 39	59	57	65	37	39	32	2	4	3
Aged 40 to 49	55	60	60	42	34	38	2	4	3
Aged 50 to 59	63	64	64	34	32	34	2	3	2
Aged 60 to 69	71	70	67	27	26	31	2	3	2
Aged 70 or older	63	74	78	35	26	19	1	0	3
Not high school grad.	60	61	60	36	36	37	2	2	3
High school graduate	61	63	70	36	33	27	2	4	2
Bachelor's degree	64	71	68	33	24	31	2	4	1
Graduate degree	62	62	70	35	30	28	2	4	2

Note: Asked of people who were married at the time of the survey. Numbers may not add to 100 because "don't know" and no answer are not included.
Source: General Social Surveys, National Opinion Research Center, University of Chicago

Happiness of Romantic Relationships

Happy couples get married.

People in romantic relationships are almost evenly divided between those who say their relationships are pretty happy and those who say they are very happy. In contrast, the solid majority (61 percent) of married couples say their marriages are very happy. The explanation for this difference is that the happiest romantic relationships quickly lead to marriage.

Women and men have similar perspectives on their romantic relationships, although women are more likely than men to say their relationship is not too happy (8 percent of women versus 3 percent of men).

Blacks are considerably less likely than whites to report very happy romantic relationships. Only 35 percent of blacks say their relationship is very happy compared with 50 percent of whites. Ten percent of blacks say their romantic relationship is not too happy.

Older Americans are far more likely than younger adults to say their romantic relationship is not too happy. Fully 15 percent of people in their 60s say their relationship is not too happy compared with 3 to 4 percent of those under age 40. This is hardly surprising. Older singles have a smaller pool of people to choose from, driving many into less-than-ideal relationships. Women are especially disadvantaged since the ratio of women to men rises with age.

Happiness of Romantic Relationship, 1996

"Taking all things together, how would you describe your romantic relationship? Would you say that your relationship is very happy, pretty happy, or not too happy?"

(percent responding by sex, race, age, and education, 1996)

	very happy	pretty happy	not too happy
Total	**46%**	**48%**	**5%**
Men	47	50	3
Women	45	47	8
Black	35	54	10
White	50	45	4
Aged 18 to 29	50	47	3
Aged 30 to 39	45	51	4
Aged 40 to 49	47	46	7
Aged 50 to 59	37	53	10
Aged 60 to 69	46	38	15
Aged 70 or older	33	56	11
Not a high school graduate	41	49	8
High school graduate	43	53	5
Bachelor's degree	46	46	8
Graduate degree	65	35	0

Note: Asked of single persons involved in a romantic relationship at the time of the survey. Numbers may not add to 100 because "don't know" is not included.
Source: General Social Survey, National Opinion Research, University of Chicago

Success in Family Life

Most people feel very or completely successful in family life.

In spite of all the talk about the deteriorating state of the American family, most people say their family life is very or completely successful. Few believe that their families are not very or not at all successful.

Whites are far more likely than blacks to feel successful in their family life. Fully 57 percent of whites say they are very or completely successful compared with only 37 percent of blacks. Blacks don't feel that they are failing at this task, however. Half say they are somewhat successful in their family life.

People aged 50 or older are more likely than younger people to say they are very or completely successful in their family life. While 58 to 62 percent of the older age groups feel successful, only 47 to 53 percent of those under age 50 feel the same way. Indeed, 8 to 10 percent of younger Americans say they are not very or not at all successful, double the 4 to 5 percent share among those aged 50 to 69.

Feeling successful in one's family life increases with education. Among those without a high school diploma, only 46 percent say they are very or completely successful, but the figure rises to 64 percent among those with graduate degrees.

Success in Family Life, 1996

"How successful do you feel in your family life?"

(percent responding by sex, race, age, and education, 1996)

	completely successful	very successful	somewhat successful	not very successful	not at all successful
Total	**13%**	**40%**	**38%**	**7%**	**2%**
Men	13	38	40	6	2
Women	13	42	36	7	2
Black	9	28	50	7	4
White	14	43	35	6	1
Aged 18 to 29	10	39	41	9	1
Aged 30 to 39	8	39	42	7	3
Aged 40 to 49	13	40	37	6	2
Aged 50 to 59	15	43	36	4	0
Aged 60 to 69	21	41	33	5	0
Aged 70 or older	17	42	29	4	4
Not a high school graduate	19	27	42	7	2
High school graduate	12	40	38	7	2
Bachelor's degree	12	46	33	5	1
Graduate degree	10	54	28	7	0

Note: Numbers may not add to 100 because "don't know" and no answer are not included.
Source: General Social Survey, National Opinion Research, University of Chicago

Balancing Work and Family

Most people feel at least somewhat successful at juggling work and family.

Most people would agree that it has become more difficult to balance work and family than it once was. But nearly half (48 percent) of Americans say they are somewhat successful at it. Thirty-one percent think they are very successful at the juggling act.

Women are more likely than men to say they are very or completely successful at balancing work and family (39 percent of women compared with 33 percent of men). Some differences by race exist as well. While 37 percent of whites say they are very or completely successful, only 33 percent of blacks do. On the other hand, whites are more likely than blacks to feel not very or not at all successful at balancing work and family (14 percent of whites versus 9 percent of blacks).

The proportion of those who feel very or completely successful at balancing work and family is lowest in the 30-to-39 age group, when people are most likely to have young children at home. This age group is also most likely to feel not very or not at all successful in balancing work and family, with nearly one in five (18 percent) feeling this way.

There are also important differences in response to this question by education. The proportion of Americans who feel very successful in balancing work and family rises with education. Only 31 percent of people who did not complete high school (most of whom are low-wage earners) say they are very or completely successful at balancing work and family. This compares with 41 percent of people with graduate degrees.

Balancing Work and Family, 1996

"How successful do you feel at balancing your paid work and family life?"

(percent responding by sex, race, age, and education, 1996)

	completely successful	very successful	somewhat successful	not very successful	not at all successful	completely/ very successful	not very/ not at all successful
Total	5%	31%	48%	11%	2%	36%	13%
Men	5	28	50	12	2	33	14
Women	5	34	46	10	3	39	13
Black	4	29	56	6	3	33	9
White	5	32	47	12	2	37	14
Aged 18 to 29	5	31	50	12	1	36	13
Aged 30 to 39	4	25	50	14	4	29	18
Aged 40 to 49	4	37	45	10	2	41	12
Aged 50 to 59	7	31	51	8	2	38	10
Aged 60 to 69	11	32	40	14	0	43	14
Aged 70 or older	4	38	50	4	0	42	4
Not high school grad.	11	20	52	11	3	31	14
High school graduate	4	31	50	12	2	35	14
Bachelor's degree	5	34	47	10	1	39	11
Graduate degree	5	36	42	12	2	41	14

Note: Asked of people who were working or temporarily out of work at the time of the survey. Numbers may not add to 100 because "don't know" and no answer are not included.
Source: General Social Survey, National Opinion Research, University of Chicago

Work Versus Family

Job responsibilities cut into family time for many.

Half of working Americans have missed a family occasion or holiday because of their job responsibilities. Almost half (47 percent) have been unable to keep up with their usual work around the house. But there are limits to the family sacrifices people will make for work. Only 17 percent say work has prevented them from caring for a sick child or relative.

When choosing whether to sacrifice family time for work or work time for family, work is the hands-down winner. A larger proportion of workers have taken on additional work because of family responsibilities (39 percent) than have cut back on their work (23 percent) to spend more time with their family.

Men are much more likely than women to have missed a family occasion or holiday because of work (59 percent compared with 42 percent of women). People in their 30s and 40s are most likely to say they have missed family events. These age groups are also more likely to have been unable to care for a sick family member and to have neglected their chores because of work. Not surprisingly, these age groups are also the most likely to have taken on additional work because of their family responsibilities.

The percentage of people saying they have been unable to do their household chores because of work rises with educational attainment. Only 36 percent of people who did not complete high school say they have been unable to do chores because of work, a figure that rises to 58 percent among those with graduate degrees. Interestingly, however, the most educated workers are least likely to have taken on additional work to meet family responsibilities.

Work Versus Family, 1996

"In your present/most recent job, have you ever done any of
the following because of your responsibilities to the job?"

(percent responding yes by sex, race, age, and education, 1996)

	missed a family occasion or holiday	been unable to care for a sick child or relative	been unable to do the work you usually do around the house
Total	**50%**	**17%**	**47%**
Men	59	16	47
Women	42	19	47
Black	48	17	42
White	51	16	48
Aged 18 to 29	49	13	47
Aged 30 to 39	56	20	57
Aged 40 to 49	50	22	51
Aged 50 to 59	48	19	46
Aged 60 to 69	44	15	37
Aged 70 or older	43	10	22
Not a high school graduate	49	23	36
High school graduate	50	15	46
Bachelor's degree	47	17	51
Graduate degree	45	22	58

Note: Not asked of persons who have never been employed.
Source: General Social Survey, National Opinion Research, University of Chicago

Family Versus Work, 1996

"In your present/most recent job, have you ever done any of
the following because of your responsibilities to members of your family?"

(percent responding yes by sex, race, age, and education, 1996)

	refused a job promotion	taken on additional paid work	refused to work overtime or extra hours	cut back on your work
Total	**11%**	**39%**	**22%**	**23%**
Men	11	46	20	22
Women	11	33	24	24
Black	7	39	19	17
White	12	39	23	24
Aged 18 to 29	9	34	23	22
Aged 30 to 39	12	42	29	28
Aged 40 to 49	13	42	26	25
Aged 50 to 59	10	40	18	22
Aged 60 to 69	7	37	13	16
Aged 70 or older	13	32	12	17
Not a high school graduate	9	42	14	17
High school graduate	11	41	24	21
Bachelor's degree	8	29	21	28
Graduate degree	16	38	27	30

Note: Not asked of persons who have never been employed.
Source: General Social Survey, National Opinion Research, University of Chicago

Do Families Suffer When Men Work Too Much?

Most Americans think men can be too dedicated to their jobs.

Nearly three-quarters of Americans believe family life often suffers because men concentrate too much on their work. Only 15 percent disagree.

Although one might expect this to be a point of contention between men and women, there is only a small difference of opinion. Seventy percent of women and 75 percent of men agree that family life is often the victim of men's focus on work.

Slight differences by age exist in response to this question. Only 69 percent of people under age 30 believe men often focus too much on work to the detriment of family. This figure rises to between 71 and 73 percent among people aged 30 to 59. Among those aged 60 or older, 76 to 78 percent agree. These differences may be the result of differing work experiences or they may reflect a different way in which younger men approach work.

The college educated are more likely than those with less education to believe family life often suffers because men concentrate too much on their work. Among people who did not complete high school, 66 percent agree. This compares with 78 to 79 percent among the college educated.

Do Families Suffer When Men Work Too Much? 1996

"Family life often suffers because men concentrate
too much on their work—do you agree or disagree?"

(percent responding by sex, race, age, and education, 1996)

	strongly agree	agree	neither	disagree	strongly disagree	agree, total	disagree, total
Total	**16%**	**57%**	**12%**	**14%**	**1%**	**73%**	**15%**
Men	15	60	13	9	2	75	11
Women	16	54	11	17	1	70	18
Black	22	48	9	18	1	70	19
White	15	59	11	13	2	74	15
Aged 18 to 29	14	55	13	14	2	69	16
Aged 30 to 39	18	55	11	15	1	73	16
Aged 40 to 49	17	56	13	13	1	73	14
Aged 50 to 59	15	56	14	14	2	71	16
Aged 60 to 69	12	66	10	11	1	78	12
Aged 70 or older	19	57	8	11	2	76	13
Not high school grad.	19	47	13	16	1	66	17
High school graduate	15	56	12	14	2	71	16
Bachelor's degree	15	64	10	10	1	79	11
Graduate degree	15	63	11	10	0	78	10

Note: Numbers may not add to 100 because "can't choose" and no answer are not included.
Source: General Social Survey, National Opinion Research Center, University of Chicago

Will Children Have Happier Family Lives in the Future?

The largest percentage of people think future families will be as happy as they are today.

Americans worry about the future of the family, but only about one-third think children growing up today will have a worse chance of having a happy family life than adults do today. The largest proportion think it will be about the same.

Blacks are more hopeful than whites. Twenty-two percent of blacks think boys have a better chance of having a happy family in the future. Only 16 percent of whites agree. Twenty-seven percent of blacks think girls' future families will be happier than today's compared with 18 percent of whites. But blacks are also more likely than whites to think the chances for a happy family life for boys will be worse in the future than they are today (42 percent of blacks versus 33 percent of whites).

Older Americans are more pessimistic than younger people, and more of them think that children are less likely to have happy families in the future. Younger people are more likely to believe things will stay the same.

People who did not complete high school have more hope for future families than do those with more education. Twenty-seven percent say boys' chances of a happy family life will be better compared with only 14 to 18 percent of those with more education. Girls will have a better shot at a happy family life, according to 28 percent of those without a high school diploma and 16 to 18 percent of those with more education.

Will Children Have Happier Family Lives in the Future? 1996

"Think about girls/boys growing up today. Do you think their chances for a happy family life will be better than yours, about the same, or worse than yours?"

(percent responding by sex, race, age, and education, 1996)

	boys			girls		
	better	*same*	*worse*	*better*	*same*	*worse*
Total	**17%**	**45%**	**34%**	**19%**	**43%**	**35%**
Men	16	49	34	18	45	35
Women	19	43	35	21	41	36
Black	22	31	42	27	30	39
White	16	47	33	18	45	35
Aged 18 to 29	9	57	31	14	54	29
Aged 30 to 39	18	48	32	19	48	32
Aged 40 to 49	22	42	34	22	40	35
Aged 50 to 59	20	44	33	22	41	33
Aged 60 to 69	22	38	37	23	32	42
Aged 70 or older	17	33	42	17	28	51
Not a high school graduate	27	31	37	28	29	40
High school graduate	15	47	35	18	44	36
Bachelor's degree	18	51	27	19	52	27
Graduate degree	14	53	33	16	45	35

Note: Numbers may not add to 100 because "don't know" and no answer are not included.
Source: General Social Survey, National Opinion Research, University of Chicago

Ideal Number of Children

Two is the most popular number.

American families have been shrinking for decades, and this trend is reflected in the number of children people believe is ideal. For the majority of Americans (55 percent), the ideal family has two children. Twenty-one percent think three is best. Only 10 percent think four or more children is ideal. Regardless of sex, race, age, or education, however, people were less likely in 1996 than in 1976 to say four children is the ideal number.

Men and women have similar opinions about the ideal number of children. But blacks and whites differ considerably, with blacks preferring larger families. The majority of whites (57 percent) say two children is ideal, but only 45 percent of blacks agree. Four or more children is ideal according to 17 percent of blacks, compared with only 8 percent of whites.

Both blacks and whites are less likely to favor large families than they were in 1976. The change has been especially pronounced among blacks. The share of blacks who say two is the best number rose by 14 percentage points between 1976 and 1996.

Older Americans still cling to the ideal of a large family. Fully 20 percent of people aged 70 or older believe four or more children is ideal, compared with only 7 percent of those under age 30. In every age group, the proportion favoring large families was smaller in 1996 than in 1976.

People who did not complete high school are less likely than those with more education to say two is the perfect number of children. Only 47 percent of those lacking a high school diploma favor two children compared with 54 to 57 percent of people with at least a high school education.

Ideal Number of Children, 1996

"What do you think is the ideal number of children for a family to have?"

(percent responding by sex, race, age, and education, 1996)

	none	one	two	three	four	five or more	"as many as you want"
Total	1%	3%	55%	21%	8%	2%	6%
Men	2	3	53	22	7	1	6
Women	1	2	56	20	9	2	6
Black	2	2	45	22	12	5	7
White	1	3	57	20	7	1	6
Aged 18 to 29	1	4	59	21	6	1	5
Aged 30 to 39	1	4	54	23	8	2	6
Aged 40 to 49	2	3	58	19	7	2	6
Aged 50 to 59	1	1	61	17	7	0	7
Aged 60 to 69	1	2	49	24	10	4	5
Aged 70 or older	1	1	40	23	18	2	9
Not high school grad.	3	2	47	21	11	5	7
High school graduate	1	2	56	21	9	1	5
Bachelor's degree	1	4	57	20	6	1	7
Graduate degree	0	3	54	21	4	2	11

Note: Numbers may not add to 100 because "don't know" and no answer are not included.
Source: General Social Survey, National Opinion Research Center, University of Chicago

Ideal Number of Children, 1976 to 1996

"What do you think is the ideal number of children for a family to have?"

(percent responding by sex, race, age, and education, 1976–96)

	two			three			four		
	1996	*1986*	*1976*	*1996*	*1986*	*1976*	*1996*	*1986*	*1976*
Total	**55%**	**50%**	**50%**	**21%**	**24%**	**20%**	**8%**	**13%**	**13%**
Men	53	50	49	22	26	21	7	10	11
Women	56	51	52	20	23	19	9	14	14
Black	45	42	31	22	22	17	12	19	18
White	57	52	52	20	25	20	7	11	12
Aged 18 to 29	59	52	55	21	29	22	6	10	9
Aged 30 to 39	54	59	56	23	20	17	8	11	10
Aged 40 to 49	58	50	52	19	20	19	7	14	9
Aged 50 to 59	61	49	46	17	22	23	7	12	16
Aged 60 to 69	49	45	45	24	26	20	10	16	18
Aged 70 or older	40	40	39	23	30	18	18	14	22
Not high school grad.	47	45	41	21	23	19	11	17	20
High school graduate	56	52	54	21	25	21	9	12	10
Bachelor's degree	57	52	60	20	27	20	6	10	7
Graduate degree	54	54	62	21	24	13	4	9	7

Note: Numbers will not add to 100 because not all answers are shown.
Source: General Social Surveys, National Opinion Research Center, University of Chicago

Most Important Qualities in Children

Most Americans want kids to be independent.

We are a nation of individualists, and our children are being raised to carry on this tradition. Half of Americans (51 percent) say it is most important that children learn to think for themselves. People are far more likely to rank independent thinking first than other qualities such as obedience, hard work, helping others, or being popular.

Women are more likely than men to put the highest value on independent thinking (56 versus 44 percent). Whites are more likely than blacks to say thinking for oneself is most important (53 versus 44 percent). Blacks are more likely than whites to say it is most important for children to learn to obey (29 percent of blacks compared with 16 percent of whites).

Substantial differences by age exist in the rankings of obedience and independent thinking. People aged 30 to 59 are more likely than older or younger age groups to say teaching children to think for themselves is most important (53 to 58 percent compared with 45 percent of people under age 30 and 38 to 45 percent of people aged 60 or older). Older Americans are far more likely to say obedience is most important (26 to 29 percent compared with 13 to 18 percent of those under age 60), while people under age 30 are more likely than other age groups to believe children need to learn to work hard. Within each age group, the percentage of those who rank the ability to work hard as the most important quality has grown since 1986. The proportion of those who say obedience is most important has declined in almost every age group.

People with different levels of education have substantially different views on what children need to succeed. Only one-third of people who did not complete high school (many of whom are older) rank independent thinking as the most important quality in children. This rises to 71 percent among those with graduate degrees. The proportion saying hard work is most important is highest (19 percent) among those with the least education.

Most Important Qualities in Children, 1996

"If you had to choose, which thing on this list would you pick as
the most important for a child to learn to prepare him or her for life?"

(percent choosing a quality as most important, by sex, race, age, and education, 1996)

	to think for himself or herself	to obey	to work hard	to help others	to be popular
Total	**51%**	**18%**	**17%**	**13%**	**1%**
Men	44	20	20	14	1
Women	56	16	15	11	0
Black	39	29	20	11	0
White	53	16	16	13	1
Aged 18 to 29	45	16	24	13	0
Aged 30 to 39	53	13	16	16	0
Aged 40 to 49	58	15	14	11	1
Aged 50 to 59	57	18	14	9	0
Aged 60 to 69	45	29	13	10	1
Aged 70 or older	38	26	19	14	2
Not a high school graduate	33	28	19	17	1
High school graduate	48	20	18	12	1
Bachelor's degree	62	8	16	13	1
Graduate degree	71	10	8	7	0

Note: Numbers may not add to 100 because of rounding.
Source: General Social Survey, National Opinion Research Center, University of Chicago

Most Important Qualities in Children, 1986 to 1996

"If you had to choose, which thing on this list would you pick as the most important for a child to learn to prepare him or her for life?"

(percent choosing a quality as most important, by sex, race, age, and education, 1986–96)

	to think for himself or herself		to obey		to work hard		to help others		to be popular	
	1996	*1986*	*1996*	*1986*	*1996*	*1986*	*1996*	*1986*	*1996*	*1986*
Total	**51%**	**51%**	**18%**	**23%**	**17%**	**11%**	**13%**	**14%**	**1%**	**1%**
Men	44	50	20	18	20	14	14	16	1	1
Women	56	52	16	26	15	9	11	12	0	0
Black	39	48	29	23	20	14	11	14	0	1
White	53	52	16	23	16	10	13	13	1	0
Aged 18 to 29	45	49	16	18	24	14	13	18	0	0
Aged 30 to 39	53	61	13	13	16	13	16	11	0	1
Aged 40 to 49	58	59	15	24	14	10	11	7	1	0
Aged 50 to 59	57	46	18	26	14	10	9	15	0	1
Aged 60 to 69	45	46	29	35	13	5	10	13	1	1
Aged 70 or older	38	34	26	31	19	12	14	20	2	1
Not a high school graduate	33	28	28	36	19	14	17	18	1	2
High school graduate	48	53	20	22	18	10	12	13	1	0
Bachelor's degree	62	67	8	11	16	11	13	11	1	0
Graduate degree	71	88	10	2	8	6	7	2	0	0

Note: Numbers may not add to 100 because of rounding.
Source: General Social Surveys, National Opinion Research Center, University of Chicago

Spanking Children

Most people still believe in spanking, but the number is down from a decade ago.

While "time out" has become the discipline of choice for many parents in recent years, spanking still remains popular. Seventy-one percent of Americans say a good, hard spanking is sometimes necessary for disciplining children. Studies by social researchers indicating that spanking may do more harm than good may be influencing parents, however. The proportion of the public that favors spanking is down from 83 percent in 1986.

Blacks are far more likely than whites to believe in spanking. Fully 82 percent of blacks say a spanking is sometimes necessary compared with 70 percent of whites.

People 18 to 29 and 40 to 49 are less likely than other age groups to feel a spanking is sometimes necessary (67 to 68 percent compared with 72 to 81 percent of other age groups).

College graduates are less enthusiastic about spanking than those with less education. Among people who did not complete high school, 79 percent say children sometimes need a spanking. Among college graduates, however, only 63 to 64 percent agree.

The proportion of people who believe in spanking is down since 1986 for all demographic groups. The biggest declines came among people under age 30 (down 16 percentage points since 1986) and the college educated (down 16 to 20 percentage points).

Spanking Children, 1996

"It is sometimes necessary to discipline a child with a good, hard spanking—do you agree or disagree?"

(percent responding by sex, race, age, and education, 1996)

	strongly agree	agree	disagree	strongly disagree	agree, total	disagree, total
Total	**26%**	**45%**	**18%**	**8%**	**71%**	**26%**
Men	28	45	18	7	73	25
Women	24	46	18	10	70	28
Black	39	43	12	5	82	17
White	24	46	19	9	70	28
Aged 18 to 29	22	46	19	10	68	29
Aged 30 to 39	25	48	17	7	73	24
Aged 40 to 49	25	42	21	11	67	32
Aged 50 to 59	29	44	17	9	73	26
Aged 60 to 69	34	47	15	3	81	18
Aged 70 or older	27	45	17	7	72	24
Not a high school graduate	37	42	14	6	79	20
High school graduate	27	46	17	8	73	25
Bachelor's degree	21	42	25	10	63	35
Graduate degree	16	48	20	14	64	34

Note: Numbers may not add to 100 because "don't know" and no answer are not included.
Source: General Social Survey, National Opinion Research Center, University of Chicago

Spanking Children, 1986 to 1996

"It is sometimes necessary to discipline a child with a good,
hard spanking—do you agree or disagree?"

(percent responding by sex, race, age, and education, 1986-96)

| | agree/strongly agree | | disagree/strongly disagree | |
	1996	1986	1996	1986
Total	**71%**	**83%**	**26%**	**16%**
Men	73	84	25	15
Women	70	83	28	17
Black	82	89	17	10
White	70	82	28	17
Aged 18 to 29	68	84	29	15
Aged 30 to 39	73	84	24	16
Aged 40 to 49	67	79	32	19
Aged 50 to 59	73	87	26	11
Aged 60 to 69	81	83	18	16
Aged 70 or older	72	80	24	20
Not a high school graduate	79	86	20	14
High school graduate	73	83	25	17
Bachelor's degree	63	79	35	21
Graduate degree	64	84	34	14

Note: Numbers may not add to 100 because "don't know" and no answer are not included.
Source: General Social Surveys, National Opinion Research Center, University of Chicago

Is Freedom More Important than Marriage?

Most people value marriage more than freedom.

Fully 69 percent of Americans do not consider freedom more important than marriage. Only 14 percent say it is.

Most likely to feel freedom outweighs the companionship of marriage are blacks and people who did not complete high school (29 percent and 20 percent, respectively). Among other demographic groups, between 11 and 16 percent agree.

Contrary to the stereotype of the man who is unwilling to make a commitment, men favor marriage over freedom more than women. Seventy-four percent of men, but only 65 percent of women, think marriage is more important than freedom. Seventy-one percent of whites see marriage as more important than freedom compared with only 59 percent of blacks.

The proportion of people saying marriage is more important than freedom rises slightly with age, from 65 percent of those aged 18 to 29 to 75 percent of those in their 60s.

For most demographic groups, the proportion of those who say freedom is more important than marriage hasn't changed appreciably since 1988. But there has been a shift away from a neutral position to disagreement. In 1988 55 percent of Americans said they did not value freedom more than the companionship of marriage. By 1996 the share had increased to 69 percent.

The largest changes came about among blacks and among people under age 30. The proportion of those who say they do not believe freedom is more important than marriage increased by 20 percentage points in both these groups.

Is Freedom More Important than Marriage? 1996

"Personal freedom is more important than the companionship
of marriage—do you agree or disagree?"

(percent responding by sex, race, age, and education, 1996)

	strongly agree	agree	neither	disagree	strongly disagree	agree, total	disagree, total
Total	**4%**	**10%**	**15%**	**48%**	**21%**	**14%**	**69%**
Men	3	9	13	51	23	12	74
Women	5	11	17	45	20	16	65
Black	10	19	9	40	19	29	59
White	3	9	15	49	22	12	71
Aged 18 to 29	4	10	21	47	18	14	65
Aged 30 to 39	4	11	16	45	23	15	68
Aged 40 to 49	3	13	14	47	21	16	68
Aged 50 to 59	3	11	14	46	24	14	70
Aged 60 to 69	2	10	10	54	21	12	75
Aged 70 or older	9	6	8	53	19	15	72
Not high school grad.	8	12	9	45	22	20	67
High school graduate	4	10	15	47	23	14	70
Bachelor's degree	4	12	15	49	19	16	68
Graduate degree	1	10	25	48	13	11	61

Note: Numbers may not add to 100 because "can't choose" and no answer are not included.
Source: General Social Survey, National Opinion Research, University of Chicago

Is Freedom More Important than Marriage? 1988 to 1996

"Personal freedom is more important than the companionship
of marriage—do you agree or disagree?"

(percent responding by sex, race, age, and education, 1988–96)

	agree/ strongly agree		neither		disagree/ strongly disagree	
	1996	*1988*	*1996*	*1988*	*1996*	*1988*
Total	**14%**	**15%**	**15%**	**24%**	**69%**	**55%**
Men	12	16	13	21	74	58
Women	16	14	17	27	65	52
Black	29	31	9	26	59	39
White	12	13	15	24	71	57
Aged 18 to 29	14	20	21	32	65	45
Aged 30 to 39	15	16	16	25	68	55
Aged 40 to 49	16	13	14	22	68	61
Aged 50 to 59	14	18	14	22	70	57
Aged 60 to 69	12	10	10	24	75	59
Aged 70 or older	15	12	8	16	72	58
Not a high school graduate	20	18	9	22	67	51
High school graduate	14	14	15	26	70	56
Bachelor's degree	16	12	15	20	68	63
Graduate degree	11	18	25	27	61	52

Note: Numbers may not add to 100 because "can't choose" and no answer are not included.
Source: General Social Surveys, National Opinion Research, University of Chicago

Traditional or Modern Relationship?

Traditional families are a thing of the past.

Fully 70 percent of Americans say they prefer a relationship in which responsibilities for making money and caring for home and family are shared by husband and wife. This strong support reflects the life styles of the baby-boom and younger generations of Americans.

Men cling to traditional roles more than women do. About one-third of men say they prefer the traditional arrangement compared with 28 percent of women.

Black women historically have been more likely to work than white women. This may be why there is such a difference by race in preferences for a traditional relationship. Thirty-one percent of whites, but only 21 percent of blacks, say they prefer having the husband earn the money while the wife takes care of home and family.

The biggest differences in opinion are by age. Only 20 percent of people under age 30 prefer a traditional relationship. Among people aged 30 to 59, 27 to 29 percent prefer a traditional arrangement. But this proportion jumps to 40 percent among people in their 60s and 45 percent among those aged 70 or older.

People without a college degree (many of whom are older Americans) are also more likely to prefer a traditional division of labor (32 to 33 percent compared with 20 to 27 percent for those with college degrees).

Preference for Traditional or Modern Relationship? 1996

"Which type of relationship with a spouse or partner would you prefer?
One in which the man has the main responsibility for providing the household
income and the woman has the main responsibility for taking care of home and
family or one in which the man and woman equally share responsibilities?"

(percent responding by sex, race, age, and education, 1996)

	man provides income, woman cares for home and family	responsibilities are shared
Total	**30%**	**70%**
Men	32	68
Women	28	71
Black	21	78
White	31	68
Aged 18 to 29	20	79
Aged 30 to 39	27	72
Aged 40 to 49	28	71
Aged 50 to 59	29	71
Aged 60 to 69	40	60
Aged 70 or older	45	53
Not a high school graduate	33	67
High school graduate	32	68
Bachelor's degree	27	72
Graduate degree	20	80

Note: Numbers may not add to 100 because "don't know" and no answer are not included.
Source: General Social Survey, National Opinion Research, University of Chicago

Shared or Separate Social Lives

Most people want to socialize with their spouse or partner.

Americans value their independence, but in relationships they want to share their lives. Three-quarters of Americans say they prefer a relationship in which the spouses or partners do most things in their social life together. Only 22 percent prefer to pursue separate interests.

Whites are only slightly more likely than blacks to prefer pursuing separate interests (23 percent of whites compared with 19 percent of blacks). A bigger difference exists between people by age. Life stage probably accounts for these differences. People under age 30 are still building their relationships and are more likely than most other age groups to prefer a joint social life. Most of those aged 40 to 59, however, have been married for some time. This age group is less likely to want to spend most of their free time together. The early years of retirement boost interest in togetherness, but this falls off slightly among those aged 70 or older.

The biggest difference in opinion on this question is by education. While 74 to 79 percent of people without college degrees think husband and wife should do most things in their social life together, only 65 to 69 percent of those with college degrees agree.

Should Spouses Have Shared or Separate Social Lives? 1996

"Which type of relationship with a spouse or partner would you prefer?
A relationship where the man and woman do most things in their social life
together or one in which they do separate things that interest them?"

(percent responding by sex, race, age, and education, 1996)

	do most things together	pursue separate interests
Total	**75%**	**22%**
Men	74	23
Women	76	22
Black	78	19
White	75	23
Aged 18 to 29	79	18
Aged 30 to 39	78	21
Aged 40 to 49	72	24
Aged 50 to 59	71	27
Aged 60 to 69	78	21
Aged 70 or older	71	25
Not a high school graduate	74	22
High school graduate	79	19
Bachelor's degree	69	28
Graduate degree	65	32

Note: Numbers may not add to 100 because "don't know" and no answer are not included.
Source: General Social Survey, National Opinion Research, University of Chicago

Should Both Spouses Contribute to Household Income?

Most people now believe bringing home the bacon is a joint responsibility.

Women's incomes are no longer viewed as pin money, something to save for a rainy day. Fully two-thirds of Americans believe both husband and wife should make a financial contribution to the household. This share is up significantly from 48 percent in 1988.

The incomes of blacks are generally lower than those of whites, which probably explains the large difference of opinion by race on this issue. Fully 87 percent of blacks believe both spouses should contribute to the income of the household compared with 63 percent of whites.

An income disparity is probably also behind the difference in response by education. People who did not graduate from high school have considerably lower incomes than those with more education. Nongraduates are also most likely to say both husband and wife should be responsible for the household income (76 percent compared with 61 to 66 percent of those with more education).

Generational differences are apparent on this issue. Fully 80 percent of Generation Xers (under age 30) believe both members of a couple should contribute. This drops to 66 to 68 percent among boomers (aged 30 to 49) and 62 percent among people in their 50s. Only 55 to 59 percent of the oldest Americans feel both husband and wife have an obligation to contribute.

Should Both Spouses Contribute to Household Income? 1996

"Do you agree or disagree with this statement: Both the husband and wife should contribute to the household income."

(percent responding by sex, race, age, and education, 1996)

	agree strongly	agree	neither	disagree	disagree strongly	agree, total	disagree, total
Total	**30%**	**37%**	**21%**	**9%**	**2%**	**67%**	**11%**
Men	27	39	21	10	2	66	12
Women	32	35	20	9	2	67	11
Black	51	36	10	1	1	87	2
White	26	37	23	11	2	63	13
Aged 18 to 29	42	38	13	5	1	80	6
Aged 30 to 39	30	38	21	6	3	68	9
Aged 40 to 49	27	39	24	9	1	66	10
Aged 50 to 59	29	33	26	11	1	62	12
Aged 60 to 69	22	33	26	15	3	55	18
Aged 70 or older	22	37	17	17	2	59	19
Not high school grad.	36	40	10	10	1	76	11
High school graduate	30	36	21	10	2	66	12
Bachelor's degree	28	34	25	10	2	62	12
Graduate degree	25	36	30	5	4	61	9

Note: Numbers may not add to 100 because "can't choose" and no answer are not included.
Source: General Social Survey, National Opinion Research, University of Chicago

Should Both Spouses Contribute to Household Income? 1988 to 1996

"Do you agree or disagree with this statement: Both the husband and wife should contribute to the household income."

(percent responding by sex, race, age, and education, 1988–96)

	agree/ strongly agree		neither		disagree/ strongly disagree	
	1996	1988	1996	1988	1996	1988
Total	**67%**	**48%**	**21%**	**29%**	**11%**	**19%**
Men	66	46	21	32	12	19
Women	67	49	20	27	11	18
Black	87	73	10	12	2	8
White	63	44	23	32	13	20
Aged 18 to 29	80	58	13	26	6	14
Aged 30 to 39	68	45	21	35	9	16
Aged 40 to 49	66	41	24	31	10	23
Aged 50 to 59	62	48	26	30	12	20
Aged 60 to 69	55	41	26	28	18	23
Aged 70 or older	59	48	17	23	19	23
Not a high school graduate	76	54	10	20	11	19
High school graduate	66	46	21	30	12	19
Bachelor's degree	62	41	25	37	12	20
Graduate degree	61	41	30	44	9	13

Note: Numbers may not add to 100 because "can't choose" and no answer are not included.
Source: General Social Surveys, National Opinion Research, University of Chicago

How Married Couples Organize Their Finances

The largest share of couples pool their money.

When husbands were breadwinners and wives were homemakers, many women received an allowance while their husbands managed the family's money. This arrangement suits only 9 percent of married couples now. The most common arrangement is that of one pool of money with each spouse taking out whatever he or she needs (37 percent). The second most common arrangement (28 percent) is that of a wife who manages the family's money—except for the husband's personal spending money.

Blacks are much more likely than whites to have an arrangement in which the wife has a housekeeping allowance while the husband manages the rest of the money (20 percent of blacks versus 7 percent of whites). Only 20 percent of blacks say they pool their money compared with 38 percent of whites.

People with college degrees are considerably more likely than those with less education to pool their money. While 42 to 43 percent of the college educated say they pool their money, this is true for only 30 to 34 percent of people who do not have a college diploma. For people without a college degree, it is more common for the wife to manage the family's money (31 to 34 percent compared with 16 to 25 percent of those with college degrees).

How Married Couples Organize Their Finances, 1996

"Which of the following comes closest to describing the system that you and your husband/wife use to organize your finances?"

(percent responding by sex, race, age, and education, 1996)

	wife manages money, except husband's personal spending money	husband manages money, except wife's personal spending money	wife has housekeeping allowance, husband manages rest of money	all money pooled, each takes out what he/she needs	some money pooled, each partner has some separate	keep finances completely separate
Total	**28%**	**9%**	**8%**	**37%**	**13%**	**5%**
Men	28	10	6	36	14	5
Women	28	7	10	37	12	4
Black	23	9	20	20	18	11
White	29	8	7	38	13	4
Aged 18 to 29	26	10	3	45	12	4
Aged 30 to 39	28	8	10	38	13	3
Aged 40 to 49	28	9	9	33	15	4
Aged 50 to 59	28	9	6	37	13	5
Aged 60 to 69	29	10	11	35	8	6
Aged 70 or older	35	4	6	33	10	10
Not a high school graduate	31	14	10	30	9	4
High school graduate	34	6	8	34	13	4
Bachelor's degree	16	15	8	42	14	4
Graduate degree	25	6	8	43	12	6

Note: Asked of people who were married at the time of the survey. Numbers may not add to 100 because no answer is not included.
Source: General Social Survey, National Opinion Research, University of Chicago

Chapter 7

Women's Roles

Attitudes towards the roles of women have changed dramatically over the past two decades—perhaps more so than opinions about any other topic. Most Americans no longer believe women should be homemakers who leave business and politics to men.

Solid majorities are comfortable with women in the workplace. They do not believe a husband's career is more important than his wife's, nor do they think there is anything wrong with women working even if they don't need the money. Two decades ago, however, most people believed a husband's career came first and that it was better for everyone if the woman was a homemaker. And although most people don't want to be called feminists, solid majorities credit the women's movement with improving the lives of working women.

Although one might assume that women and men would disagree on women's issues, this is not the case for most of the questions examined here. The opinions of men and women do diverge, however, on working mothers and on affirmative action for women.

Women are less likely than men to believe young children suffer if their mothers work. Far more women than men believe working mothers can have just as good a relationship with their children as nonworking mothers.

There is also a big gap between the percentages of men and women who support affirmative action. Predictably, women are more supportive than men. But women are also more likely to believe a woman will be passed over for a job or promotion in favor of an equally or less qualified man. The solid majority of women, but not quite half of men, attribute the earnings gap between men and women to the tendency of employers to give better-paying jobs to men.

Blacks and whites disagree on women's issues about as much as men and women do. Blacks are far more supportive than whites of affirmative action for women. They also consider women's rights a more important issue than do whites, and they are more likely to believe the women's movement has benefited homemakers. Perhaps because black mothers have historically had to work, blacks think more highly of working mothers.

Many older Americans still hold traditional attitudes towards women's roles. Most people aged 60 or older believe it is better for everyone if women take care of the home and family while men earn the money, an opinion shared by only a small minority of people under age 50. Older Americans are more inclined to believe preschoolers suffer if their mother works and are more skeptical of a working mother's ability to establish a good relationship with her children.

Most people under age 60 do not believe men are better suited than women for political life or that women should let men run the country. But among those aged 60 or older, sizable minorities still believe women and politics don't mix.

Considerable disagreement exists among segments with differing educational attainments about the appropriate roles for women. People who did not complete high school (a group that includes a disproportionately large number of older people) are especially likely to favor traditional roles for women. This group is far more likely to believe a husband's career is more important than a wife's and to think women should leave running the country up to men. Those without a high school diploma are also less likely to believe a working mother's relationship with her children can be as good as that of a nonworking mother.

College graduates are more likely than those with less education to disagree that the best arrangement is that of female homemaker and male breadwinner. But they are less likely than those with less education to support affirmative action for women.

Should Only Men Run the Country?

Few people believe running the country is only a man's job.

Should women stick to running their homes and leave running the country up to men? The majority of Americans (80 percent) say no, up substantially from 1975 when only 62 percent said no.

Men and women are about equally likely to say there is no reason why women can't be in the house—and the Senate. The proportions of both sexes who believe women should leave running the country up to men has declined since 1975.

People aged 60 or older have more difficulty accepting changes in the roles of women. While 82 to 85 percent of people under age 60 disagree with the idea that men alone should run the country, this is true for only 72 percent of people in their 60s and 53 percent of people aged 70 or older. Each age group was more likely to disagree with this statement in 1996 than it was in 1975, however.

Only 59 percent of people who did not finish high school disagree with the idea that women should let men run the country. In contrast, 90 to 92 percent of those with college degrees disagree with this statement.

Should Only Men Run the Country? 1996

"Do you agree or disagree with this statement? Women should take care of running their homes and leave running the country up to men."

(percent responding by sex, race, age, and education, 1996)

	agree	*disagree*
Total	**16%**	**80%**
Men	16	80
Women	15	81
Black	17	77
White	15	81
Aged 18 to 29	12	85
Aged 30 to 39	12	85
Aged 40 to 49	10	88
Aged 50 to 59	15	82
Aged 60 to 69	24	72
Aged 70 or older	36	53
Not a high school graduate	34	59
High school graduate	15	81
Bachelor's degree	6	92
Graduate degree	8	90

Note: Numbers may not add to 100 percent because "not sure" and no answer are not included.
Source: General Social Survey, National Opinion Research Center, University of Chicago

Should Only Men Run the Country? 1975 to 1996

"Do you agree or disagree with this statement? Women should take care
of running their homes and leave running the country up to men."

(percent responding by sex, race, age, and education, 1975–96)

	agree			disagree		
	1996	**1986**	**1975**	**1996**	**1986**	**1975**
Total	**16%**	**23%**	**35%**	**80%**	**73%**	**62%**
Men	16	21	34	80	76	63
Women	15	25	35	81	71	62
Black	17	29	40	77	65	58
White	15	22	34	81	75	63
Aged 18 to 29	12	14	20	85	84	77
Aged 30 to 39	12	14	32	85	84	65
Aged 40 to 49	10	20	30	88	77	67
Aged 50 to 59	15	25	42	82	73	56
Aged 60 to 69	24	37	50	72	59	48
Aged 70 or older	36	46	56	53	48	41
Not a high school graduate	34	47	51	59	48	46
High school graduate	15	17	30	81	80	67
Bachelor's degree	6	8	11	92	91	87
Graduate degree	8	6	6	90	91	92

Note: Numbers may not add to 100 percent because "not sure" and no answer are not included.
Source: General Social Surveys, National Opinion Research Center, University of Chicago

Are Men Better Suited for Politics?

Once divided on this question, a solid majority of the public now says "no."

The supposed emotionalism of women historically has been used to exclude them from the public arena. But this belief has lost ground over the years. Three-quarters of Americans say they do not believe men are better suited emotionally for politics than are women. In 1974, the nation was about evenly divided on this question.

There is little disagreement between men and women and between blacks and whites on this issue, but a generation gap lingers. Among people under age 60, 75 to 80 percent don't believe men are better suited emotionally for politics. But the proportion drops to 64 percent among people in their 60s and to 56 percent among people aged 70 or older.

A difference of opinion also exists by education. Only 60 percent of people who did not complete high school disagree that men are better suited emotionally for politics, but this figure rises to 83 percent among people with bachelor's degrees.

Are Men Better Suited for Politics? 1996

"Most men are better suited emotionally for politics than are most women—do you agree or disagree?"

(percent responding by sex, race, age, and education, 1996)

	agree	disagree
Total	**21%**	**74%**
Men	21	73
Women	21	76
Black	19	75
White	21	75
Aged 18 to 29	16	80
Aged 30 to 39	17	79
Aged 40 to 49	17	78
Aged 50 to 59	19	75
Aged 60 to 69	32	64
Aged 70 or older	37	56
Not a high school graduate	31	60
High school graduate	21	75
Bachelor's degree	15	83
Graduate degree	18	77

Note: Numbers may not add to 100 because "not sure" and no answer are not included.
Source: General Social Survey, National Opinion Research Center, University of Chicago

Are Men Better Suited for Politics? 1975 to 1996

"Most men are better suited emotionally for politics than are
most women—do you agree or disagree?"

(percent responding by sex, race, age, and education, 1975–96)

	agree			disagree		
	1996	**1986**	**1975**	**1996**	**1986**	**1975**
Total	**21%**	**36%**	**48%**	**74%**	**60%**	**48%**
Men	21	33	44	73	62	50
Women	21	38	51	76	59	47
Black	19	36	55	75	59	42
White	21	36	47	75	61	49
Aged 18 to 29	16	28	38	80	67	58
Aged 30 to 39	17	27	44	79	71	52
Aged 40 to 49	17	28	42	78	68	54
Aged 50 to 59	19	40	58	75	56	39
Aged 60 to 69	32	51	60	64	46	38
Aged 70 or older	37	56	58	56	38	33
Not a high school graduate	31	49	56	60	46	40
High school graduate	21	33	48	75	64	48
Bachelor's degree	15	27	29	83	69	69
Graduate degree	18	25	20	77	71	76

Note: Numbers may not add to 100 because "not sure" and no answer are not included.
Source: General Social Surveys, National Opinion Research Center, University of Chicago

Female Presidential Candidate

Few Americans say they would not vote for a female presidential candidate.

Nine in 10 Americans say if their political party nominated a woman for president, they would vote for her. In 1975, however, a far lower 78 percent said they would vote for a female presidential candidate.

There is solid agreement among people under age 60, with 91 to 93 percent saying they would vote for a woman for president. But older Americans are not as willing to accept a President and First Gentleman. A slightly lower 88 percent of people in their 60s say they would vote for a woman, and this drops to 81 percent among people aged 70 or older. But this is a big change from 1975 when only 62 percent of people aged 70 or older said they would vote for a woman.

Fully 91 to 96 percent of people with at least a high school diploma say they would vote for a woman for president. Among people who did not complete high school, however, only 82 percent say they would do so.

Female Presidential Candidate, 1996

"If your party nominated a woman for president,
would you vote for her if she were qualified for the job?"

(percent of respondents by sex, race, age, and education, 1996)

	yes	no
Total	**90%**	**7%**
Men	88	8
Women	92	6
Black	94	3
White	90	7
Aged 18 to 29	91	5
Aged 30 to 39	92	6
Aged 40 to 49	93	4
Aged 50 to 59	92	6
Aged 60 to 69	88	11
Aged 70 or older	81	15
Not a high school graduate	82	14
High school graduate	91	7
Bachelor's degree	96	2
Graduate degree	92	5

Note: Numbers may not add to 100 because "don't know" and no answer are not included.
Source: General Social Survey, National Opinion Research Center, University of Chicago

Female Presidential Candidate, 1975 to 1996

"If your party nominated a woman for president,
would you vote for her if she were qualified for the job?"

(percent responding by sex, race, age, and education, 1975–96)

	yes			no		
	1996	**1986**	**1975**	**1996**	**1986**	**1975**
Total	**90%**	**84%**	**78%**	**7%**	**13%**	**19%**
Men	88	86	80	8	11	17
Women	92	82	76	6	15	20
Black	94	86	75	3	11	22
White	90	83	78	7	13	18
Aged 18 to 29	91	89	87	5	9	10
Aged 30 to 39	92	90	82	6	8	15
Aged 40 to 49	93	90	80	4	8	17
Aged 50 to 59	92	81	76	6	16	22
Aged 60 to 69	88	79	65	11	19	31
Aged 70 or older	81	64	62	15	30	31
Not a high school graduate	82	73	67	14	23	28
High school graduate	91	86	82	7	12	15
Bachelor's degree	96	92	88	2	6	10
Graduate degree	92	95	94	5	4	6

Note: Numbers may not add to 100 because "don't know" and no answer are not included.
Source: General Social Surveys, National Opinion Research Center, University of Chicago

Female Homemakers and Male Breadwinners

Americans have reversed their opinions on traditional sex roles.

Once upon a time, life was neatly divided into two separate spheres: his and hers. The woman's domain was the home while the man's was everything else. Most Americans believed this was the best arrangement. In 1977, 65 percent supported separate roles for men and women. By 1996, a 60 percent majority did not.

As with most questions regarding appropriate roles for men and women, there is little disagreement by sex and race, but there is sharp disagreement by age and education.

The different generations could hardly disagree more. Three-quarters of Generation Xers (under age 30) do not favor traditional sex roles, nor do 66 to 67 percent of baby boomers (aged 30 to 49). In contrast, only a small majority of people in their 50s (57 percent) disagree with the idea that men should be breadwinners and women homemakers. Among people aged 70 or older, only 23 percent disagree. While there was disagreement among the generations in 1977, the gap was even wider in 1996.

There is also disagreement by education. Those with less education (many of whom are older) are more likely to believe traditional sex roles are better. The majority (56 percent) of people without a high school diploma say traditional sex roles are best. Only 22 to 27 percent of those with college degrees agree.

Female Homemakers and Male Breadwinners, 1996

"It is much better for everyone involved if the man is the achiever outside the home and the woman takes care of the home and family—do you agree or disagree?"

(percent responding by sex, race, age, and education, 1996)

	strongly agree	agree	disagree	strongly disagree	agree, total	disagree, total
Total	**7%**	**30%**	**43%**	**17%**	**37%**	**60%**
Men	7	33	45	12	40	57
Women	8	27	41	21	35	62
Black	7	26	47	14	33	61
White	8	30	42	18	38	60
Aged 18 to 29	3	22	53	21	25	74
Aged 30 to 39	7	23	45	22	30	67
Aged 40 to 49	5	26	45	21	31	66
Aged 50 to 59	6	33	42	15	39	57
Aged 60 to 69	13	39	37	7	52	44
Aged 70 or older	16	56	19	4	72	23
Not a high school graduate	15	41	31	9	56	40
High school graduate	7	31	45	14	38	59
Bachelor's degree	5	22	45	26	27	71
Graduate degree	4	18	47	27	22	74

Note: Numbers may not add to 100 because "don't know" and no answer are not included.
Source: General Social Survey, National Opinion Research Center, University of Chicago

Female Homemakers and Male Breadwinners, 1977 to 1996

"It is much better for everyone involved if the man is the achiever outside the home and the woman takes care of the home and family—do you agree or disagree?"

(percent responding by sex, race, age, and education, 1977–96)

	agree/strongly agree			disagree/strongly disagree		
	1996	*1986*	*1977*	*1996*	*1986*	*1977*
Total	**37%**	**47%**	**65%**	**60%**	**51%**	**34%**
Men	40	47	68	57	51	31
Women	35	47	62	62	52	36
Black	33	46	60	61	51	37
White	38	47	65	60	52	33
Aged 18 to 29	25	32	45	74	67	54
Aged 30 to 39	30	31	51	67	69	47
Aged 40 to 49	31	44	67	66	54	30
Aged 50 to 59	39	57	79	57	42	21
Aged 60 to 69	52	63	83	44	33	15
Aged 70 or older	72	80	88	23	18	11
Not a high school graduate	56	68	79	40	30	19
High school graduate	38	43	61	59	55	38
Bachelor's degree	27	34	45	71	65	54
Graduate degree	22	24	45	74	75	54

Note: Numbers may not add to 100 because "don't know" and no answer are not included.
Source: General Social Surveys, National Opinion Research Center, University of Chicago

Should Women Work If They Don't Have To?

Most people don't believe women should work only if the family needs money.

A solid majority (81 percent) of Americans say it is fine for a married woman to work even if her husband makes enough to support the family. In 1975 a somewhat smaller proportion of people felt this way (70 percent).

Whites are more likely than blacks to approve of a married woman working when her family doesn't need the money. Fully 83 percent of whites approve compared with 74 percent of blacks.

People of all ages were more likely in 1996 than in 1975 to approve of married women working even if they don't need the money. In both years, younger people were more likely than their elders to find this acceptable, but the gap was much smaller in 1996. In 1975, only 42 percent of people aged 70 or older approved. This figure had risen to 65 percent by 1996.

The more education people have, the more likely they are to approve of wives working even if they don't need the money. Fully 88 to 89 percent of college graduates approve, compared with 81 percent of high school graduates and 70 percent of people who did not complete high school.

Should Women Work If They Don't Have To? 1996

"Do you approve or disapprove of a married woman earning money in business or industry if she has a husband capable of supporting her?"

(percent responding by sex, race, age, and education, 1996)

	approve	disapprove
Total	**81%**	**16%**
Men	82	15
Women	81	17
Black	74	23
White	83	15
Aged 18 to 29	84	13
Aged 30 to 39	83	15
Aged 40 to 49	85	14
Aged 50 to 59	83	16
Aged 60 to 69	80	17
Aged 70 or older	65	30
Not a high school graduate	70	27
High school graduate	81	17
Bachelor's degree	89	10
Graduate degree	88	11

Note: Numbers may not add to 100 because "don't know" and no answer are not included.
Source: General Social Survey, National Opinion Research Center, University of Chicago

Should Women Work If They Don't Have To? 1975 to 1996

"Do you approve or disapprove of a married woman earning money in business or industry if she has a husband capable of supporting her?"

(percent responding by sex, race, age, and education, 1975–96)

	approve			disapprove		
	1996	*1986*	*1975*	*1996*	*1986*	*1975*
Total	**81%**	**76%**	**70%**	**16%**	**22%**	**28%**
Men	82	78	68	15	21	30
Women	81	76	71	17	22	27
Black	74	78	66	23	19	31
White	83	76	70	15	22	28
Aged 18 to 29	84	87	85	13	12	14
Aged 30 to 39	83	86	78	15	14	20
Aged 40 to 49	85	81	75	14	16	23
Aged 50 to 59	83	71	57	16	27	39
Aged 60 to 69	80	68	56	17	30	42
Aged 70 or older	65	49	42	30	45	55
Not a high school graduate	70	61	52	27	36	45
High school graduate	81	80	76	17	19	22
Bachelor's degree	89	90	91	10	10	8
Graduate degree	88	84	92	11	14	8

Note: Numbers may not add to 100 because "don't know" and no answer are not included.
Source: General Social Surveys, National Opinion Research Center, University of Chicago

Is a Husband's Career More Important?

Older Americans still believe a husband's career is more important.

In the past, if a wife worked her career was assumed to be secondary to that of her husband. In 1977, a majority of Americans (55 percent) agreed it was more important for a wife to help her husband's career than to have one herself. But in 1996, more than three-quarters of Americans disagreed with this statement.

A substantial percentage of older people still believe a wife's career should take a back seat to her husband's. Among people under age 60, 79 to 84 percent say they do not agree that a husband's career is more important. Among people in their 60s, however, 60 percent disagree while 36 percent say a wife's career should be secondary to her husband's. Among people aged 70 or older, half say a husband's career is more important, and only 42 percent disagree.

Forty-one percent of people who did not complete high school agree with the idea that a husband's career takes precedence over his wife's. Among people who completed high school, only 19 percent agree. Just 12 percent of college graduates agree.

Is a Husband's Career More Important? 1996

"It is more important for a wife to help her husband's career than to have one herself—do you agree or disagree?"

(percent responding by sex, race, age, and education, 1996)

	strongly agree	agree	disagree	strongly disagree	agree, total	disagree, total
Total	**3%**	**17%**	**53%**	**24%**	**20%**	**77%**
Men	3	18	59	16	21	75
Women	3	17	47	30	20	77
Black	3	14	55	24	17	79
White	3	18	52	24	21	76
Aged 18 to 29	2	11	54	29	13	83
Aged 30 to 39	3	11	54	30	14	84
Aged 40 to 49	2	11	57	27	13	84
Aged 50 to 59	2	17	56	23	19	79
Aged 60 to 69	7	29	49	11	36	60
Aged 70 or older	6	45	37	5	51	42
Not a high school graduate	8	33	43	12	41	55
High school graduate	2	17	56	21	19	77
Bachelor's degree	1	11	52	34	12	86
Graduate degree	2	10	47	36	12	83

Note: Numbers may not add to 100 because "don't know" and no answer are not included.
Source: General Social Survey, National Opinion Research Center, University of Chicago

Is a Husband's Career More Important? 1977 to 1996

"It is more important for a wife to help her husband's career
than to have one herself—do you agree or disagree?"

(percent responding by sex, race, age, and education 1977–96)

	agree/strongly agree			disagree/strongly disagree		
	1996	*1986*	*1977*	*1996*	*1986*	*1977*
Total	**21%**	**35%**	**55%**	**77%**	**62%**	**41%**
Men	21	33	51	75	64	45
Women	20	37	59	77	62	38
Black	17	31	52	79	66	44
White	21	36	55	76	63	41
Aged 18 to 29	13	21	35	83	77	62
Aged 30 to 39	14	21	43	84	77	53
Aged 40 to 49	13	30	58	84	68	37
Aged 50 to 59	19	40	64	79	59	32
Aged 60 to 69	36	52	75	60	42	21
Aged 70 or older	51	68	79	42	29	17
Not a high school graduate	41	59	67	55	40	30
High school graduate	19	28	53	77	70	43
Bachelor's degree	12	23	33	86	73	66
Graduate degree	12	22	29	83	75	64

Note: Numbers may not add to 100 because "don't know" and no answer are not included.
Source: General Social Surveys, National Opinion Research Center, University of Chicago

Is a Working Mother as Good?

A large generation gap exists around the issue of working mothers.

Two-thirds of Americans believe a working mother can establish as warm and secure a relationship with her children as a mother who does not work. This was not always the case, however. Two decades ago, when mothers of young children were pouring into the labor force for the first time, many Americans worried that children would be neglected. At that time, people were divided on this issue, with half believing a working mother's relationship with her children would not be as good as that of a nonworking mother.

Women are more likely than men to believe working mothers can maintain a good relationship with their children (73 percent compared with 55 percent of men). While both men and women are more likely to feel this way now than they were in 1977, the gap between the sexes was larger in 1996 than in 1977.

More blacks than whites believe a working mother can be as close to her children as a nonworking mother (77 percent of blacks compared with 63 percent of whites). This attitudinal gap is explained by the different experiences of blacks and whites. Historically, black women have been in the labor force in greater proportions than white women.

A wide generation gap still exists on this question. Fully 71 to 74 percent of people under age 40 believe a working mother can have as good a relationship with her children as one who does not work. The figure drops slightly to two-thirds among people in their 40s and 50s. But older Americans are much more skeptical, with only 54 percent of those in their 60s and 45 percent of those aged 70 or older agreeing.

In 1977, the college-educated were much more likely than those with less education to believe working mothers could have as good a relationship with their children as nonworking mothers. By 1996, however, the gap by education had narrowed considerably. Still, only 57 percent of those without a high school diploma say working mothers can have as warm and secure a relationship with their children as nonworking mothers. This compares with two-thirds of people with more education.

Is a Working Mother as Good? 1996

"A working mother can establish just as warm and secure a relationship with her children as a mother who does not work—do you agree or disagree?"

(percent responding by sex, race, age, and education, 1996)

	strongly agree	agree	disagree	strongly disagree	agree, total	disagree, total
Total	**24%**	**42%**	**26%**	**7%**	**66%**	**33%**
Men	13	42	33	9	55	42
Women	32	41	20	6	73	26
Black	33	44	16	5	77	21
White	22	41	27	8	63	35
Aged 18 to 29	25	49	21	3	74	24
Aged 30 to 39	30	41	20	7	71	27
Aged 40 to 49	26	40	24	9	66	33
Aged 50 to 59	24	43	23	8	67	31
Aged 60 to 69	17	37	36	9	54	45
Aged 70 or older	11	34	43	9	45	52
Not a high school graduate	18	39	34	8	57	42
High school graduate	24	42	25	7	66	32
Bachelor's degree	27	40	23	7	67	30
Graduate degree	26	41	25	6	67	31

Note: Numbers may not add to 100 because "don't know" and no answer are not included.
Source: General Social Survey, National Opinion Research Center, University of Chicago

Is a Working Mother as Good? 1977 to 1996

"A working mother can establish just as warm and secure a relationship with her children as a mother who does not work—do you agree or disagree?"

(percent responding by sex, race, age, and education, 1977–1996)

	agree/strongly agree			disagree/strongly disagree		
	1996	1986	1977	1996	1986	1977
Total	**66%**	**62%**	**48%**	**33%**	**38%**	**50%**
Men	55	55	41	42	44	58
Women	73	67	54	26	32	45
Black	77	68	56	21	29	44
White	63	61	47	35	38	51
Aged 18 to 29	74	70	60	24	30	38
Aged 30 to 39	71	75	60	27	26	38
Aged 40 to 49	66	69	45	33	30	54
Aged 50 to 59	67	58	43	31	41	57
Aged 60 to 69	54	51	32	45	47	67
Aged 70 or older	45	33	29	52	66	68
Not a high school graduate	57	47	37	42	52	61
High school graduate	66	66	52	32	33	47
Bachelor's degree	67	67	61	30	33	39
Graduate degree	67	77	63	31	23	31

Note: Numbers may not add to 100 because "don't know" and no answer are not included.
Source: General Social Surveys, National Opinion Research Center, University of Chicago

Do Young Children Suffer If Mother Works?

Americans have changed their minds in the last two decades.

Over half of Americans (52 percent) do not agree that preschool children suffer if their mother works. This figure is much higher than in 1977, when only 32 percent disagreed.

Women are more likely than men to disagree that preschoolers suffer when their mother works (58 percent of women compared with 44 percent of men). While both men and women are more likely to disagree with this statement than they once were, the gap between the sexes was wider in 1996 than in 1977.

A solid majority of blacks (67 percent) disagree that preschoolers suffer if their mother works. Whites, however, are divided on this issue; 47 percent say preschoolers suffer and 49 percent say they do not.

The generations were more sharply divided in 1996 than in 1977. The percentage of people who do not think preschoolers suffer if their mother works falls with age. Sixty-seven percent of people under age 30 disagree compared with only 28 percent of those aged 70 or older.

The gap in opinions on this issue between those who did not complete high school and those with more education narrowed between 1996 and 1977. In 1996, slightly more than half of people with at least a high school diploma disagreed that preschoolers suffer if their mothers work, compared with 45 percent of people who did not complete high school.

Do Young Children Suffer If Mother Works? 1996

"A preschool child is likely to suffer if his or her mother works—
do you agree or disagree?"

(percent responding by sex, race, age, and education, 1996)

	strongly agree	agree	disagree	strongly disagree	agree, total	disagree, total
Total	**8%**	**36%**	**41%**	**11%**	**44%**	**52%**
Men	9	42	38	6	51	44
Women	8	31	44	14	39	58
Black	5	24	53	14	29	67
White	9	38	39	10	47	49
Aged 18 to 29	3	26	55	12	29	67
Aged 30 to 39	10	33	42	13	43	55
Aged 40 to 49	9	35	40	13	44	53
Aged 50 to 59	6	43	38	9	49	47
Aged 60 to 69	13	44	35	6	57	41
Aged 70 or older	13	50	24	4	63	28
Not a high school graduate	10	39	37	8	49	45
High school graduate	8	36	43	10	44	53
Bachelor's degree	8	35	41	12	43	53
Graduate degree	6	37	41	11	43	52

Note: Numbers may not add to 100 because "don't know" and no answer are not included.
Source: General Social Survey, National Opinion Research Center, University of Chicago

Do Young Children Suffer If Mother Works? 1977 to 1996

"A preschool child is likely to suffer if his or her mother works—
do you agree or disagree?"

(percent responding by sex, race, age, and education, 1977–96)

	agree/strongly agree			disagree/strongly disagree		
	1996	**1986**	**1977**	**1996**	**1986**	**1977**
Total	**44%**	**51%**	**66%**	**52%**	**48%**	**32%**
Men	51	57	71	44	42	26
Women	39	46	61	58	52	36
Black	29	36	52	67	63	46
White	47	52	68	49	46	31
Aged 18 to 29	29	40	55	67	58	44
Aged 30 to 39	43	38	56	55	61	43
Aged 40 to 49	44	48	68	53	51	29
Aged 50 to 59	49	56	72	47	41	25
Aged 60 to 69	57	63	82	41	36	16
Aged 70 or older	63	75	78	28	22	19
Not a high school graduate	49	63	73	45	35	24
High school graduate	44	46	63	53	53	35
Bachelor's degree	43	42	60	53	55	39
Graduate degree	43	45	56	52	49	39

Note: Numbers may not add to 100 because "don't know" and no answer are not included.
Source: General Social Surveys, National Opinion Research Center, University of Chicago

Discrimination against Women and Men

Americans seem to think both sexes are discriminated against.

Asked whether they think a woman will be passed over for a job or promotion in favor of an equally or less qualified man, most Americans (65 percent) say it is somewhat or very likely. But at the same time, 51 percent say it is somewhat or very likely that a man will lose a job or promotion to a less qualified woman. Some people, apparently, believe the work world is unfair to both sexes.

It is clear, however, that people are more likely to believe women will be the ones to suffer from sex discrimination. Most demographic segments respond similarly to the question of whether a woman will lose a job or promotion to a man. The sexes, however, see things differently. Almost three-quarters of women believe it is at least somewhat likely that a woman will not get a job or promotion while an equally or less qualified man gets one instead. In contrast, only 58 percent of men say this is at least somewhat likely. When the question is reversed, however, 60 percent of men say it is at least somewhat likely that a man will get passed over for an equally or less qualified woman compared with only 43 percent of women.

By age, there is a great deal of variation in attitudes. Those most likely to think a man will lose a job or promotion to an equally or less qualified woman are people under age 30. Least likely to believe this are people in their 50s.

About half of people who have at least a high school diploma feel that men are at least somewhat likely to be discriminated against in favor of a woman. But among people who did not complete high school, only 40 percent agree.

Discrimination Against Men, 1996

"What do you think the chances are these days that a man won't get a job or promotion while an equally or less qualified woman gets one instead? Is this very likely, somewhat likely, somewhat unlikely, or very unlikely these days?"

(percent responding by sex, race, age, and education, 1996)

	very likely	somewhat likely	somewhat unlikely	very unlikely	likely, total	unlikely, total
Total	**14%**	**37%**	**28%**	**15%**	**51%**	**43%**
Men	16	44	22	10	60	32
Women	12	31	31	18	43	49
Black	17	29	22	20	46	42
White	13	39	29	13	52	42
Aged 18 to 29	12	44	29	10	56	39
Aged 30 to 39	15	34	32	15	49	47
Aged 40 to 49	12	39	28	14	51	42
Aged 50 to 59	19	26	27	19	45	46
Aged 60 to 69	15	37	24	16	52	40
Aged 70 or older	12	37	20	16	49	36
Not a high school graduate	11	29	22	21	40	43
High school graduate	15	37	29	13	52	42
Bachelor's degree	13	38	30	14	51	44
Graduate degree	6	44	23	23	50	46

Note: Numbers may not add to 100 because "don't know" and no answer are not included.
Source: General Social Survey, National Opinion Research, University of Chicago

Discrimination Against Women, 1996

"What do you think the chances are these days that a woman won't get a job or promotion while an equally or less qualified man gets one instead? Is this very likely, somewhat likely, somewhat unlikely, or very unlikely these days?"

(percent responding by sex, race, age, and education, 1996)

	very likely	somewhat likely	somewhat unlikely	very unlikely	likely, total	unlikely, total
Total	17%	48%	20%	9%	65%	29%
Men	13	45	26	11	58	37
Women	22	51	15	7	73	22
Black	18	50	17	10	68	27
White	17	48	21	8	65	29
Aged 18 to 29	16	53	19	9	69	28
Aged 30 to 39	15	48	21	10	63	31
Aged 40 to 49	18	51	20	7	69	27
Aged 50 to 59	22	39	26	7	61	33
Aged 60 to 69	16	49	16	12	65	28
Aged 70 or older	20	43	18	8	63	26
Not a high school graduate	24	39	15	12	63	27
High school graduate	17	48	20	8	65	28
Bachelor's degree	15	50	25	7	65	32
Graduate degree	15	53	19	10	68	29

Note: Numbers may not add to 100 because "don't know" and no answer are not included.
Source: General Social Survey, National Opinion Research, University of Chicago

Why Women Earn Less

It's not for lack of trying, say most Americans.

It is a well-known fact that women earn less than men, on average. What's less clear in the minds of most people is why this is so.

The majority of Americans (62 percent) do not believe men earn more than women because they work harder. Only 9 percent say this is a very important reason for the earning disparity. People are more likely to believe the "Mommy Track" is a factor, with 39 percent saying this is an important or very important reason. Only 29 percent say women's family responsibilities are not an important reason for the earning disparity between men and women.

Most people do believe, however, that discrimination is a primary factor. Over half (56 percent) say an important or very important reason why women earn less is that employers give men better-paying jobs than they give women. Only 18 percent say this is not an important reason.

Women give more weight to discrimination than do men, with 37 percent of women saying it is a very important reason compared with just 22 percent of men. Men are more likely to believe the reason is that they work harder than women. While 66 percent of women say this is not at all important in explaining the earning disparity, only 56 percent of men agree.

Blacks and whites are not far apart in their opinions about the earning disparity between men and women—with one exception. Whites are more likely than blacks to say they don't believe men earn more because they work harder (64 percent of whites compared with 53 percent of blacks).

While clear generational differences exist on many women's issues, that is not the case here. There are noticeable differences by education, however. Three-quarters of college graduates say they don't believe men earn more because they work harder. This compares with 59 percent of high school graduates and only 46 percent of people who did not complete high school. Twenty percent of those with the least education say women's family responsibilities are a very important reason for their lower earnings compared with only 15 to 16 percent of those with at least a high school diploma. While 63 to 65 percent of college graduates say an important or very important reason for the earning disparity is that employers give men better jobs, only 54 to 55 percent of those without college degrees say this is an important or very important reason.

Why Women Earn Less: Men Get Better-Paying Jobs, 1996

"On average, women who are employed full time earn less than men earn.
I'm going to read several reasons why this might be so. Please tell me
how important you think each reason is. Employers tend to give men
better paying jobs than they give women."

(percent responding by sex, race, age, and education, 1996)

	very important	important	somewhat important	not at all important
Total	**30%**	**26%**	**20%**	**18%**
Men	22	27	26	20
Women	37	25	16	17
Black	31	28	17	21
White	31	26	21	18
Aged 18 to 29	30	26	24	17
Aged 30 to 39	29	26	25	18
Aged 40 to 49	30	25	17	24
Aged 50 to 59	29	29	19	17
Aged 60 to 69	38	26	12	16
Aged 70 or older	28	24	19	15
Not a high school graduate	31	24	17	18
High school graduate	29	25	21	20
Bachelor's degree	35	28	21	15
Graduate degree	30	35	16	15

Note: Numbers may not add to 100 because "don't know" and no answer are not included.
Source: General Social Survey, National Opinion Research, University of Chicago

Why Women Earn Less: Family Responsibilities, 1996

"On average, women who are employed full time earn less than men earn. I'm going to read several reasons why this might be so. Please tell me how important you think each reason is. Women's family responsibilities keep them from putting as much time and effort into their jobs as men do."

(percent responding by sex, race, age, and education, 1996)

	very important	important	somewhat important	not at all important
Total	**16%**	**23%**	**28%**	**29%**
Men	16	23	30	26
Women	16	22	27	32
Black	18	23	25	29
White	15	22	29	30
Aged 18 to 29	15	25	30	28
Aged 30 to 39	16	20	32	29
Aged 40 to 49	16	23	30	28
Aged 50 to 59	12	20	27	34
Aged 60 to 69	19	24	25	28
Aged 70 or older	18	23	19	29
Not a high school graduate	20	22	27	24
High school graduate	15	23	27	29
Bachelor's degree	16	21	28	33
Graduate degree	15	21	35	28

Note: Numbers may not add to 100 because "don't know" and no answer are not included.
Source: General Social Survey, National Opinion Research, University of Chicago

Why Women Earn Less: Men Work Harder, 1996

"On average, women who are employed full time earn less than men earn. I'm going to read several reasons why this might be so. Please tell me how important you think each reason is. Men work harder on the job than women do."

(percent responding by sex, race, age, and education, 1996)

	very important	important	somewhat important	not at all important
Total	**9%**	**12%**	**14%**	**62%**
Men	10	13	15	56
Women	7	11	12	66
Black	13	14	14	53
White	8	11	14	64
Aged 18 to 29	10	15	19	53
Aged 30 to 39	9	10	16	63
Aged 40 to 49	5	11	12	69
Aged 50 to 59	6	9	7	73
Aged 60 to 69	12	10	12	61
Aged 70 or older	13	15	13	47
Not a high school graduate	15	20	13	46
High school graduate	9	12	16	59
Bachelor's degree	5	8	9	75
Graduate degree	3	9	10	75

Note: Numbers may not add to 100 because "don't know" and no answer are not included.
Source: General Social Survey, National Opinion Research, University of Chicago

Consider Self a Feminist?

"Feminist" has taken on a negative connotation.

Even though to most people women's rights is an important issue, few people are willing to be labeled a feminist. The term suffers from too many negative connotations.

Predictably, women are more likely than men to think of themselves as feminists. Only 12 percent of men identify themselves as feminists compared with 27 percent of women.

People aged 40 to 59 and—surprisingly—those aged 70 or older are more likely than other age groups to say they are feminists. About one-quarter of Americans in these age groups accept the designation compared with 15 to 19 percent of those in other age groups.

People with college degrees are more comfortable with being labeled feminists. Only 19 percent of people without college degrees say they are feminists compared with 25 to 28 percent of college graduates.

Consider Self a Feminist? 1996

"Do you think of yourself as a feminist or not?"

(percent responding by sex, race, age, and education, 1996)

	yes	*no*	*don't know*
Total	**20%**	**74%**	**5%**
Men	12	83	5
Women	27	67	5
Black	22	70	8
White	20	75	5
Aged 18 to 29	19	74	7
Aged 30 to 39	16	79	5
Aged 40 to 49	24	71	4
Aged 50 to 59	25	74	1
Aged 60 to 69	15	81	5
Aged 70 or older	25	65	10
Not a high school graduate	19	71	10
High school graduate	19	76	5
Bachelor's degree	25	71	4
Graduate degree	28	68	4

Note: Numbers may not add to 100 because no answer is not included.
Source: General Social Survey, National Opinion Research, University of Chicago

Effect of Women's Movement

Working women are seen as the primary beneficiaries of the women's movement.

Americans clearly view the women's movement as beneficial to working women, especially those with managerial and professional jobs. Fully 81 percent say the women's movement has improved the lives of those women. Three-quarters believe it has improved the lives of women with working-class jobs. The public is divided, however, on the effect of the women's movement on homemakers, children, and men.

Interestingly, women and men hold similar attitudes towards the impact of the women's movement on working women and homemakers. Men and women differ on the impact on men and children, however. One-third of women, but only one-quarter of men, say the women's movement has made things worse for men. Men are more likely than women to feel children are worse off (one-third of men compared with one-quarter of women).

Whites are more likely than blacks to believe working women have benefited from the women's movement. But a larger percentage of blacks say homemakers, children, and men have benefited from changes brought about by the women's movement.

People of different ages have mixed views on the effects of the women's movement. People under age 30, those in their 40s, and those aged 70 or older are more likely than other age groups to believe homemakers have benefited from the women's movement—although the differences of opinion are not large. People under age 50 are considerably more likely than those aged 50 or older to believe the lives of working-class women are better because of the women's movement.

People who did not complete high school do not share the opinions of those with more education about the effect of the women's movement on working women. Only 68 percent say working-class women are better off, compared with 74 to 79 percent of those with at least a high school diploma. Only 67 percent believe women in managerial and professional jobs have benefited from the women's movement, compared with 81 to 90 percent of those with more education.

The college educated have a more negative view of the effect of the women's movement on homemakers. While 25 to 29 percent of this group say the women's movement has made the lives of homemakers worse, only 14 to 19 percent of people without college degrees share that opinion.

Effect of the Women's Movement, 1996

"How has the women's movement affected the following groups?
Has it improved their lives, made their lives worse, or had no effect?"

(percent responding by sex, race, age, and education, 1996)

	better					worse					no effect				
	home-maker	working class	mgmt./ prof.	men	children	home-maker	working class	mgmt./ prof.	men	children	home-maker	working class	mgmt./ prof.	men	children
Total	39%	74%	81%	29%	39%	20%	6%	4%	30%	29%	33%	13%	8%	33%	21%
Men	40	76	80	30	38	19	7	6	25	33	35	13	8	38	21
Women	38	73	81	29	40	22	5	3	33	26	32	14	7	29	22
Black	48	68	76	39	49	10	5	3	18	16	33	17	9	33	21
White	38	76	82	27	37	23	6	4	32	32	33	13	7	33	21
Aged 18 to 29	41	79	82	29	42	14	3	1	24	23	36	13	10	37	26
Aged 30 to 39	37	77	80	27	36	25	8	6	34	31	30	11	8	33	24
Aged 40 to 49	42	81	88	35	48	23	5	5	30	29	28	10	3	28	14
Aged 50 to 59	35	70	82	28	35	21	5	4	31	32	36	18	8	34	20
Aged 60 to 69	34	68	80	23	31	22	5	5	27	29	38	21	10	40	28
Aged 70 or older	42	61	67	30	35	13	8	6	28	31	35	12	9	29	17
Not high school grad.	45	68	67	35	40	14	6	6	18	23	30	13	11	32	20
High school graduate	37	74	81	25	36	19	6	4	33	31	36	13	8	34	23
Bachelor's degree	41	79	90	34	48	25	3	2	31	28	31	14	6	32	17
Graduate degree	39	77	87	37	44	29	7	6	26	29	24	14	5	31	18

Note: Numbers may not add to 100 because "don't know" and no answer are not included.
Source: General Social Survey, National Opinion Research, University of Chicago

Importance of Women's Rights Issue

More Americans now say women's rights is an important issue.

The percentage of people who say women's rights is important or one of the most important issues to them was higher in 1996 than in 1983. Sixty-three percent of people say it is important or one of the most important issues to them, up from 58 percent in 1983.

Most people say it is an important issue, rather than one of the most important issues. Women are more than twice as likely as men to say women's rights is one of the most important issues, with 15 percent of women and 6 percent of men saying so.

Blacks are far more likely than whites to say women's rights is one of the most important issues (22 percent of blacks compared with 10 percent of whites). Twenty-seven percent of whites, but only 18 percent of blacks, say women's rights is not a very important issue.

People under age 30 are most likely to say women's rights is an important issue. Among young adults, 58 percent say it is important to them, as do 55 percent of people in their 30s. A smaller 45 percent of people in their 60s agree. The percentage of people saying women's rights is not an important issue rises with age. But the oldest Americans were far more likely to believe women's rights was important in 1996 than they were in 1983.

Importance of Women's Rights Issue, 1996

"How important is the women's rights issue to you—one of the most important issues, important, not very important, or not important at all?"

(percent responding by sex, race, age, and education, 1996)

	one of most important	important	not very important	not at all important
Total	**11%**	**52%**	**25%**	**10%**
Men	6	53	26	13
Women	15	51	24	7
Black	22	51	18	7
White	10	52	27	10
Aged 18 to 29	11	58	22	7
Aged 30 to 39	10	55	26	8
Aged 40 to 49	12	50	27	10
Aged 50 to 59	12	49	27	12
Aged 60 to 69	12	45	27	14
Aged 70 or older	10	50	21	12
Not a high school graduate	15	51	18	11
High school graduate	10	51	26	10
Bachelor's degree	11	54	28	7
Graduate degree	12	57	21	10

Note: Numbers may not add to 100 because "don't know" and no answer are not included.
Source: General Social Survey, National Opinion Research, University of Chicago

Importance of Women's Rights Issue, 1983 to 1996

"How important is the women's rights issue to you—one of the most important issues, important, not very important, or not important at all?"

(percent responding by sex, race, age, and education, 1983–96)

	one of most important /important		not very/not at all important	
	1996	*1983*	*1996*	*1983*
Total	**63%**	**58%**	**35%**	**41%**
Men	59	53	39	44
Women	66	65	31	34
Black	73	81	25	18
White	62	56	37	43
Aged 18 to 29	69	57	29	42
Aged 30 to 39	65	64	34	35
Aged 40 to 49	62	60	37	38
Aged 50 to 59	61	57	39	40
Aged 60 to 69	57	58	41	38
Aged 70 or older	60	44	33	53
Not a high school graduate	66	58	29	40
High school graduate	61	58	36	41
Bachelor's degree	65	62	35	36
Graduate degree	69	60	31	39

Note: Numbers may not add to 100 because "don't know" and no answer are not included.
Source: General Social Surveys, National Opinion Research, University of Chicago

Chapter 8

Personal Outlook

Most Americans are quite happy and healthy. But they are almost as likely to say that their life is routine as that their life is exciting. One reason for this so-so attitude may be a lack of time to do what they want—most Americans say they feel rushed at least some of the time.

Lack of time is undoubtedly one of the factors behind the relatively small percentages of Americans who volunteer for a variety of causes from youth development to the arts. Americans are most likely to devote time to religious organizations, but substantial numbers have also volunteered in education and working with young people.

When Americans don't feel happy, they are not afraid to let other people know about it. And when they are angry, most say they will let others know. They are unlikely to trust many people with their confidences, however, since the majority believes that one can't be too careful in dealing with others. Americans are also inclined to believe most people are selfish rather than helpful, although they are willing to give others the benefit of the doubt. A slightly larger number says most people try to be helpful rather than take advantage.

Most Americans believe they have control over the bad things that happen to them and they don't blame their ill fortune on bad breaks. Nor do they believe it is simply good luck when things go their way.

Women are less likely than men to say their lives are exciting. They are also less likely to feel they have control over the bad things that happen to them. One reason for this difference may be that women are more likely than men to feel rushed all the time.

While women and men are similar in their opinions of the fairness of others, blacks and whites are far apart on this issue. Blacks are far more likely than whites to believe people would take advantage of them rather than be fair. They are also more likely to believe people look out for themselves rather than try to be helpful, and that it is better to be careful than to trust others. It is no surprise, then, that blacks are far more likely to agree that one should take care of oneself first.

Baby boomers (aged 30 to 49) are considerably more likely than older or younger people to say they are always in a rush. While this doesn't keep life from being exciting for them, it might be the reason they are not as happy as their elders.

The older people are, the more likely they are to believe people are generally trustworthy, fair, and helpful. Generations Xers (under age 30) are particularly cynical. They are also most likely to blame their problems on bad breaks.

On all the questions examined here, the biggest differences are found by education. College graduates are happier, healthier, and more excited about life than those with less education. They have a much better opinion of other people and are far more likely to volunteer their time for a variety of causes.

People who did not complete high school are struggling with an economy that has not been favorable to them. It is understandable that they are the ones most likely to believe they have little control over the bad things that happen to them, and that good and bad things happen because of luck or bad breaks.

Personal Happiness

College graduates are happier than those with less education.

Americans are neither dancing in the streets nor wallowing in despair. The majority (57 percent) says they are pretty happy. Thirty percent say they are very happy, while only 12 percent say they are not too happy.

About one-third of men and 29 percent of women say they are very happy. Women are less likely to say this than they were in 1976, however, when 35 percent said they were very happy.

Of all demographic segments, blacks are most likely to say they are not too happy. Twenty percent of blacks say this compared with 11 percent of whites. Only 24 percent of blacks, compared with 31 percent of whites, say they are very happy.

Older people are more likely than younger generations to say they are very happy. Among people aged 60 or older, 35 to 36 percent say they are very happy, as do 32 percent of those in their 50s. In contrast, a smaller 27 to 29 percent of people aged 18 to 49 say they are very happy. In 1976, there was little variation by age in the proportions of people saying they were very happy.

As was true in earlier years, the percentage of people saying they are very happy rises with education. While 27 percent of people who did not complete high school say they are very happy, the figure rises to 35 to 39 percent among college graduates. Eighteen percent of people who do not have a high school diploma are not too happy. The proportion drops to 12 percent among people who graduated from high school and 9 percent among college graduates.

Personal Happiness, 1996

"Taken all together, how would you say things are these days—
would you say that you are very happy, pretty happy, or not too happy?"

(percent responding by sex, race, age, and education, 1996)

	very happy	pretty happy	not too happy
Total	**30**%	**57**%	**12**%
Men	32	56	11
Women	29	58	13
Black	24	56	20
White	31	58	11
Aged 18 to 29	27	62	10
Aged 30 to 39	28	59	12
Aged 40 to 49	29	58	13
Aged 50 to 59	32	55	12
Aged 60 to 69	36	50	11
Aged 70 or older	35	52	14
Not a high school graduate	27	54	18
High school graduate	29	59	12
Bachelor's degree	35	55	9
Graduate degree	39	51	9

Note: Numbers may not add to 100 because "don't know" and no answer are not included.
Source: General Social Survey, National Opinion Research Center, University of Chicago

Personal Happiness, 1976 to 1996

"Taken all together, how would you say things are these days—
would you say that you are very happy, pretty happy, or not too happy?"

(percent responding by sex, race, age, and education, 1976–96)

	very happy			pretty happy			not too happy		
	1996	**1986**	**1976**	**1996**	**1986**	**1976**	**1996**	**1986**	**1976**
Total	**30%**	**32%**	**34%**	**57%**	**56%**	**53%**	**12%**	**11%**	**13%**
Men	32	30	33	56	57	54	11	11	13
Women	29	33	35	58	54	53	13	11	12
Black	24	22	16	56	59	53	20	17	30
White	31	33	36	58	55	53	11	10	11
Aged 18 to 29	27	28	33	62	59	53	10	11	14
Aged 30 to 39	28	30	36	59	63	55	12	6	9
Aged 40 to 49	29	31	34	58	57	57	13	10	9
Aged 50 to 59	32	31	32	55	52	55	12	16	13
Aged 60 to 69	36	40	33	50	45	50	11	13	17
Aged 70 or older	35	35	37	52	49	49	14	15	14
Not high school grad.	27	31	30	54	52	54	18	16	16
High school graduate	29	31	35	59	57	52	12	11	13
Bachelor's degree	35	40	36	55	52	58	9	6	6
Graduate degree	39	34	46	51	58	49	9	5	5

Note: Numbers may not add to 100 because "don't know" and no answer are not included.
Source: General Social Surveys, National Opinion Research Center, University of Chicago

Is Life Exciting?

Few Americans say life is dull.

Americans are divided between those who find life exciting (49 percent) and those who find it routine (45 percent). Almost no one says life is dull.

Life is more exciting for men than for women. Over half of men (54 percent) say life is exciting compared with 46 percent of women. Women are more likely to say their lives are routine—48 percent compared with 42 percent of men.

Whites are considerably more likely than blacks to say life is exciting (51 percent compared with 41 percent of blacks). But the proportion of blacks who say life is exciting is up sharply from 27 percent in 1976.

People in their postretirement years have more time to do what they want, but this doesn't seem to make life more exciting. Only 40 percent of people aged 70 or older say life is exciting. People aged 30 to 59 are more likely than those older or younger to say life is exciting (51 to 52 percent).

The proportion of people who say life is exciting rises sharply with education. This was true in earlier years as well. Only 35 percent of people who did not complete high school say their lives are exciting, but the proportion rises to 46 percent among high school graduates and peaks at 66 to 70 percent among college graduates. Eleven percent of people without a high school diploma say their lives are dull. This compares with no more than 4 percent of people with more education.

Is Life Exciting? 1996

"In general, do you find life exciting, pretty routine, or dull?"

(percent responding by sex, race, age, and education, 1996)

	exciting	pretty routine	dull
Total	**49%**	**45%**	**4%**
Men	54	42	4
Women	46	48	4
Black	41	51	6
White	51	45	4
Aged 18 to 29	48	47	4
Aged 30 to 39	51	45	3
Aged 40 to 49	52	43	4
Aged 50 to 59	52	42	5
Aged 60 to 69	48	48	3
Aged 70 or older	40	51	9
Not a high school graduate	35	52	11
High school graduate	46	49	4
Bachelor's degree	66	33	1
Graduate degree	70	30	0

Note: Numbers may not add to 100 because "no opinion" and no answer are not included.
Source: General Social Survey, National Opinion Research Center, University of Chicago

Is Life Exciting? 1976 to 1996

"In general, do you find life exciting, pretty routine, or dull?"

(percent responding by sex, race, age, and education, 1976–96)

	exciting			pretty routine			dull		
	1996	*1985*	*1976*	*1996*	*1985*	*1976*	*1996*	*1985*	*1976*
Total	**49%**	**46%**	**44%**	**45%**	**46%**	**51%**	**4%**	**6%**	**4%**
Men	54	48	47	42	46	50	4	5	3
Women	46	45	42	48	47	52	4	7	4
Black	41	36	27	51	48	63	6	14	9
White	51	47	46	45	46	49	4	6	3
Aged 18 to 29	48	56	53	47	40	43	4	3	2
Aged 30 to 39	51	46	50	45	50	45	3	4	3
Aged 40 to 49	52	48	36	43	48	60	4	4	2
Aged 50 to 59	52	41	37	42	49	60	5	8	2
Aged 60 to 69	48	41	39	48	50	52	3	8	6
Aged 70 or older	40	37	37	51	44	54	9	15	7
Not high school grad.	35	34	31	52	52	61	11	13	7
High school graduate	46	46	47	49	48	49	4	5	2
Bachelor's degree	66	58	63	33	37	36	1	4	0
Graduate degree	70	70	70	30	26	28	0	2	0

Note: Numbers may not add to 100 because "no opinion" and no answer are not included.
Source: General Social Surveys, National Opinion Research Center, University of Chicago

Health Status

Most Americans say they are in good or excellent health.

The large majority of Americans (80 percent) rate their health as excellent or good. A plurality of 49 percent rates their health as good, while 31 percent say it is excellent. Since 1976, the percentage of people who say their health is good has grown despite the continued aging of the population.

Whites are more likely than blacks to say they are in excellent health (32 percent compared with 22 percent of blacks). Almost one-quarter of blacks say their health is only fair compared with 14 percent of whites. Both blacks and whites are less likely to say their health is only fair than they were in 1976.

As one would expect, the percentage of people rating their health as excellent declines with age. More than one-third of people younger than 50 say they are in excellent health, but the proportion declines to 23 percent among those in their 60s and to 17 percent among those aged 70 or older. Of the oldest Americans, 29 percent say they are in only fair health, a far higher proportion than among younger people.

A smaller share of people under age 40 said they were in excellent health in 1996 than in 1976. In contrast, among the middle aged (aged 40 to 59), the proportion of those who say they are in excellent health increased.

The college educated are far more likely than those with less education to say they are in excellent health (46 percent compared with 29 percent of high school graduates and 14 percent of people with less education). Those with little education generally have lower incomes and less access to health care than the better educated. In addition, many less-educated Americans are older people with age-related health problems.

Health Status, 1996

"Would you say your own health, in general, is excellent, good, fair, or poor?"

(percent responding by sex, race, age, and education, 1996)

	excellent	good	fair	poor
Total	**31%**	**49%**	**16%**	**4%**
Men	31	48	17	3
Women	30	49	15	5
Black	22	50	23	5
White	32	49	14	4
Aged 18 to 29	36	49	14	1
Aged 30 to 39	35	52	10	2
Aged 40 to 49	32	50	15	3
Aged 50 to 59	30	44	19	7
Aged 60 to 69	23	49	18	9
Aged 70 or older	17	46	29	8
Not a high school graduate	14	40	33	12
High school graduate	29	52	16	3
Bachelor's degree	46	46	6	1
Graduate degree	46	44	8	1

Note: Numbers may not add to 100 because no answer is not included.
Source: General Social Survey, National Opinion Research Center, University of Chicago

Health Status, 1976 to 1996

"Would you say your own health, in general, is excellent, good, fair, or poor?"

(percent responding by sex, race, age, and education, 1976–96)

	excellent			good			fair			poor		
	1996	*1985*	*1976*	*1996*	*1985*	*1976*	*1996*	*1985*	*1976*	*1996*	*1985*	*1976*
Total	**31%**	**32%**	**31%**	**49%**	**43%**	**42%**	**16%**	**18%**	**20%**	**4%**	**7%**	**7%**
Men	31	33	35	48	43	42	17	17	17	3	6	6
Women	30	31	28	49	43	42	15	18	22	5	7	8
Black	22	25	19	50	42	40	23	20	30	5	11	12
White	32	33	32	49	43	42	14	17	19	4	7	7
Aged 18 to 29	36	42	44	49	44	44	14	12	10	1	1	2
Aged 30 to 39	35	35	41	52	52	44	10	10	11	2	3	3
Aged 40 to 49	32	36	27	50	47	47	15	14	19	3	3	7
Aged 50 to 59	30	30	23	44	33	44	19	23	23	7	13	9
Aged 60 to 69	23	19	18	49	44	32	18	26	37	9	11	12
Aged 70 or older	17	18	17	46	34	37	29	30	31	8	17	15
Not a high school graduate	14	18	18	40	35	38	33	32	32	12	15	13
High school graduate	29	32	35	52	48	46	16	15	14	3	5	4
Bachelor's degree	46	43	49	46	44	38	6	10	11	1	4	2
Graduate degree	46	55	49	44	40	38	8	3	11	1	2	2

Note: Numbers may not add to 100 because no answer is not included.
Source: General Social Surveys, National Opinion Research Center, University of Chicago

Trustworthiness of People

Most Americans say you can't be too careful in dealing with other people.

Americans are less trusting than they used to be. Only 34 percent say most people can be trusted, while 61 percent say you can't be too careful. Twenty years earlier, a larger 44 percent said most people could be trusted, while 52 percent said you can't be too careful.

Blacks are far more wary than whites. Fully 81 percent of blacks say you can't be too careful compared with 57 percent of whites. Only 15 percent of blacks believe most people can be trusted compared with 37 percent of whites.

People in their 50s are more likely than other age groups to believe you can trust other people. Forty-six percent of 50-to-59-year-olds say you can trust others, as do 41 percent of people in their 40s. But only 31 to 35 percent of people aged 60 or older and of those in their 30s agree. People under age 30 are least likely to believe you can trust others (21 percent).

College graduates are more trusting than those with less education. The majority of college graduates (51 to 53 percent) say most people can be trusted, but only 31 percent of high school graduates and 16 percent of those without a high school diploma agree.

Trustworthiness of People, 1996

"Generally speaking, would you say that most people can be trusted
or that you can't be too careful in dealing with people?"

(percent responding by sex, race, age, and education, 1996)

	most people can be trusted	you can't be too careful
Total	**34%**	**61%**
Men	36	58
Women	32	62
Black	15	81
White	37	57
Aged 18 to 29	21	74
Aged 30 to 39	31	63
Aged 40 to 49	41	55
Aged 50 to 59	46	49
Aged 60 to 69	35	56
Aged 70 or older	32	60
Not a high school graduate	16	78
High school graduate	31	64
Bachelor's degree	51	43
Graduate degree	53	40

*Note: Numbers may not add to 100 because "depends," "don't know," and no answer are not included. "Depends"
was not included because it was a volunteered response.*
Source: General Social Survey, National Opinion Research Center, University of Chicago

Trustworthiness of People, 1976 to 1996

"Generally speaking, would you say that most people can be trusted
or that you can't be too careful in dealing with people?"

(percent responding by sex, race, age, and education, 1976–96)

	most people can be trusted			you can't be too careful		
	1996	1986	1976	1996	1986	1976
Total	**34%**	**37%**	**44%**	**61%**	**60%**	**52%**
Men	36	41	45	58	57	51
Women	32	35	43	62	61	52
Black	15	15	13	81	83	82
White	37	41	47	57	56	49
Aged 18 to 29	21	34	34	74	62	63
Aged 30 to 39	31	38	45	63	59	50
Aged 40 to 49	41	41	51	55	57	45
Aged 50 to 59	46	40	47	49	58	48
Aged 60 to 69	35	38	50	56	61	45
Aged 70 or older	32	36	46	60	60	50
Not a high school graduate	16	23	30	78	75	65
High school graduate	31	36	48	64	61	49
Bachelor's degree	51	62	70	43	35	25
Graduate degree	53	65	62	40	31	28

*Note: Numbers may not add to 100 because "depends," "don't know" and no answer are not included. "Depends"
was not included because it was a volunteered response.*
Source: General Social Surveys, National Opinion Research Center, University of Chicago

Fairness of People

Americans are less likely than they once were to think others are fair.

One-half of Americans say most people try to be fair, down from 59 percent who felt this way in 1976. Forty-two percent believe most people will try to take advantage of them if they get a chance, up from 36 percent in 1976.

Blacks are much less inclined than whites to believe most people try to be fair. Only 29 percent of blacks believe in people's fairness compared with 53 percent of whites.

Young people have always been less trusting than their elders, but the gap was wider in 1996 than in 1976. In the earlier year, 52 percent of people under age 30 believed most people try to be fair. This figure dropped to just 36 percent in 1996. In contrast, 58 percent of people aged 60 or older feel most people are fair, a decline of only 5 to 6 percentage points since 1976.

Well-educated people are far more likely than those with less education to have faith in the motives of others. While 62 to 67 percent of college graduates say most people try to be fair, only 48 percent of high school graduates and 33 percent of those who did not complete high school agree.

Fairness of People, 1996

"Do you think most people would try to take advantage of you
if they got a chance, or would they try to be fair?"

(percent responding by sex, race, age, and education, 1996)

	would try to be fair	would take advantage
Total	**50%**	**42%**
Men	49	42
Women	50	42
Black	29	63
White	53	38
Aged 18 to 29	36	56
Aged 30 to 39	46	44
Aged 40 to 49	49	40
Aged 50 to 59	62	32
Aged 60 to 69	58	34
Aged 70 or older	58	33
Not a high school graduate	33	60
High school graduate	48	44
Bachelor's degree	62	28
Graduate degree	67	24

Note: Numbers may not add to 100 because "depends," "don't know" and no answer are not included. "Depends" was not included because it was a volunteered response.
Source: General Social Survey, National Opinion Research Center, University of Chicago

Fairness of People, 1976 to 1996

"Do you think most people would try to take advantage of you
if they got a chance, or would they try to be fair?"

(percent responding by sex, race, age, and education, 1976–96)

	try to be fair			would take advantage		
	1996	*1986*	*1976*	*1996*	*1986*	*1976*
Total	**50%**	**62%**	**59%**	**42%**	**33%**	**36%**
Men	49	59	56	42	37	40
Women	50	64	62	42	31	33
Black	29	33	23	63	62	70
White	53	67	62	38	29	33
Aged 18 to 29	36	56	52	56	40	43
Aged 30 to 39	46	61	59	44	36	37
Aged 40 to 49	49	60	62	40	34	35
Aged 50 to 59	62	65	61	32	30	33
Aged 60 to 69	58	68	63	34	28	33
Aged 70 or older	58	68	64	33	26	28
Not a high school graduate	33	51	52	60	44	42
High school graduate	48	62	61	44	34	36
Bachelor's degree	62	78	74	28	17	21
Graduate degree	67	78	70	24	16	25

*Note: Numbers may not add to 100 because "depends," "don't know" and no answer are not included. "Depends"
was not included because it was a volunteered response.*
Source: General Social Surveys, National Opinion Research Center, University of Chicago

Helpfulness of People

Older generations still believe most people try to be helpful.

Americans are more likely to believe people are just looking out for themselves (49 percent) than trying to be helpful (43 percent).

Blacks are more likely than whites to believe most people are just looking out for themselves. Only 31 percent of blacks believe people try to be helpful most of the time, while 60 percent say people are just looking out for themselves. Whites, on the other hand, are divided. Forty-six percent say people try to be helpful and 47 percent say people are selfish.

Younger generations are more cynical than their elders. The majority of people aged 50 or older believe most people try to be helpful (54 to 59 percent). In contrast, most people under age 50 say most people are just looking out for themselves (51 to 62 percent).

The more education people have, the higher their opinion of others. Only 39 to 40 percent of people with a high school diploma or less education think most people try to be helpful compared with 51 to 54 percent of college graduates.

Helpfulness of People, 1996

"Would you say that most of the time people try to be helpful,
or that they are mostly just looking out for themselves?"

(percent responding by sex, race, age, and education, 1996)

	try to be helpful	just look out for themselves
Total	**43%**	**49%**
Men	42	50
Women	45	48
Black	31	60
White	46	47
Aged 18 to 29	31	62
Aged 30 to 39	38	54
Aged 40 to 49	41	51
Aged 50 to 59	54	38
Aged 60 to 69	59	36
Aged 70 or older	54	36
Not a high school graduate	39	55
High school graduate	40	52
Bachelor's degree	54	38
Graduate degree	51	39

Note: Numbers may not add to 100 because "depends," "don't know" and no answer are not included. "Depends" was not included because it was a volunteered response.
Source: General Social Survey, National Opinion Research Center, University of Chicago

Helpfulness of People, 1976 to 1996

"Would you say that most of the time people try to be helpful,
or that they are mostly just looking out for themselves?"

(percent responding by sex, race, age, and education, 1976–96)

	try to be helpful			just looking out for themselves		
	1996	*1986*	*1976*	*1996*	*1986*	*1976*
Total	**43%**	**56%**	**43%**	**49%**	**38%**	**50%**
Men	42	52	40	50	43	55
Women	45	58	46	48	35	47
Black	31	38	20	60	57	72
White	46	59	45	47	35	48
Aged 18 to 29	31	48	36	62	44	56
Aged 30 to 39	38	53	46	54	43	49
Aged 40 to 49	41	56	48	51	35	47
Aged 50 to 59	54	58	43	38	38	50
Aged 60 to 69	59	63	40	36	33	54
Aged 70 or older	54	62	50	36	31	42
Not a high school graduate	39	43	34	55	51	59
High school graduate	40	57	45	52	39	50
Bachelor's degree	54	70	61	38	22	30
Graduate degree	51	68	54	39	21	38

Note: Numbers may not add to 100 because "depends," "don't know" and no answer are not included. "Depends" was not included because it was a volunteered response.
Source: General Social Surveys, National Opinion Research Center, University of Chicago

Take Care of Self First

Altruism rises with education.

Americans are divided on whether or not to put themselves first. Forty-four percent agree with the statement, "You have to take care of yourself first, and if you have any energy left over, then help other people." But 42 percent disagree with that statement.

Blacks are far more likely than whites to say that one has to take care of oneself first. A solid majority of blacks (61 percent) say that one has to look out for oneself compared with 42 percent of whites.

People under age 60 are fairly evenly divided on this issue. But people aged 60 or older are more likely to agree than to disagree with the statement.

The biggest difference is found by education. Fully 60 percent of people who did not complete high school agree that one has to take care of oneself first. This share drops to 45 percent among high school graduates and just 35 to 38 percent among college graduates.

Take Care of Self First, 1996

"You have to take care of yourself first, and if you have
any energy left over, then help other people."

(percent responding by sex, race, age, and education, 1996)

	strongly agree	agree	neither	disagree	strongly disagree	agree, total	disagree, total
Total	**10%**	**34%**	**12%**	**33%**	**9%**	**44%**	**42%**
Men	10	32	13	36	9	42	45
Women	11	36	11	31	9	47	40
Black	18	43	11	22	6	61	28
White	9	33	12	36	9	42	45
Aged 18 to 29	12	33	14	33	9	45	42
Aged 30 to 39	10	32	12	35	11	42	46
Aged 40 to 49	11	34	10	36	9	45	45
Aged 50 to 59	8	35	9	37	11	43	48
Aged 60 to 69	9	38	17	29	6	47	35
Aged 70 or older	12	40	14	26	5	52	31
Not high school grad.	20	40	11	20	6	60	26
High school graduate	10	35	13	33	8	45	41
Bachelor's degree	8	30	9	38	15	38	53
Graduate degree	3	32	15	38	12	35	50

Note: Numbers may not add to 100 because "don't know" and no answer are not included.
Source: General Social Survey, National Opinion Research Center, University of Chicago

Feeling Rushed

Baby boomers are most likely to say they always feel rushed.

Thirty percent of Americans say they always feel rushed, up from 24 percent in 1982. Half say they sometimes feel rushed, while 18 percent say they almost never feel rushed—down from 24 percent in 1982.

In 1982, one-quarter of women said they were always pressed for time. By 1996 the proportion was nearly one-third. Men are less likely than women to say they feel rushed all the time (27 percent). Both men and women are less likely than they once were to say they almost never feel rushed.

Blacks are more likely than whites to say they almost never feel rushed (27 percent compared with 17 percent of whites). Conversely, whites are more likely than blacks to always feel rushed (31 percent compared with 23 percent of blacks).

Baby boomers (aged 30 to 49) are more likely than other age groups to say they always feel rushed. Not until people reach the age of 60 does a substantial proportion say they almost never feel rushed. One-third of people in their 60s and 53 percent of those aged 70 or older almost never feel rushed compared with 9 to 16 percent of younger people.

People who did not complete high school (many of whom are older) are less likely than those with more education to say they always feel rushed. Only 25 percent of them say they are always rushed compared with 30 to 33 percent of people with at least a high school diploma.

Feeling Rushed, 1996

"In general how do you feel about your time—would you say you feel rushed even to do things you have to do, only sometimes feel rushed, or almost never feel rushed?"

(percent responding by sex, race, age, and education, 1996)

	always	sometimes	almost never
Total	**30%**	**52%**	**18%**
Men	27	55	17
Women	32	49	19
Black	23	49	27
White	31	52	17
Aged 18 to 29	29	60	11
Aged 30 to 39	37	53	9
Aged 40 to 49	38	50	11
Aged 50 to 59	31	52	16
Aged 60 to 69	14	52	34
Aged 70 or older	12	36	53
Not a high school graduate	25	41	33
High school graduate	30	53	17
Bachelor's degree	32	54	13
Graduate degree	33	55	11

Note: Numbers may not add to 100 because "don't know" and no answer are not included.
Source: General Social Survey, National Opinion Research Center, University of Chicago

Feeling Rushed, 1982 to 1996

"In general how do you feel about your time—would you say
you feel rushed even to do things you have to do, only sometimes
feel rushed, or almost never feel rushed?"

(percent responding by sex, race, age, and education, 1982–96)

	always		sometimes		almost never	
	1996	1982	1996	1982	1996	1982
Total	**30%**	**24%**	**52%**	**52%**	**18%**	**24%**
Men	27	22	55	52	17	25
Women	32	25	49	51	19	24
Black	23	22	49	53	27	25
White	31	24	52	52	17	24
Aged 18 to 29	29	29	60	57	11	14
Aged 30 to 39	37	28	53	63	9	10
Aged 40 to 49	38	32	50	51	11	17
Aged 50 to 59	31	24	52	49	16	26
Aged 60 to 69	14	12	52	48	34	39
Aged 70 or older	12	9	36	29	53	61
Not a high school graduate	25	19	41	42	33	38
High school graduate	30	26	53	54	17	19
Bachelor's degree	32	24	54	64	13	11
Graduate degree	33	28	55	66	11	6

Note: Numbers may not add to 100 because "don't know" and no answer are not included.
Source: General Social Surveys, National Opinion Research Center, University of Chicago

Good Luck

Most people don't believe good things happen just because of luck.

Three-quarters of Americans disagree or strongly disagree that the really good things that happen are mostly due to luck. Only 16 percent agree or strongly agree.

There are big differences of opinion on this question by education, however. People with more education are far less likely to believe good fortune is just a matter of luck. Fully 86 to 90 percent of college graduates say good things don't happen just because of luck compared with 76 percent of high school graduates and only 49 percent of those with less education. Thirty-eight percent of those without a high school diploma believe good things happen because of luck, but this drops to 16 percent among high school graduates and to just 3 to 7 percent among college graduates.

Whites are more likely than blacks to disagree that good things happen because of luck (78 percent compared with 65 percent of blacks). Twenty-one percent of blacks feel luck is the reason for good fortune compared with 15 percent of whites.

Good Luck, 1996

"Do you agree or disagree with this statement:
The really good things that happen to me are mostly luck?"

(percent responding by sex, race, age, and education, 1996)

	strongly agree	agree	neither	disagree	strongly disagree	agree, total	disagree, total
Total	**3%**	**13%**	**8%**	**59%**	**17%**	**16%**	**76%**
Men	2	13	7	62	16	15	78
Women	3	13	8	57	18	16	75
Black	6	15	12	53	12	21	65
White	2	13	6	60	18	15	78
Aged 18 to 29	4	16	10	56	14	20	70
Aged 30 to 39	3	14	6	60	15	17	75
Aged 40 to 49	1	12	9	59	18	13	77
Aged 50 to 59	1	7	6	65	20	8	85
Aged 60 to 69	5	10	5	60	19	15	79
Aged 70 or older	4	19	10	50	15	23	65
Not high school grad.	8	30	9	40	9	38	49
High school graduate	3	13	8	61	15	16	76
Bachelor's degree	0	7	6	64	22	7	86
Graduate degree	0	3	7	59	31	3	90

Note: Numbers may not add to 100 because "don't know" and no answer are not included.
Source: General Social Survey, National Opinion Research Center, University of Chicago

Bad Breaks

People with less education are more likely to say bad breaks cause their problems.

Nearly three-quarters of Americans say their problems can't be written off as nothing more than bad breaks. Only 17 percent think their problems are the result of bad breaks.

Blacks are more likely than whites to think bad breaks cause their problems. Twenty-eight percent of blacks blamed bad breaks compared with 15 percent of whites. Three-quarters of whites don't believe that bad breaks cause most of their problems compared with 56 percent of blacks.

Generation Xers (under age 30) are more likely than their elders to blame their problems on bad breaks. About one-quarter of Xers say bad breaks cause their problems compared with 11 to 17 percent of older people.

There are large differences by education in the proportions of people who blame bad breaks for their problems. One-third of people who did not complete high school think that most of their problems come from bad breaks. In contrast, only 17 percent of high school graduates and 8 to 9 percent of college graduates agree.

Bad Breaks, 1996

"Do you agree or disagree with this statement:
Most of my problems are due to bad breaks."

(percent responding by sex, race, age, and education, 1996)

	strongly agree	agree	neither	disagree	strongly disagree	agree, total	disagree, total
Total	**3%**	**14%**	**9%**	**54%**	**19%**	**17%**	**73%**
Men	3	15	9	55	17	18	72
Women	3	14	9	52	20	17	72
Black	8	20	14	47	9	28	56
White	2	13	8	55	21	15	76
Aged 18 to 29	5	21	14	46	14	26	60
Aged 30 to 39	2	15	6	59	17	17	76
Aged 40 to 49	2	14	10	52	21	16	73
Aged 50 to 59	1	10	9	54	26	11	80
Aged 60 to 69	5	8	6	60	19	13	79
Aged 70 or older	3	12	8	54	21	15	75
Not high school grad.	7	27	9	46	8	34	54
High school graduate	3	14	9	56	17	17	73
Bachelor's degree	1	8	10	53	28	9	81
Graduate degree	2	6	7	48	36	8	84

Note: Numbers may not add to 100 because "don't know" and no answer are not included.
Source: General Social Survey, National Opinion Research Center, University of Chicago

Control over Bad Things

People with more education feel more in control of their lives.

Only 30 percent of Americans believe they have little control over the bad things that happen to them, while a majority of 61 percent believes they do have control.

The largest differences of opinion on this question exist by education. The less educated people are, the more they believe the bad things that happen to them are beyond their control. Half of people who did not complete high school believe this compared with 30 percent of high school graduates and 14 to 17 percent of college graduates.

People aged 70 or older are more likely than younger people to believe they have little control over the bad things that happen (49 percent compared with 24 to 29 percent of younger people). For many of the elderly, this belief may be grounded in reality. The primary problems facing the oldest Americans are health related and are, in fact, largely out of their control. One-third of women say bad things are out of their control compared with 27 percent of men.

Blacks are more likely than whites to believe they have little control over bad things that happen to them. Forty percent of blacks agree with this statement compared with 27 percent of whites.

Control over Bad Things, 1996

"Do you agree or disagree with this statement:
I have little control over the bad things that happen to me."

(percent responding by sex, race, age, and education, 1996)

	strongly agree	agree	neither	disagree	strongly disagree	agree, total	disagree, total
Total	**5%**	**25%**	**8%**	**49%**	**12%**	**30%**	**61%**
Men	5	22	8	51	13	27	64
Women	5	27	8	47	12	32	59
Black	8	32	10	41	6	40	47
White	4	23	7	50	14	27	64
Aged 18 to 29	4	24	10	49	12	28	61
Aged 30 to 39	4	25	6	54	9	29	63
Aged 40 to 49	3	22	8	51	13	25	64
Aged 50 to 59	3	21	8	51	15	24	66
Aged 60 to 69	5	24	8	50	12	29	62
Aged 70 or older	12	37	9	28	12	49	40
Not high school grad.	11	40	7	33	7	51	40
High school graduate	5	25	8	49	11	30	60
Bachelor's degree	1	16	9	56	16	17	72
Graduate degree	2	12	7	63	16	14	79

Note: Numbers may not add to 100 because "don't know" and no answer are not included.
Source: General Social Survey, National Opinion Research Center, University of Chicago

Hide Emotions

College graduates are less likely to keep feelings to themselves.

Forty-six percent of Americans say they don't keep their emotions to themselves. But nearly as many (41 percent) say they keep their feelings hidden.

Not surprisingly, men are more likely than women to keep their emotions hidden. Nearly half of men (46 percent) say they keep their feelings to themselves compared with 38 percent of women. Half of women say they don't hide their emotions compared with 42 percent of men.

Older generations were raised to hide their feelings. The majority (55 to 56 percent) of people aged 60 or older keep their emotions to themselves. Among people under age 60, however, 46 to 54 percent say they do not keep their emotions to themselves.

The majority (55 percent) of people who did not complete high school (many of whom are older Americans) say they keep their emotions to themselves. High school graduates, on the other hand, are more likely to say they do not hide their feelings (47 percent). Among college graduates, 52 to 55 percent say they don't keep their feelings hidden.

Hide Emotions, 1996

"Do you agree or disagree with this statement: I keep my emotions to myself."

(percent responding by sex, race, age, and education, 1996)

	strongly agree	agree	neither	disagree	strongly disagree	agree, total	disagree, total
Total	**7%**	**34%**	**10%**	**37%**	**9%**	**41%**	**46%**
Men	8	38	11	34	8	46	42
Women	7	31	9	40	10	38	50
Black	11	31	5	42	11	42	53
White	7	35	10	37	9	42	46
Aged 18 to 29	6	33	4	43	11	39	54
Aged 30 to 39	7	36	7	38	10	43	48
Aged 40 to 49	5	30	18	37	9	35	46
Aged 50 to 59	7	29	7	43	11	36	54
Aged 60 to 69	11	44	15	23	8	55	31
Aged 70 or older	14	42	9	31	1	56	32
Not high school grad.	13	42	8	26	6	55	32
High school graduate	8	34	10	38	9	42	47
Bachelor's degree	6	29	10	41	11	35	52
Graduate degree	2	34	10	40	15	36	55

Note: Numbers may not add to 100 because "don't know" and no answer are not included.
Source: General Social Survey, National Opinion Research Center, University of Chicago

Show Feelings

Most people are not afraid to let others know how they feel.

Two-thirds of Americans say they aren't afraid to let other people know how they feel. This doesn't necessarily mean people freely share their emotions, however, since about two in five adults say they keep their emotions to themselves.

Men may not be known for freely sharing their feelings, but they are just as likely as women to say they aren't afraid to show how they feel. Two-thirds of men and women are not afraid to let people know how they feel while only 20 percent say they don't want others to know their feelings.

Blacks are more likely than whites to say they are not afraid to show their feelings (75 percent compared with 65 percent of whites). By education, similar proportions of people say they are not afraid to let people know their feelings. But people who did not complete college are more likely than those with college degrees to hide their feelings.

Show Feelings, 1996

"Do you agree or disagree with this statement:
I'm not afraid to let people know my feelings."

(percent responding by sex, race, age, and education, 1996)

	strongly agree	agree	neither	disagree	strongly disagree	agree, total	disagree, total
Total	**19%**	**47%**	**12%**	**16%**	**4%**	**66%**	**20%**
Men	17	49	13	16	4	66	20
Women	21	46	11	16	4	67	20
Black	25	50	7	14	3	75	17
White	18	47	12	17	4	65	21
Aged 18 to 29	25	42	13	15	4	67	19
Aged 30 to 39	16	51	8	21	3	67	24
Aged 40 to 49	17	49	20	11	3	66	14
Aged 50 to 59	23	46	8	15	3	69	18
Aged 60 to 69	20	44	9	20	7	64	27
Aged 70 or older	12	53	12	15	8	65	23
Not high school grad.	19	47	8	20	4	66	24
High school graduate	22	46	11	17	4	68	21
Bachelor's degree	18	51	15	12	3	69	15
Graduate degree	10	56	16	11	5	66	16

Note: Numbers may not add to 100 because "don't know" and no answer are not included.
Source: General Social Survey, National Opinion Research Center, University of Chicago

Show Anger

Most people say they let others know when they are angry.

Most Americans (61 percent) agree with the statement, "When I'm angry I let people know." Only 29 percent disagree.

Blacks are more likely than whites to say they let others know when they are angry. Seventy percent of blacks say this compared with 59 percent of whites.

People under age 40 feel freer than their elders to express their anger. Seventy percent of 18-to-29-year-olds say they let people know when they are angry, as do 62 percent of people in their 30s. This share drops to 58 to 59 percent among people aged 40 to 69 and to 51 percent among those aged 70 or older.

People with less education are more likely to say they let people know when they are angry. Among people with a high school diploma or less, 61 to 64 percent say they let people know when they are angry. But the figure drops to 49 to 56 percent among college graduates, who are more likely than those with less education to say they neither agree nor disagree with the statement.

Show Anger, 1996

"Do you agree or disagree with this statement: When I'm angry I let people know."

(percent responding by sex, race, age, and education, 1996)

	strongly agree	agree	neither	disagree	strongly disagree	agree, total	disagree, total
Total	**16%**	**45%**	**9%**	**24%**	**5%**	**61%**	**29%**
Men	15	44	8	28	5	59	33
Women	17	45	10	21	5	62	26
Black	23	47	9	15	5	70	20
White	15	44	9	26	5	59	31
Aged 18 to 29	19	51	9	18	3	70	21
Aged 30 to 39	14	48	8	24	5	62	29
Aged 40 to 49	15	44	13	24	2	59	26
Aged 50 to 59	17	41	7	29	5	58	34
Aged 60 to 69	19	40	9	23	8	59	31
Aged 70 or older	15	36	8	31	9	51	40
Not high school grad.	24	37	6	24	8	61	32
High school graduate	17	47	8	23	4	64	27
Bachelor's degree	10	46	15	25	4	56	29
Graduate degree	10	39	12	31	6	49	37

Note: Numbers may not add to 100 because "don't know" and no answer are not included.
Source: General Social Survey, National Opinion Research Center, University of Chicago

Volunteer Work

College graduates are most likely to volunteer their time.

One-quarter of Americans say they have volunteered for a religious organization in the past year. This is considerably higher than the proportion of those who volunteered for any other kind of organization. Eighteen percent of Americans have volunteered in the field of education and 16 percent in youth development activities.

Women are more likely than men to have done volunteer work for a religious organization (28 percent compared with 22 percent of men). They are also more likely to have volunteered in an educational setting (20 percent compared with 15 percent of men) and in the area of health (13 percent compared with 8 percent of men).

Baby boomers (aged 30 to 49) have less free time than most other age groups, but this has not prevented them from volunteering. One reason for this volunteer spirit is that most boomers have school-aged children, which explains why they are more likely than other age groups to volunteer in education and youth development.

College graduates are considerably more likely than those with less education to volunteer their time. While 33 to 40 percent of college graduates volunteered for religious organizations, only 15 to 22 percent of those with less education did. College graduates are also far more likely than those with less education to volunteer in the areas of education, youth development, health, the arts, and the environment.

Volunteer Work, 1996

Here are examples of the many different areas in which people do volunteer activity. Volunteer activity means not just belonging to a service organization, but actually working in some way to help others for no monetary pay. In which, if any, of these areas have you done some volunteer work in the past twelve months?"

(percent responding by sex, race, age, and education, 1996)

	religious organiza- tions	education	youth develop- ment	health	environ- ment	recreation (adults)	arts, culture, humanities	political organiza- tions or campaigns
Total	**25%**	**18%**	**16%**	**11%**	**7%**	**7%**	**7%**	**5%**
Men	22	15	17	8	9	9	7	8
Women	28	20	15	13	6	5	7	3
Black	26	15	13	9	7	6	6	3
White	25	18	16	11	8	7	7	6
Aged 18 to 29	18	15	16	9	10	10	7	4
Aged 30 to 39	28	23	21	15	7	8	5	5
Aged 40 to 49	30	25	21	14	7	7	11	6
Aged 50 to 59	31	15	13	6	9	4	9	7
Aged 60 to 69	24	9	4	8	4	5	9	5
Aged 70 or older	17	6	3	7	5	2	3	4
Not a high school graduate	15	5	7	5	3	5	2	2
High school graduate	22	16	14	9	7	7	4	4
Bachelor's degree	40	30	26	16	13	8	17	11
Graduate degree	33	29	20	17	13	4	17	7

Note: Numbers may not add to 100 because "don't know" and no answer are not included.
Source: General Social Survey, National Opinion Research Center, University of Chicago

Chapter 9

Sexual Attitudes and Behavior

The sexual mores of Americans have changed dramatically over the past 20 years. The public has grown more accepting of premarital sex, more tolerant of homosexual sex, and more supportive of sex education in the schools. But Americans have not become more permissive across the board. They are more likely than they once were to say adultery is always wrong. Most also think prostitution is wrong, and they think teens should not be having sex or buying pornography.

Conventional wisdom says that men are more libertine than woman in the sexual arena, and the attitudes examined here largely support that view. Women are more likely than men to believe it is always wrong for young teens to have sex and they are more likely to want pornography outlawed entirely. Men are far more likely than women to say there is nothing wrong with premarital sex. They are also more likely to have committed adultery and paid someone for sex.

Blacks are more conservative than whites about some sexual issues. More blacks than whites say homosexual and premarital sex are always wrong. But whites are more likely to say pornography should be outlawed entirely, while blacks are more likely to favor restricting its distribution to adults.

The generations differ strongly in their opinions about many sexual issues. They are worlds apart on the issue of homosexual sex, with fewer than half of the youngest adults, but three-quarters of the oldest, saying it is always wrong. Younger generations are far more likely to see nothing wrong with premarital sex, and they are less likely to believe it is always wrong for young teens to have sex. While most people aged 60 or older would outlaw pornography entirely, younger people are far more likely to favor simply restricting it to adults.

The attitudes of college graduates resemble those of younger generations. This is due, in part, to the fact that younger people are overrepresented among college graduates while older generations make up a larger share of the less educated. The proportions of people saying homosexual and premarital sex are always wrong decline with more education. College graduates are more likely to favor restricting pornography to adults while those who went no further than high school are more likely to want it outlawed entirely. Most people, regardless of education, believe sex between young teens and adultery are always wrong, but college graduates are less absolute on these issues, with a significant share saying they are almost always wrong.

Sex Education

An overwhelming majority of Americans favor sex education in the public schools.

For a topic that ignites so much controversy, Americans are remarkably united in their opinions about sex education—85 percent favor sex education in the public schools. And, unlike with so many of the hot-button issues confronting the nation today, men and women, blacks and whites, are in agreement on this topic. Support for sex education in school was higher in 1996 than in 1975.

This is not to say there are no dissenters. By age and education, there are differences of opinion on whether schools are the proper arena for teaching young people about sex. The proportion of those who support sex education falls substantially among older people. Ninety-three percent of people under age 30 support sex education, as do 87 to 88 percent of those aged 30 to 49. Support is slightly lower among those aged 50 to 69 (81 to 82 percent). Least likely to support sex education are those aged 70 or older—only 68 percent favor it.

People who did not complete high school are less likely than those with more education to support sex education. While 86 to 89 percent of people with at least a high school diploma favor sex education, only 74 percent of those who did not complete high school agree.

Sex Education, 1996

"Would you be for or against sex education in the public schools?"

(percent responding by sex, race, age, and education, 1996)

	for	*against*
Total	**85%**	**12%**
Men	85	13
Women	85	12
Black	87	10
White	85	13
Aged 18 to 29	93	5
Aged 30 to 39	88	11
Aged 40 to 49	87	11
Aged 50 to 59	81	14
Aged 60 to 69	82	17
Aged 70 or older	68	25
Not a high school graduate	74	22
High school graduate	86	11
Bachelor's degree	89	10
Graduate degree	88	9

Note: Numbers may not add to 100 because "don't know" and no answer are not included.
Source: General Social Survey, National Opinion Research Center, University of Chicago

Sex Education, 1975 to 1996

"Would you be for or against sex education in the public schools?"

(percent responding by sex, race, age, and education, 1975–96)

	favor			oppose		
	1996	1986	1975	1996	1986	1975
Total	**85%**	**82%**	**76%**	**12%**	**16%**	**20%**
Women	85	84	73	13	13	22
Men	85	80	79	12	17	18
Black	87	77	74	10	20	21
White	85	82	77	13	15	20
Aged 18 to 29	93	90	89	5	9	9
Aged 30 to 39	88	88	82	11	9	15
Aged 40 to 49	87	88	82	11	11	13
Aged 50 to 59	81	80	76	14	17	22
Aged 60 to 69	82	73	60	17	23	36
Aged 70 or older	68	58	44	25	35	45
Not a high school graduate	74	67	62	22	29	33
High school graduate	86	85	82	11	13	15
Bachelor's degree	89	93	92	10	6	5
Graduate degree	88	90	90	9	8	8

Note: Numbers may not add to 100 because "don't know" and no answer are not included.
Source: General Social Surveys, National Opinion Research Center, University of Chicago

Teens and Sex

Most people disapprove of young teens having sex before marriage.

Americans are far more accepting of premarital sex than they used to be, but sex between minors has not gained acceptance. Two-thirds of adults say it is always wrong for young teens to have premarital sex. Another 16 percent say it is almost always wrong. Only 4 percent say it is not wrong at all.

Women are more likely than men to say it is always wrong for young teens to have sex (71 percent compared with 65 percent of men). A larger proportion of blacks (73 percent) than whites (68 percent) says it is always wrong. Blacks were far more likely to say this in 1996 than in 1986.

There is a big difference of opinion by age. Those closest to their early teens, the 18-to-29-year-olds, are least likely to say it is always wrong for young teens to have sex before marriage (53 percent). Fully 21 percent of them say it is only wrong sometimes and 8 percent say it is not wrong at all. People aged 60 or older are more likely than younger age groups to say it is always wrong.

The proportion of those who say it is always wrong for young teens to have sex declines with education. Among people with a high school diploma or less education, 70 to 72 percent say it is always wrong. This falls to 55 to 60 percent among college graduates.

Teens and Sex, 1996

"What about sexual relations before marriage between people
in their early teens, say 14 to 16 years old? Is it always wrong,
almost always wrong, wrong only sometimes, or not wrong at all?"

(percent responding by sex, race, age, and education, 1996)

	always wrong	almost always wrong	wrong only sometimes	not wrong at all
Total	**68%**	**16%**	**10%**	**4%**
Men	65	16	12	5
Women	71	17	8	3
Black	73	12	7	6
White	68	17	10	4
Aged 18 to 29	53	18	21	8
Aged 30 to 39	71	15	8	4
Aged 40 to 49	64	22	8	4
Aged 50 to 59	74	16	6	3
Aged 60 to 69	79	12	4	3
Aged 70 or older	83	8	6	2
Not a high school graduate	70	12	8	7
High school graduate	72	14	10	3
Bachelor's degree	60	23	11	5
Graduate degree	55	28	11	4

Note: Numbers may not add to 100 because "don't know" and no answer are not included.
Source: General Social Survey, National Opinion Research Center, University of Chicago

Teens and Sex, 1986 to 1996

"What about sexual relations before marriage between people in their early teens, say 14 to 16 years old? Is it always wrong, almost always wrong, wrong only sometimes, or not wrong at all?"

(percent responding by sex, race, age, and education, 1986–96)

	always wrong		almost always wrong		sometimes wrong		not wrong at all	
	1996	*1986*	*1996*	*1986*	*1996*	*1986*	*1996*	*1986*
Total	**68%**	**66%**	**16%**	**19%**	**10%**	**11%**	**4%**	**3%**
Men	65	60	16	19	12	14	5	5
Women	71	70	17	18	8	9	3	2
Black	73	61	12	17	7	13	6	7
White	68	66	17	19	10	10	4	3
Aged 18 to 29	53	49	18	26	21	21	8	3
Aged 30 to 39	71	58	15	22	8	14	4	5
Aged 40 to 49	64	66	22	23	8	8	4	3
Aged 50 to 59	74	74	16	15	6	4	3	3
Aged 60 to 69	79	81	12	8	4	5	3	3
Aged 70 or older	83	85	8	9	6	4	2	0
Not a high school graduate	70	74	12	10	8	11	7	4
High school graduate	72	65	14	18	10	12	3	3
Bachelor's degree	60	57	23	31	11	8	5	2
Graduate degree	55	59	28	26	11	10	4	4

Note: Numbers may not add to 100 because "don't know" and no answer are not included.
Source: General Social Surveys, National Opinion Research Center, University of Chicago

Opinion of Premarital Sex

Fewer than one-quarter of Americans think premarital sex is always wrong.

Since the "sexual revolution" of the 1960s, attitudes about sex have changed. A plurality of 42 percent of Americans now say there is nothing wrong with sex before marriage. Fewer than one-quarter believe premarital sex is always wrong. In 1975, Americans were much more divided on this issue, with 30 percent saying premarital sex was always wrong and 31 percent saying it was not wrong.

Men and women don't entirely agree on this issue. Both sexes were more likely in 1996 than in 1975 to think premarital sex is OK, but women are still less accepting than men. While nearly half of men think it's not wrong, only 38 percent of women agree.

Age is a strong predictor of attitudes about premarital sex. Over half of people under age 30 say there is nothing wrong with sex before marriage, but fewer than 30 percent of those aged 60 or older agree. The proportion saying premarital sex is OK rose in every age group between 1975 and 1996.

There are only small differences by education in attitudes towards premarital sex. Those with less education are more likely to say premarital sex is always wrong. Only 18 to 20 percent of college graduates say it is always wrong, but this share rises to 30 percent among people who did not complete high school.

Opinion of Premarital Sex, 1996

"If a man and woman have sex relations before marriage, do you think it is always wrong, almost always wrong, wrong only sometimes, or not wrong at all?"

(percent responding by sex, race, age, and education, 1996)

	always wrong	almost always wrong	wrong only sometimes	not wrong at all
Total	**23%**	**9%**	**22%**	**42%**
Men	19	7	22	48
Women	26	11	22	38
Black	31	8	18	41
White	22	9	22	43
Aged 18 to 29	14	6	24	54
Aged 30 to 39	22	9	23	44
Aged 40 to 49	20	7	19	49
Aged 50 to 59	25	9	19	44
Aged 60 to 69	31	13	25	29
Aged 70 or older	38	18	23	16
Not a high school graduate	30	7	15	41
High school graduate	23	11	22	42
Bachelor's degree	20	7	25	44
Graduate degree	18	8	25	47

Note: Numbers may not add to 100 because "don't know" and no answer are not included.
Source: General Social Survey, National Opinion Research Center, University of Chicago

Opinion of Premarital Sex, 1975 to 1996

"If a man and woman have sex relations before marriage, do you think it is always wrong, almost always wrong, wrong only sometimes, or not wrong at all?"

(percent responding by sex, race, age, and education, 1975–96)

	always wrong			almost always wrong			sometimes wrong			not wrong at all		
	1996	*1986*	*1975*	*1996*	*1986*	*1975*	*1996*	*1986*	*1975*	*1996*	*1986*	*1975*
Total	23%	27%	30%	9%	9%	12%	22%	22%	23%	42%	39%	31%
Men	19	20	25	7	9	10	22	22	23	48	47	38
Women	26	32	33	11	8	14	22	22	23	38	33	26
Black	31	26	20	8	7	9	18	15	16	41	46	48
White	22	27	31	9	9	12	22	23	24	43	38	29
Aged 18 to 29	14	11	13	6	7	6	24	31	28	54	50	50
Aged 30 to 39	22	18	26	9	8	12	23	20	23	44	52	38
Aged 40 to 49	20	26	31	7	6	11	19	22	24	49	44	29
Aged 50 to 59	25	31	33	9	10	21	19	20	22	44	34	19
Aged 60 to 69	31	39	42	13	13	16	25	19	18	29	23	17
Aged 70 or older	38	55	57	18	9	10	23	19	15	16	11	11
Not a high school graduate	30	37	37	7	11	12	15	15	20	41	33	25
High school graduate	23	25	29	11	8	13	22	24	21	42	39	33
Bachelor's degree	20	19	13	7	6	11	25	26	35	44	48	37
Graduate degree	18	20	14	8	5	4	25	29	44	47	43	36

Note: Numbers may not add to 100 because "don't know" and no answer are not included.
Source: General Social Surveys, National Opinion Research Center, University of Chicago

Opinion of Extramarital Sex

Americans are more likely now than they were 20 years ago to condemn adultery.

The sexual mores of Americans are more liberal than they were a few decades ago. But on one issue, Americans are stricter than ever. Extramarital sexual activity (adultery) was more likely to be condemned in 1996 than it was in 1976. Three-quarters of adults say extramarital sex is always wrong. Only 2 percent say it is not wrong.

In 1976, the more education people had the less likely they were to say adultery was always wrong. In that year, 76 percent of people who had not completed high school said adultery was always wrong, but this share dropped to only 39 percent among people with graduate degrees. Those with more education were most likely to hedge a little, saying it was almost always wrong.

By 1996, the gap in opinion had narrowed considerably, however. Sixty to 68 percent of college graduates say it is always wrong to have extramarital sex compared with 81 to 83 percent of people with a high school diploma or less.

People aged 40 to 59 are slightly less likely than those younger or older to say adultery is always wrong. They are also more likely to admit they have committed adultery. But the differences by age are small, especially compared with the results from 1976. In that year, the proportion of those who said adultery was always wrong rose sharply with age, from only 55 percent of people under age 30 to 88 percent of those aged 70 or older. In 1996, the largest difference by age was only 7 percentage points.

Opinion of Extramarital Sex, 1996

"What is your opinion about a married person having sexual relations with someone other than the marriage partner—is it always wrong, almost always wrong, wrong only sometimes, or not wrong at all?"

(percent responding by sex, race, age, and education, 1996)

	always wrong	almost always wrong	wrong only sometimes	not wrong at all
Total	**76%**	**15%**	**5%**	**2%**
Men	74	16	6	2
Women	78	14	4	1
Black	76	11	7	5
White	77	15	5	1
Aged 18 to 29	76	16	7	1
Aged 30 to 39	79	13	4	2
Aged 40 to 49	73	17	7	2
Aged 50 to 59	74	16	5	4
Aged 60 to 69	81	15	3	1
Aged 70 or older	80	13	3	2
Not a high school graduate	83	8	5	2
High school graduate	81	13	4	2
Bachelor's degree	68	21	7	2
Graduate degree	60	27	6	3

Note: Numbers may not add to 100 because "don't know" and no answer are not included.
Source: General Social Survey, National Opinion Research Center, University of Chicago

Opinion of Extramarital Sex, 1976 to 1996

"What is your opinion about a married person having sexual relations with someone other than the marriage partner—is it always wrong, almost always wrong, wrong only sometimes, or not wrong at all?"

(percent responding by sex, race, age, and education, 1976–96)

	always wrong			almost always wrong			sometimes wrong			not wrong at all		
	1996	1985	1976	1996	1985	1976	1996	1985	1976	1996	1985	1976
Total	76%	74%	68%	15%	13%	15%	5%	9%	11%	2%	3%	4%
Men	74	71	64	16	13	17	6	10	13	2	4	5
Women	78	77	71	14	13	14	4	7	10	1	2	4
Black	76	71	56	11	10	14	7	11	19	5	5	6
White	77	75	69	15	13	16	5	8	11	1	2	4
Aged 18 to 29	76	69	55	16	18	20	7	10	18	1	2	7
Aged 30 to 39	79	66	61	13	18	19	4	12	11	2	3	6
Aged 40 to 49	73	67	69	17	15	17	7	12	9	2	5	3
Aged 50 to 59	74	84	73	16	7	11	5	4	11	4	2	4
Aged 60 to 69	81	83	76	15	8	11	3	6	9	1	1	2
Aged 70 or older	80	85	88	13	6	6	3	3	3	2	2	1
Not a high school graduate	83	85	76	8	6	10	5	4	9	2	3	3
High school graduate	81	74	68	13	13	15	4	8	12	2	3	4
Bachelor's degree	68	65	48	21	19	28	7	14	16	2	3	7
Graduate degree	60	48	39	27	30	34	6	20	16	3	1	8

Note: Numbers may not add to 100 because "don't know" and no answer are not included.
Source: General Social Surveys, National Opinion Research Center, University of Chicago

Opinion of Homosexual Sex

Attitudes about gays are changing.

A small majority (56 percent) of Americans say that sex between two adults of the same sex is always wrong. But a growing minority says it is not wrong. In 1976 only 15 percent of adults said homosexual sex is not wrong at all, but this proportion had risen to 26 percent by 1996.

Blacks are more likely than whites to say sexual relations between people of the same sex is always wrong (68 percent of blacks compared with 54 percent of whites). Blacks were about as likely to say this in 1996 as in 1976, but the percentage of whites who say it is always wrong dropped substantially.

Strong differences of opinion exist among people of different ages. Fewer than half (45 percent) of Generation Xers (under age 30) say homosexual sex is always wrong and fully 38 percent say it is not wrong at all. Among people aged 30 to 49, a slim majority (52 to 54 percent) says homosexual sex is always wrong. This figure rises to 58 percent among people in their 50s. People aged 60 or older are resolutely opposed to homosexual sex, with 70 to 76 percent saying it is always wrong.

The percentage of people who say homosexual sex is always wrong declines with education while the proportion of those who say it is not wrong at all rises. Fully 70 percent of people who did not complete high school say homosexual sex is always wrong, but this drops to only 37 percent among people with graduate degrees. College graduates are most likely to say it is never wrong (37 to 39 percent compared with only 15 percent of those who did not complete high school).

Opinion of Homosexual Sex, 1996

"What about sexual relations between two adults of the same sex—
do you think it is it is always wrong, almost always wrong,
wrong only sometimes, or not wrong at all?"

(percent responding by sex, race, age, and education, 1996)

	always wrong	almost always wrong	wrong only sometimes	not wrong at all
Total	**56%**	**5%**	**6%**	**26%**
Men	58	6	7	24
Women	54	4	5	28
Black	68	2	4	19
White	54	5	6	27
Aged 18 to 29	45	3	7	38
Aged 30 to 39	54	4	6	28
Aged 40 to 49	52	6	7	26
Aged 50 to 59	58	4	4	27
Aged 60 to 69	70	8	3	15
Aged 70 or older	76	6	6	7
Not a high school graduate	70	5	4	15
High school graduate	60	5	5	24
Bachelor's degree	42	5	8	37
Graduate degree	37	4	12	39

Note: Numbers may not add to 100 because "don't know" and no answer are not included.
Source: General Social Survey, National Opinion Research Center, University of Chicago

Opinion of Homosexual Sex, 1976 to 1996

"What about sexual relations between two adults of the same sex—do you think it is always wrong, almost always wrong, wrong only sometimes, or not wrong at all?"

(percent responding by sex, race, age, and education, 1976–96)

	always wrong			almost always wrong			sometimes wrong			not wrong at all		
	1996	1985	1976	1996	1985	1976	1996	1985	1976	1996	1985	1976
Total	**56%**	**72%**	**67%**	**5%**	**4%**	**6%**	**6%**	**7%**	**7%**	**26%**	**14%**	**15%**
Men	58	72	67	6	4	6	7	7	9	24	13	14
Women	54	72	66	4	4	6	5	7	6	28	15	16
Black	68	83	70	2	3	1	4	3	7	19	7	16
White	54	71	66	5	4	6	6	7	8	27	15	15
Aged 18 to 29	45	68	52	3	5	9	7	8	10	38	17	25
Aged 30 to 39	54	61	64	4	3	6	6	12	8	28	24	18
Aged 40 to 49	52	67	66	6	8	9	7	7	9	26	16	12
Aged 50 to 59	58	80	73	4	3	4	4	5	6	27	7	13
Aged 60 to 69	70	83	74	8	1	4	3	4	5	15	9	9
Aged 70 or older	76	84	86	6	3	2	6	1	3	7	3	3
Not a high school graduate	70	84	80	5	2	2	4	2	4	15	7	7
High school graduate	60	75	66	5	3	8	5	6	7	24	14	15
Bachelor's degree	42	51	41	5	8	7	8	16	11	37	23	34
Graduate degree	37	41	34	4	13	5	12	15	25	39	27	34

Note: Numbers may not add to 100 because "don't know" and no answer are not included.
Source: General Social Surveys, National Opinion Research Center, University of Chicago

Pornography Laws

The generations divide sharply on restricting pornography.

A majority of Americans (58 percent) believe the best approach to pornography is simply to keep it out of the hands of minors. Another 37 percent would have it outlawed entirely. Support for laws against the distribution of pornography to minors has grown slightly since 1976. Few people are libertarian regarding pornography—wanting no restrictions placed on its distribution. In 1976 there was more support for this approach among some segments of the population.

Women are far more likely than men to support making the distribution of pornography completely illegal (47 percent compared with 25 percent of men). Men (who are the primary consumers of pornography) are more likely than women to say that only the distribution of pornography to minors should be illegal.

The proportion of people who would outlaw pornography entirely rises sharply with age, from 25 percent of people under age 30 to 65 percent of those aged 70 or older. Younger people are more likely to believe it should be restricted to adults rather than outlawed entirely.

By education, those with the least schooling are more supportive of laws making all pornography illegal. Nearly half of people who did not complete high school would outlaw it entirely. This view drops to 38 percent among high school graduates and to 29 to 30 percent among college graduates. The proportion of college graduates who favor no laws against pornography dropped from 11 to 15 percent in 1976 to only 3 to 6 percent in 1996.

Pornography Laws, 1996

"Which of these statements comes closest to your feelings about pornography laws?
There should be laws against the distribution of pornography whatever the age.
There should be laws against the distribution of pornography to persons under 18.
There should be no laws forbidding the distribution of pornography."

(percent responding by sex, race, age, and education, 1996)

	illegal for all ages	illegal under age 18	legal
Total	37%	58%	4%
Men	25	70	4
Women	47	48	4
Black	31	64	4
White	39	56	4
Aged 18 to 29	25	72	3
Aged 30 to 39	28	69	3
Aged 40 to 49	34	63	3
Aged 50 to 59	42	52	4
Aged 60 to 69	55	38	6
Aged 70 or older	65	25	7
Not a high school graduate	48	42	6
High school graduate	38	58	3
Bachelor's degree	30	66	3
Graduate degree	29	65	6

Note: Numbers may not add to 100 because "don't know" and no answer are not included.
Source: General Social Survey, National Opinion Research Center, University of Chicago

Pornography Laws, 1976 to 1996

"Which of these statements comes closest to your feelings about pornography laws? There should be laws against the distribution of pornography whatever the age. There should be laws against the distribution of pornography to persons under 18. There should be no laws forbidding the distribution of pornography."

(percent responding by sex, race, age, and education, 1976–96)

	illegal for all ages			illegal under age 18			legal		
	1996	*1986*	*1976*	*1996*	*1986*	*1976*	*1996*	*1986*	*1976*
Total	**37%**	**43%**	**40%**	**58%**	**53%**	**50%**	**4%**	**4%**	**8%**
Men	25	30	31	70	64	57	4	4	10
Women	47	51	47	48	44	44	4	4	6
Black	31	36	26	64	55	53	4	5	17
White	39	43	42	56	53	49	4	3	7
Aged 18 to 29	25	25	17	72	71	69	3	2	12
Aged 30 to 39	28	33	32	69	63	60	3	4	7
Aged 40 to 49	34	39	42	63	56	51	3	4	6
Aged 50 to 59	42	49	48	52	47	43	4	2	5
Aged 60 to 69	55	59	56	38	35	32	6	5	11
Aged 70 or older	65	72	71	25	22	20	7	5	3
Not high school grad.	48	51	49	42	43	40	6	4	7
High school graduate	38	41	38	58	55	53	3	3	7
Bachelor's degree	30	36	33	66	60	55	3	3	11
Graduate degree	29	39	16	65	54	69	6	6	15

Note: Numbers may not add to 100 because "don't know" and no answer are not included.
Source: General Social Surveys, National Opinion Research Center, University of Chicago

Is Prostitution Wrong?

The majority of Americans say prostitution is wrong, but many think sex between consenting adults is nobody else's business.

Many Americans take a libertarian stance towards the behavior of consenting adults. This is true with attitudes towards prostitution, with 45 percent of the public saying that if consenting adults exchange money for sex, it's their business. A slim majority of 52 percent believes prostitution is wrong.

There are no real differences of opinion by education or race. Men and women, however, do not see eye-to-eye on this question. Half of men, but only 42 percent of women, say it's nobody else's business if adults want to buy and sell sex. Fifty-six percent of women disagree compared with only 47 percent of men. Fully 40 percent of women say they strongly disagree versus only 25 percent of men.

There are some generational differences as well. Younger people are more likely to take a libertarian stance on prostitution. While 47 to 49 percent of people under age 50 agree that there's nothing inherently wrong with prostitution, only 41 to 44 percent of people aged 50 or older agree.

Is Prostitution Wrong? 1996

"There is nothing inherently wrong with prostitution, so long as the health risks can be minimized. If consenting adults agree to exchange money for sex, that is their business. Do you agree or disagree?"

(percent responding by sex, race, age, and education, 1996)

	strongly agree	somewhat agree	somewhat disagree	strongly disagree	agree, total	disagree, total
Total	**25%**	**20%**	**19%**	**33%**	**45%**	**52%**
Men	25	25	22	25	50	47
Women	26	16	16	40	42	56
Black	29	17	15	36	46	51
White	26	21	19	32	47	51
Aged 18 to 29	30	19	18	32	49	50
Aged 30 to 39	24	22	22	30	46	52
Aged 40 to 49	23	24	22	30	47	52
Aged 50 to 59	24	17	18	38	41	56
Aged 60 to 69	24	20	12	40	44	52
Aged 70 or older	27	16	14	38	43	52
Not a high school graduate	27	17	12	37	44	49
High school graduate	26	20	20	32	46	52
Bachelor's degree	21	24	21	33	45	54
Graduate degree	25	18	22	35	43	57

Note: Numbers may not add to 100 because "don't know" and no answer are not included.
Source: General Social Survey, National Opinion Research Center, University of Chicago

Ever Paid or Been Paid for Sex?

Seventeen percent of men admit they have paid for sex.

Although fully 45 percent of Americans say there is nothing inherently wrong with prostitution, few have actually participated in it. Only 9 percent admit to having paid or been paid for sex at least once since their 18th birthday. It's important to note that on questions about sexual behavior, it is not uncommon for people to lie or refuse to answer. Twelve percent of people aged 70 or older, for example, refused to say whether or not they had ever paid for sex.

Not surprisingly, the largest difference is found by sex. Only 2 percent of women say they have paid or been paid for sex. A substantial 17 percent of men, however, say they have exchanged money for sex.

People aged 50 to 69 are most likely to have paid or been paid for sex (or to admit it). Thirteen percent say they have exchanged money for sex, as have 10 percent of those in their 40s. Only 5 to 7 percent of older and younger age groups admit to having done so.

Ever Paid or Been Paid for Sex? 1996

"Thinking about the time since your 18th birthday, have you ever had sex with a person you paid or who paid you for sex?"

(percent responding by sex, race, age, and education, 1996)

	yes	no
Total	**9%**	**88%**
Men	17	79
Women	2	95
Black	10	83
White	8	89
Aged 18 to 29	5	92
Aged 30 to 39	7	91
Aged 40 to 49	10	88
Aged 50 to 59	13	84
Aged 60 to 69	13	84
Aged 70 or older	6	82
Not a high school graduate	8	85
High school graduate	9	88
Bachelor's degree	7	91
Graduate degree	7	90

Note: Numbers may not add to 100 because "don't know" and no answer are not included.
Source: General Social Survey, National Opinion Research Center, University of Chicago

Ever Committed Adultery?

Men are more likely than women to say they have had extramarital sex.

Eighteen percent of Americans who are or have been married admit to having committed adultery. As is the case with any question about a sensitive topic, the percentage of those who are willing to admit an extramarital affair probably understates the proportion of those who have actually committed adultery.

Men are more likely than women to say they have committed adultery. Nearly one-quarter of men, but only 14 percent of women, say they have had sex with someone other than their spouse while they were married.

A similar difference exists between blacks and whites. About one-quarter of blacks say they have had extramarital sexual relations compared with 18 percent of whites.

People who did not complete high school are less likely to have committed adultery (or less likely to own up to it) than those with more education. While 18 to 20 percent of people with at least a high school diploma say they have committed adultery, only 14 percent of people who did not complete high school agree.

People aged 40 to 59 are most likely to say they had sex with someone other than their spouse. Within this age group, 23 to 25 percent say they have committed adultery. This compares with 13 to 15 percent of people under age 40, 19 percent of those in their 60s, and just 9 percent of people aged 70 or older.

Ever Committed Adultery? 1996

"Have you ever had sex with someone other than
your husband or wife while you were married?"

(percent responding by sex, race, age, and education, 1996)

	yes	*no*
Total	**18%**	**79%**
Men	24	74
Women	14	83
Black	24	71
White	18	80
Aged 18 to 29	13	84
Aged 30 to 39	15	84
Aged 40 to 49	23	76
Aged 50 to 59	25	72
Aged 60 to 69	19	78
Aged 70 or older	9	83
Not a high school graduate	14	79
High school graduate	19	79
Bachelor's degree	18	81
Graduate degree	20	78

Note: Includes only people who are or have been married. Numbers may not add to 100 because "don't know" and no answer are not included.
Source: General Social Survey, National Opinion Research Center, University of Chicago

Sex Frequency

Frequency of sex diminishes with age.

Forty-five percent of Americans have sex at least once a week. But 18-to-29-year-olds are more sexually active than the average person. Sixty percent of them say they have sex at least weekly. More than 1 in 10 have sex more than three times a week.

Half of people in their 40s are still having sex once a week or more, but the proportion drops to 38 percent among people in their 50s and to 21 percent among those in their 60s. Only 7 percent of people aged 70 or older have sex at least once a week. Most of the oldest Americans (68 percent) have not had sex in the past year, in large part because many of them are widowed. Viagra, the male anti-impotence pill, may change some of these figures in the years ahead, especially among people in their 50s and 60s—the primary market for impotence medications.

Half of men say they have sex at least once a week, compared with 41 percent of women. There are several explanations for this discrepancy, including the fact that the average woman is older and more likely to be widowed than the average man, and the tendency among men to exaggerate their sexual activity.

People who did not complete high school are more likely than those with more education to say they did not have sex at all in the 12 months prior to the survey (31 percent compared with 14 to 16 percent of people with at least a high school diploma). One reason for this is the fact that older people (many of them widows) are overrepresented among those without a high school diploma.

Sex Frequency, 1996

"About how often did you have sex during the last 12 months?"

(percent responding by sex, race, age, and education, 1996)

	not at all	once or twice	about once a month	2 to 3 times a month	about once a week	2 to 3 times a week	more than 3 times a week
Total	**18%**	**7%**	**9%**	**16%**	**18%**	**21%**	**6%**
Men	12	8	10	17	21	22	7
Women	23	7	9	14	15	21	5
Black	16	8	12	15	11	24	6
White	19	7	9	15	19	20	6
Aged 18 to 29	7	9	7	14	15	31	14
Aged 30 to 39	7	6	9	16	22	29	7
Aged 40 to 49	11	7	11	18	22	23	5
Aged 50 to 59	19	9	11	18	20	15	3
Aged 60 to 69	30	8	15	18	13	6	2
Aged 70 or older	68	4	5	7	6	1	0
Not high school grad.	31	8	8	12	12	17	6
High school graduate	16	7	9	16	17	22	7
Bachelor's degree	14	7	10	15	23	23	5
Graduate degree	16	8	9	18	19	17	5

Note: Numbers may not add to 100 because "don't know" and no answer are not included.
Source: General Social Survey, National Opinion Research Center, University of Chicago

Sex Partners in Past Year

Most people had only one sex partner in the past year.

Sixty-five percent of Americans had only one sex partner in the past 12 months. Nineteen percent had no sex partners, and 13 percent had two or more. These figures are not much different from what they were in 1988.

Women are twice as likely as men to have had no sex partners in the past year (24 percent of women compared with 12 percent of men). In part, this is so because there are far more widowed women than men. Men are much more likely than women to have had more than one sexual partner during the past year (19 percent compared with 9 percent of women).

Two-thirds of whites say they had only one sex partner in the previous 12 months compared with 56 percent of blacks. Blacks are more likely to have had multiple sex partners. Twenty percent of blacks say they had two or more sex partners compared with 12 percent of whites.

As people get older, the likelihood of not having a sex partner increases. Only 7 percent of people under age 40 did not have any sex partners in the prior year, but this share rose to 20 percent among people in their 50s and 31 percent among those in their 60s. More than two-thirds (69 percent) of people aged 70 or older did not have a sex partner in the past year.

Younger people are far more likely to have had multiple sex partners. Only 2 to 6 percent of people aged 50 or older had more than one sex partner in the past 12 months compared with 19 percent of people in their 30s and 28 percent of 18-to-29-year-olds.

While 15 to 17 percent of people with at least a high school diploma had no sex partners in the past year, the figure rises to 31 percent among those who did not complete high school. One reason for this difference is the fact that many of the least educated Americans are older widows.

Sex Partners in Past Year, 1996

"How many sex partners have you had in the last 12 months?"

(percent responding by sex, race, age, and education, 1996)

	none	*one*	*two*	*three*	*four or more*
Total	**19%**	**65%**	**7%**	**3%**	**3%**
Men	12	66	8	5	6
Women	24	64	6	2	1
Black	19	56	10	5	5
White	19	66	7	3	2
Aged 18 to 29	7	60	13	7	8
Aged 30 to 39	7	72	10	5	4
Aged 40 to 49	13	76	5	3	2
Aged 50 to 59	20	72	5	1	0
Aged 60 to 69	31	64	2	0	0
Aged 70 or older	69	26	1	0	1
Not a high school graduate	31	53	5	3	5
High school graduate	17	66	8	4	2
Bachelor's degree	15	69	7	3	5
Graduate degree	18	71	7	2	0

Note: Numbers may not add to 100 because "several," "one or more," and no answer are not included.
Source: General Social Survey, National Opinion Research Center, University of Chicago

Sex Partners in Past Year, 1988 to 1996

"How many sex partners have you had in the last 12 months?"

(percent responding by sex, race, age, and education, 1988–96)

	none		one		two		three		four or more	
	1996	*1988*	*1996*	*1988*	*1996*	*1988*	*1996*	*1988*	*1996*	*1988*
Total	19%	23%	65%	63%	7%	6%	3%	4%	3%	4%
Men	12	16	66	65	8	6	5	5	6	8
Women	24	28	64	61	6	6	2	3	1	2
Black	19	15	56	58	10	9	5	7	5	10
White	19	23	66	64	7	5	3	3	2	3
Aged 18 to 29	7	9	60	60	13	12	7	7	8	7
Aged 30 to 39	7	8	72	77	10	5	5	5	4	1
Aged 40 to 49	13	12	76	76	5	5	3	4	2	0
Aged 50 to 59	20	27	72	64	5	4	1	1	0	3
Aged 60 to 69	31	39	64	57	2	2	0	2	0	0
Aged 70 or older	69	67	26	31	1	1	0	0	1	1
Not a high school graduate	31	39	53	48	5	4	3	4	5	4
High school graduate	17	19	66	67	8	7	4	2	2	2
Bachelor's degree	15	13	69	73	7	7	3	4	5	2
Graduate degree	18	14	71	74	7	5	2	6	0	0

Note: Numbers may not add to 100 because "several," "one or more," and no answer are not included.
Source: General Social Surveys, National Opinion Research Center, University of Chicago

Sex Partners in Past Five Years

One-third of Americans had at least two sex partners in the past five years.

Half of adults say they had only one sex partner in the past five years. One-third had two or more, and 22 percent had three or more.

As in all questions about sex, however, it is difficult to know how honest respondents are. Forty-one percent of men, but only 26 percent of women, say they had two or more sex partners over the past five years. The discrepancy between men and women suggests that someone isn't telling the truth.

Blacks are more likely than whites to have had multiple sex partners. Forty-five percent of blacks say they had two or more partners in the five years preceding the survey compared with 31 percent of whites.

Young adults are most likely to have had more than one sex partner. Fully 65 percent say they had more than one partner in the past five years, while 48 percent had three or more. The proportion of people who say they have had more than one partner drops steadily with age to only 3 percent among those aged 70 or older.

Sex Partners in Past Five Years, 1996

"How many sex partners have you had in the past five years?"

(percent responding by sex, race, age, and education, 1996)

	none	one	two	three	four	five to ten	eleven or more
Total	**12%**	**51%**	**10%**	**7%**	**5%**	**7%**	**3%**
Men	7	49	10	9	7	10	5
Women	17	52	11	6	4	4	1
Black	10	37	15	11	7	8	4
White	13	54	9	7	5	7	3
Aged 18 to 29	6	26	17	14	10	16	8
Aged 30 to 39	2	56	12	8	7	9	3
Aged 40 to 49	6	64	11	6	5	3	2
Aged 50 to 59	12	66	8	5	2	3	1
Aged 60 to 69	21	66	3	4	1	1	0
Aged 70 or older	55	29	1	1	1	0	0
Not high school grad.	22	47	6	8	4	3	3
High school graduate	11	50	12	7	5	7	3
Bachelor's degree	8	54	8	7	6	10	3
Graduate degree	10	63	8	7	5	3	1

Note: Numbers may not add to 100 because "several," "one or more," and no answer are not included.
Source: General Social Survey, National Opinion Research Center, University of Chicago

Index

Crime, fear of, in neighborhood, 67–69

Customs, racial and ethnic, maintain distinct, 215–216

Death penalty, support for, 61–63

Democrat, identification as, 110–113

Discrimination
  by race, 200, 202–203, 209–210
  by sex, 351–353

Earnings of women, why lower, 354–358

Economic system, U.S., 92–93

Economy, things government might do for
  control prices, 158–160
  control wages, 155–157
  cut spending, 122–124
  finance projects to create new jobs, 152–154
  protect jobs in declining industries, 146–148
  provide jobs for everyone, 149–151
  regulate business less, 161–163
  support development of new technologies, 174–175

Education
  confidence in, 14, 16, 34–35
  lack of, and socioeconomic status of blacks, 200–201, 202, 204
  sex, in schools, support for, 409–411
  volunteer work in, 404–405

Elderly, government responsibility to help, 130–132

Electric power, government or private organization should run, 172–173

Emotions, willingness to express, 398–403

Environment
  and international governmental bodies, 94–95
  volunteer work in, 404–405
  vs. development, 90–91

Extramarital sex
  ever had, 431–432
  wrong or not, 418–420

Fair housing laws, 184–186

Fairness of people, 381–383

Family life
  and work, balancing, 294–295
  children's future, likelihood it will be happy, 301–302
  success in, 292–293
  suffers when men work too much, 299–300

Family responsibilities
  as reason women earn less, 354–355, 357
  employer provide flextime for, 278–279
  vs. job responsibilities, 296–298

Feminist, consider self, 359–360

Finances
  changes in, 248–250
  of married couples, organization of, 322–323
  satisfaction with, 245–247

Flextime, should employers provide, 278–279

Genetic screening, harmful or beneficial, 83–84

Government
  control of prices, 158–160
  control of wages, 155–157
  does too much, 119–121
  finance projects to create new jobs, 152–154
  or private organizations should run
    banks, 168–169
    electric power industry, 172–173
    hospitals, 170–171
  protect jobs in declining industries, 146–148
  provide jobs for everyone, 149–151
  regulate business less, 161–163